RESTON POLYTECHNIC

274

D0413360

INNOVATIVE APPROACHES TO LANGUAGE TEACHING

Robert W. Blair, Editor

Brigham Young University

NEWBURY HOUSE PUBLISHERS, INC.
ROWLEY, MASSACHUSETTS 01969
ROWLEY • LONDON • TOKYO

1982

Library of Congress Cataloging in Publication Data
Main entry under title:

Innovative approaches to language teaching.

Bibliography: p.
1. Language and languages—Study and teaching—
Addresses, essays, lectures.   I. Blair, Robert
Wallace, 1930–
P51.I46   1982   418'.007'1   82-8236
ISBN 0-88377-247-7

Cover design by Jean Ploss

NEWBURY HOUSE PUBLISHERS, INC.

Language Science
Language Teaching
Language Learning

ROWLEY, MASSACHUSETTS 01969
ROWLEY ● LONDON ● TOKYO

ACC.   274145

CLASS NO.
418. 0071 INN

17 APR 1985

O/S   N   CATEGORY
N.L.

Copyright © 1982 by Newbury House Publishers, Inc. All rights reserved. No part
of this book may be reproduced or transmitted in any form or by any means, electronic
or mechanical, including photocopying, recording, or by any information storage and
retrieval system, without permission in writing from the Publisher.

First printing: November 1982
5   4   3   2

Printed in the U.S.A.

FOREWORD

This book is a look at a variety of ways that people gain control of a second language, both in and out of the classroom. Every approach covered in this volume departs in some way from "convention"—that is, from the way most of us learned languages in high school, college, and adult education courses.

Editor-contributor Robert Blair is eminently well suited for the task of compiling such a volume. Over the years he has not only had vast experience developing curriculum for teaching and learning languages through most if not all of the more conventional second language methods. He has also observed extensively many of these *unconventional* approaches and has incorporated elements of many of them into his own teaching repertoire.

This book represents a report by Blair on his personal quest for methods. One is struck by his enthusiastic willingness to be open to anything and everything which could produce faster, more successful language learning, and his volume offers us a wide range of such approaches.

Although many of the papers will be new to the reader, some of these writings on "departures from convention" have actually been around for a number of years. Yet, as Blair points out, even when a relatively recent article (Terrell's) first appeared, "readers were unprepared for it . . . the article was for many just 'too far out' to be taken seriously." Blair senses that at present both teachers and learners may be more willing than in the past to try such "far out" approaches, particularly if the methods are spelled out clearly.

A principal aim of the book is to accelerate change in language teaching, to encourage experimentation in alternate approaches. In my opinion, this book succeeds admirably at this endeavor. A number of opinions are expressed in this volume that language teachers, teacher trainers, and learners alike can subscribe to and utilize successfully in teaching about, teaching, or learning a second language.

Andrew D. Cohen
Jerusalem University

iii

ACKNOWLEDGMENTS

I express my sincere gratitude to the authors and publishers who have made this book possible. The following journal articles and other pieces are reprinted here by permission of the author and the publisher:

Harold R. Palmer. The principles of linguistic pedagogy. In *The Scientific Study and Teaching of Languages,* pp. 117–119, George G. Harrap & Co. Ltd., 1917.

Eugene A. Nida. Listening. Chapter Three in *Learning a Foreign Language,* Friendship Press, New York, 1957.

James J. Asher. *Learning Another Language through Actions: The Complete Teacher's Guidebook,* 1977 (pp. 36–52), Los Gatos, California: Sky Oak Productions, 19544 Sky Oaks Way, 95030.

Valerian A. Postovsky. Effects of delay in oral practice at the beginning of second language learning. *Modern Language Journal,* 58:229–239.

Robbins Burling. An introductory course in reading French. *Language Learning,* 28.1.105–128.

Leonard Newmark. How not to interfere with language learning. In Edward W. Najam, ed. *Language Learning: The Individual and the Process,* Indiana University Research Center in Anthropology, Folklore, and Linguistics, Bloomington, Indiana, 1966.

Earl W. Stevick. "B=VSP or after BC = PS + AP, What?" *Language Sciences,* August, 1969, Indiana University, Bloomington, Indiana.

Charles A. Curran. Counseling skills adapted to the learning of foreign languages." *Bulletin of the Menninger Forum,* March, 1961.

Charles A. Curran. A linguistic model for learning and living in the new age of the person. *On TESOL '78,* Washington, D.C.

Georgi Lozanov. Suggestology and suggestopedia: A report to UNESCO, Paris, 1978.

Tracy D. Terrell. A natural approach to second language acquisition and learning. *Modern Language Journal,* 60:325–337.

Beverly Galyean. A confluent design for language teaching. Unpublished paper, 1978.

Caleb Gattegno. *Teaching Foreign Languages in the Schools the Silent Way,* Educational Solutions, New York, 1963, pp. 34–39.

Caleb Gattegno. Much language and little vocabulary. In *Common Sense about Language Teaching,* Educational Solutions, New York, 1976, pp. 40–44.

John H. T. Harvey. In *Symposium Papers of the Desert Language and Linguistics Society.* Linguistics Department, Brigham Young University, Provo, Utah, 1979.

PREFACE

This book is intended for language learners and language teachers. The compiler's aim has been to select authors whose approaches to language teaching are currently attracting the interest of other professionals, and allow these primary authors to speak for themselves—with commentary from the compiler on the historical perspective and rationale of the approaches relative to each other and to more conventional methods.

This book does not pretend to report comparative research on the performance of competing methods. It does not present a critical assessment of the powers and limitations or the strengths and weaknesses of the techniques and approaches discussed. Although it would be useful to have an anthology of writings both pro and con on these approaches, with the compiler as a disinterested referee, this is not that. This book is concerned more with probing the rationale of the newer approaches than with measuring their performance or attesting to or refuting the claims of their proponents. The primary authors are allowed to state their case without rebuttal. The compiler's contributions, based on his own investigation of and informal experimentation with the various approaches discussed, support the claims of the authors that for achieving certain objectives in language teaching, these innovative approaches may be more effective than the conventional ones.

This book will not be the first, of course, to point out that the linguistics and behavioral psychology that underlie the conventional approaches and enjoyed great prestige in the 1950s have few serious proponents today. Nor will it be the first to recognize that the principles of the new methods are in conflict with the principles of the conventional methods, or that the successes of the new approaches are in no way predictable from the traditional understanding of language learning.

If the reader finds here not only food for thought but ideas and tools to help in his or her pursuit of excellence in language learning and teaching, the primary objective of the book will have been achieved.

INTRODUCTION

If we lived in a world where the development of large numbers of competent bilinguals was accepted as a goal by the majority of the citizens, where language teachers could shape things better to suit language-learning needs, and where the time and cost to achieve this goal were not primary considerations, doubtless we could bring about far more effective language teaching than we actually do. Among the variables we might attend to where change could be introduced are:

1. The students: their age, maturity, and motivation for learning; their entry skills or preparation for the learning task; the efficiency of their language study; their strategies and tactics of language learning; their attitude toward users of the language, their contact and relationship with fluent speakers of the language; their management of other matters in life, their home setting and the degree and kind of parental support for language learning, the society which helps form attitudes toward other languages and cultures, etc.

2. The materials: the method and the content; their aims and objectives, the "delivery systems" (printed matter, audiovisual aids, computer-assisted instruction, etc.), the orientation: whether teaching language per se or teaching other subject matter in the language as is done in bilingual education.

3. The teachers: the content, strategies, and tactics used in class; their personality, their fluency in the language, attitude toward the language and culture, teaching skills, linguistic and cultural sophistication, relationship to students out of class and to parents.

Although each of these (and other) variables merits attention as we look to the improvement of language teaching, in this book we look primarily at the one variable which in the long tradition of language teaching has been most subject to change: method or approach. Although this may not be the most fruitful single variable to manipulate, it seems to be the most available one; it is one which can fit into the existing academic system without necessitating the reordering of priorities. And in fact it is the one variable where change is progressive and inevitable.

The aim of this book is to accelerate that change, to encourage experimentation in alternative approaches to language teaching, to inform readers about a number of interesting and successful modern approaches to language instruction, and to promote increased understanding of the role of research in second language acquisition as a foundation for language pedagogy.

The book is based on my personal feeling that:

1. Academic programs whose purpose is to train people in the fundamental skills of foreign languages generally yield a less satisfactory product than the public has a right to expect. (The reasons for this failure are, as I have pointed out, very complex, but a good part of the responsibility for improvement rests on the profession.)

2. If language departments and language teachers do not introduce changes necessary to improve the performance of average students in basic-level courses, the generally deplorable record of foreign language education will remain a threat to the credibility of our profession.

3. Part of the blame for the current inefficiency in language training must be laid at the door of a misguided faith that stimulus-response psychology, linked with sophisticated linguistic analysis, provides a scientific basis for language pedagogy. Conventional methods of language teaching, based on what must now be regarded as outmoded and unacceptable views of learning, may actually place formidable barriers in the path of learners.

4. Creative teachers and experimentalists in the field of language teaching have demonstrated that alternative approaches are available which seem to be congruent with currently accepted views of second language acquisition and which are more effective for achieving certain major objectives than are the conventional ones used generally in the profession.

5. The major reasons these new approaches are not in wider use may be that teachers have not understood them, have doubted the results claimed for them, have not had the time, the energy, or the means to devote to them, or simply have been satisfied to continue their conventional practices, hoping for the best.

PRESENT REALITIES OF ACADEMIC LANGUAGE TEACHING

To set the stage, let's first take an honest look at some of the current realities of the language teaching scene. The facts in this case do not make a pretty picture. According to the report of the President's Commmission on the Study and Teaching of Languages in the United States, the number of students who complete a second-year language course in American secondary schools is less than 5 percent of the total students enrolled in language courses. And of those who complete the equivalent of 2 years of high school language study the average level of competence attained in speaking, aural comprehension, or even reading is hardly the pride of the nation. In fact, if the potential consequences of this situation were not so serious, it would be a joking matter.

Lest it be thought that the situation in the United States is unique, Alison d'Anglejan (1978) states:

Generations of Quebec children have spent 10 or 12 years in second language classes only to emerge functionally unilingual at the end of their schooling.

One could cite other nations such as Japan where several years of study of a foreign language for all schoolchildren admittedly results in a notoriously low achievement and even in a national "complex" about a supposed inability to learn foreign languages, but this would hardly amount to an excuse for the general debility of the language programs in many of our own schools.

On the college level in America the scene is hardly any prettier. Although competence in a foreign language is supposedly envied, college students have been "staying away from language study in droves." Academic language study has the reputation of being drudgery, and is for many novice learners a distasteful if not a painful task. Many college students take a language for the minimum number of semesters in order to fill a graduation requirement, ordinarily by simply accumulating a certain number of passing credits in a language, not by demonstrating proficiency in using the language. Few academic language programs require their students to demonstrate proficiency in speaking and understanding a language at a useful level even after 2 and 3 years of study.

Although admittedly the academic study of language does not lead many students to proficiency in speaking a language, it is claimed by some in its defense that language study is worthwhile primarily for the cultural and educational experience it provides. While there may be some validity to that defense, "cultural education" is not always what the public expects and wants out of language courses. Certainly the profession has failed to make a case for the cultural experience that is convincing to the public. Too often the public has been allowed and even encouraged to believe that language courses would lead to the ability to speak, read, write, and understand a language. While this may indeed be the ideal and the desired aim, if in fact our courses consistently fail to produce this outcome *for most students* even after two, three, or more years of study, then it seems a violation of "truth in packaging" to allow the public to believe what is in fact seldom the case.

Looking at it realistically, it is the case that in most American schools and colleges the average student in an "easy" language such as Spanish is, after four semesters, still unable to understand and speak spontaneously and fluently beyond the trivia of teacher-student exchanges. In a "hard" language such as Russian the proficiency of the average student at the end of four or even six semesters is even more limited.

If it were known publicly what level of proficiency is actually attained by the *middle half* of American students at the end of two or more years of language study in the conventional school or college setting, there would probably be a further decline in language enrollments.

(We wince, of course, at the crass claims and often simplistic methods of certain commercial language courses that promise magic at high prices, and lead the public to expect what we know they cannot deliver: fluency in a few easy lessons! And we roll our eyes when we learn that some commercial language companies are thriving, while many academic language departments are withering.)

SOME CRUCIAL QUESTIONS

Can the average person attain reasonable proficiency in a language through classroom courses? From intensive language programs of the Foreign Service Institute, the Defense Language Institute, and the Peace Corps where languages are taught under more nearly ideal conditions than in academic institutions, it has been found that *selected,* capable, highly motivated learners under the best audiolingual training conditions devised, and concentrating full time on language study alone, require (depending on the language and the student) from 800 to over 2000 "contact hours" of training to attain a level of proficiency adequate for normal use (S-3 on the FSI proficiency rating scale). That amount of hours far exceeds the time available in four or six semesters of language classes meeting for 1 hour daily. Furthermore it is recognized that the efficiency of learning in an environment of concentrated, full-time study is superior by far to that of the usual academic setting.

In the usual academic situation where language study is not nearly so concentrated or so extended in time and must compete for the learner's attention with many other pressures of the normal academic load (plus other pressures and interests in the life of a student), what amount of language learning can realistically be expected in one semester or in a year or two? Or to view that question in a different light: given the goal of training people up to a usable level of communicative competence in a language, what amount of training will do it? If that amount is unrealistically large—if the educational system is unwilling to afford students that much time, or students are unwilling to invest that much effort, what alternatives are there?

Those are rhetorical questions. Recognizing the general failure of academic language training, d'Anglejan (1979) made this despairing statement:

It is difficult to accept with any measure of confidence or composure traditional academic solutions to the urgent problems of second language learning and teaching.

We may feel that that view is overly pessimistic. Clearly, however, if the length or intensity of training needed is too much to fit our present educational priorities, and if we limit ourselves to the traditional school setting, we are left with the challenge of finding more efficient training methods that will accomplish more in less time.

MORE LANGUAGE LEARNING IN LESS TIME

The authors in this book believe that the average language learner in a language course is capable of learning at a faster rate than has been normally assumed, provided that he or she is motivated to learn and is guided by correct principles. Many of them claim, in fact, that significant acceleration of language learning for the average learner is not only theoretically possible but can be done and is being done in academic settings through one approach or another. What is particularly noteworthy is that their several approaches share certain features generally absent in the conventional methods. What is shared by those approaches, in contrast with the more conventional approaches, is the subject of this book.

Lest readers' expectations be disappointed, let it be stated here again that it is not the purpose of this book to bring forth empirical evidence for the efficacy or superiority of any given approach to language teaching—or even to claim that empirical evidence is available which would conclusively demonstrate the superiority of one method or set of methods over another. In fact, I agree with the candid assessment of David Levy, who said:

The fact of the matter is that at the present time, no existing language teaching methodology has ever been empirically demonstrated to be superior to any other methodology, or even to random language exposure.

Whether empirical evidence will eventually be adduced to prove any one approach superior to all others I do not know. I doubt it. I regard all approaches as in a sense preliminary and tentative, subject to modification, their power relative to that of other approaches yet to be demonstrated. I think, however, that evidence can show that the approaches described in this book are, in certain regards and for many learners, more effective than conventional approaches. Perhaps each one can accommodate factors of language learning that have not been accommodated quite so well in the conventional approaches.

What this book will provide to the language teacher or language learner is a basic description and a positive rationale for several innovative methods of language teaching and language learning. Since the approaches described are markedly unconventional and have attracted widespread attention, and since of course they have limitations and weaknesses, most of them have been critiqued, both positively and negatively, in the professional literature. Clearly it is just as important that attention be given to the voices of the responsible critics and opponents of these innovative approaches as to those of the originators and proponents. Nevertheless I have chosen to present each one in a positive light, to allow the originators to give the rationale for their own invention. The bibliography refers to secondary sources and commentaries of interest to the serious student.

Because I have observed and worked extensively for several years with the techniques of each of the approaches described, I speak as a witness of their value. Yet I speak not as a proponent of any one approach or of any particular eclectic "mix" of techniques, but as an advocate of experimentation with profoundly different ideas on how language teaching can achieve better results with more learners.

The authors and writings included in this book are, of course, not the only ones deserving attention. There are other people in the profession whose work with innovative approaches is as exciting as that of the pioneer experimenters selected for inclusion here. To attempt to list them would involve the risk of inadvertent omissions. I also realize that many teachers are working with innovative approaches I an unaware of. I invite their correspondence.

I believe that there is a growing awareness in the language teaching profession that change is in the wind and is inevitable—and not just change in methodology. Change in approach alone, no matter how ingenious and sophisticated, is only one avenue of approach to improving language teaching. Inadequate as it is by itself, that avenue is the subject of this book, and the contributors are prominent pioneers who have, in my opinion, broken the trail.

CONTENTS

1
BACKGROUND

A SEARCH (1950–1981)

In his excellent and well-known book, *Twenty-Five Centuries of Language Teaching,* Louis Kelly treats us to a well-researched sketch of views on language teaching in a large part of the world over a long period of time. One familiar with present-day theory and practice of language teaching might almost conclude from that book that in the past quarter century there has not been much new in either the theory or the practice of language teaching.

It has been a pastime of mine for over 30 years to study people's ideas about learning and instruction, and particularly about language learning and instruction. And for most of those years it has been a pleasant pastime to experiment with many of the ideas I have found engaging. I have experimented both as learner and as teacher. I have become acquainted with the reading method, the grammar-translation method, the Direct Method (in its Berlitz and de Sauzé transformations), programmed instruction, computer-assisted instruction, and of course the audiolingual and audiovisual methods in their various transformations in name, content, and strategy: The Mim-mem Method, the Linguistic Method, the Oral-Aural Method, the Saint Cloud Method, and others.

Raised in contact with foreign languages in the home, the son of a high school teacher of Spanish and Italian, after studying Latin, French, and Spanish in secondary school, I headed eagerly into the serious study of other European languages, Russian and Finnish in particular. To legitimize my love affair with languages and hoping to create a niche for myself in the world of language instruction, I took my Ph.D. in linguistics, convinced that a better understanding of the structure of language was a road to better comprehension of language learning and teaching.

In 1965, I finished my first major book, an audiolingual course of the Maya language of Yucatan, the subject of my dissertation. At that time, although I already had serious doubts about stimulus-response psychology in general and operant conditioning in particular, I did not yet doubt the power of linguistics to specify exactly what we wanted students to learn in a language course, nor of instructional science to engineer the desired language competence.

3

I was impressed by the dicta of noted scholars on language learning. In 1942, Leonard Bloomfield, an eminent American linguist, had written a short treatise on language learning that had enormous influence in guiding language teaching for decades. In it he stated:

It is helpful to know how language works, but this knowledge is of no avail until one has practiced the forms over and over again until he can rattle them off without effort. Copy the forms, read them out loud, get them by heart, and then practice them over and over again day after day, until they become entirely natural and familiar. Language learning is overlearning; anything less is of no use.

And two decades later (1964), Nelson Brooks, a professor of foreign language education at Yale, had written:

The single paramount fact about language learning is that it concerns, not problem-solving, but the formation and performance of habits. The learner who has been made to see only how language works has not learned any language; on the contrary, he has learned something he will have to forget before he can make any progress in that area of language.

The assumptions of these reputable scholars about language learning and language teaching seemed sound to me. Logically it followed that in classroom language instruction learning efficiency results through the teacher's tight control of the learners' time so as to keep them constantly hearing and producing properly formed sentences modeled on native speech.

Stimulus-response theory called for inducing and immediately reinforcing a high rate of correct responses. As much as possible the learner should be kept from making errors; hence patterned response drill and controlled conversation seemed to make sense. Near-native, automatic control of one pattern after another is a primary aim from the first. Reinforcement contingencies are to be programmed so as to reelicit, reinforce, and thus maintain newly acquired behavior repertoires.

In order to do this, it was thought necessary to keep students occupied a high percentage of the time in high-intensity learning activities in which a high number of stimulus-response events take place per unit of time. Robert Lado (1964), a respected spokesman for audiolingualism, emphasized this point:

In pattern practice, the student produces a sentence after each cue at normal conversational speed. A class may produce 20 to 30 different sentences per minute following as many cues supplied by the teacher. This represents 1000 to 1500 recitations in a 50-minute class. Compare this with a grammar-translation class where each student takes one minute to give his part of the translation. This gives only 50 recitations compared with 1000. If learning increased with the number of recitations (when the same utterance is not repeated more than 3 times), pattern practice must be far superior. With group recitation in pattern practice, the number of student responses in a class of 10 students would be 10 times 1000 or 10,000!

In the early 1960s, my teaching was in line with the prevailing winds of doctrine. I was an advocate of the new paradigm: dialogue memorization, recitation in class, recombination drill accompanied by manipulation of vocabulary and sentence patterns through a rich assortment of patterned response drills controlled and prompted by the teacher. I prepared carefully programmed tapes for the language lab following the suggestions of Robert

Stack, Gustav Matthieu, and Ferdnand Marty. And to the extent that seemed feasible I attempted to lead my students into communication. I sensed that genuine communication in a foreign language class is the real payoff. But with all the highly structured activities in my classroom aimed at getting ready to communicate, it turned out there was not much time left for actual communication on the part of the students.

I enjoyed my teaching, and I believe my students felt they were getting their money's worth. To this day I feel that they acquired a good foundation in the language so that if they had gone abroad they would have been ready to acquire fluency in the language. In short, I was quite satisfied that my teaching was not only effective but, equally important to me, also defensible in principle.

However, before the mid-sixties my faith in the audiolingual method was wavering. This was partly due to candid feedback from my students, whose experience in my classroom was not always what I was supposing it was. Partly it was due to my intuitive perceptions as I observed the results of my teaching. And partly it was due to the skepticism of others such as John B. Carroll, who wrote in 1964:

> The audiolingual habit theory which is so prevalent in American foreign language teaching was perhaps, 15 years ago, in step with the state of psychological thinking at that time, but it is no longer abreast of recent developments. It is ripe for major revision, particularly in the direction of joining with it some of the better elements of the cognitive code-learning theory. I would venture to predict that if this can be done then teaching based on the revised theory will yield a dramatic change in effectiveness.

I was swayed by Noam Chomsky's critique of B. F. Skinner's attempt to account for language acquisition within the stimulus-response paradigm, but though I began to pay more attention to cognitive psychology and to the emerging field of psycholinguistics, I did not see clear implications from these for language teaching theory and practice. Wilga Rivers' criticism of the psychological underpinnings of audiolingualism in her 1964 book, *The Psychologist and the Foreign Language Teacher*, coming during the zenith of American enthusiasm for audiolingualism, helped set in motion the counter-thrust of the cognitivists, and I found myself in full agreement with her argument.

Adding fuel to the fire, in 1965, Noam Chomsky gave his celebrated address to the Northeast Language Teachers' Association, in which he said:

> A good deal of the foreign language instruction that's going on now . . . is based on a concept of language . . . (which assumes) that language is a system of skills and ought to be taught through drill and by the formation of S-R associations. I think the evidence is very convincing that that view of language is entirely erroneous, and it's a very bad way—certainly an unprincipled way—to teach languages. If it happens to work, it would be an accident for some other reason. Certainly it is not a method that is based on any understanding of the nature of language. Our understanding of the nature of language seems to me to show quite convincingly that language is not a habit structure, but that it has a kind of a creative property and is based on abstract formal principles and operations of a complex kind.

By that time I had long ceased to be an advocate and defender of audiolingualism and, finding comfort in the boldness of these and other scholars,

I had moved strongly toward eclecticism. I had developed a more open mind, a willingness to question the foundations of my own notions and practices. I began to question whether the answers I sought were to be found where I was seeking them, whether language science tied with instructional science would yield the better way. But where if not in these was I to inquire?

Between 1966 and 1971, with generous support from the Peace Corps, the U.S. Office of Education, The Defense Language Institute, and Brigham Young University, I was privileged to supervise teams of capable native informants and graduate students in designing and producing course materials in eight languages. I was given the freedom of designing and experimenting with entire systems of language instruction.

It was during this period of giving and supervising instruction in these languages that I did a lot of hard thinking about language learning and teaching. I became acquainted during that time with the stimulating ideas on language learning of Leonard Newmark and David Reibel, Earl Stevick and Clelland Harris, James Asher, William Rohwer and Robert Gagne, Robert Rebert, John Francis and John Harvey, Alexander Lipson, John Rassias, Valerian Postovsky, William F. Mackey and others, and found them most engaging. Being the designer and development supervisor of a series of intensive language courses, I had the opportunity to experiment with their ideas.

For me perhaps the most important yield of these years was an increased readiness to listen, genuinely listen—not just to other linguists and instructional psychologists, but to other language learners, other language teachers, and even people who held what I might earlier have regarded as wild and woolly notions about language instruction. I was fascinated with the range and diversity of opinion on the subject of language learning and language teaching. I could pick out the charlatans, I trust, but I was willing to make a sincere effort to try to understand other viewpoints and to get informed about what others were doing or thinking of doing in language teaching.

It became clear to me at that time that lesson content as well as every teaching technique and every classroom strategy and tactic used by a teacher is, consciously or not, based on decisions that derive from the teacher's and/or the course writer's assumptions about the nature of his subject matter, about learning and pedagogy, and indeed about the nature of man and social groups. Perceiving the absence of any scientific theory capable of motivating many decisions on course design and content, and not trusting traditional practices and principles, I concluded that language teaching and course development would be best served through experimental, principled eclecticism which would explore various combinations of assumptions and approaches. I presumed that such experimentation with different combinations of "mixes" could lead to finding out eventually how to "put it all together" in an optimum program formula tailored to each learner's needs.

I was guided by principles based on assumptions drawn from my interpretation and elaboration of the ideas of the people just mentioned—

liberally mixed with my own intuitions, of course. In 1970, I set down a list of these assumptions. The exercise was a useful one at the time; now, a decade later, I find the list of historical interest, a stage in the development of my present thinking.

ASSUMPTIONS (1970)

1. A language makes use of finite means (rules and items) to generate infinite ends (the total set of sentences of the language). Though it is manifestly impossible to memorize the set of sentences one may need, it is possible to gain intuitive control of a set of rules by means of which one can generate an infinite number of well-formed sentences. (From Chomsky.)

2. The sentences a language user must generate, whether listening or speaking, cannot be acquired through course work. Most of the sentences needed cannot be practiced, much less memorized.

3. One learns a language no faster than one generates and tests—in purposeful, motivated use—one's own hypotheses about the language. This means that the learner is central in the learning process. All other things: the instructional program, the instrumental paraphernalia, even the teacher, exist only to facilitate the learner's task of generating and testing hypotheses about the language through motivated use.

4. Just as a child must derive information for his hypotheses from both his "hits" and his "misses" as he confronts actual communication situations, so the adult learner must learn language by meeting situations and problems head on, taking profit from his mistakes as well as his successes.

5. The principal job of a language program is to create a rich and varied learning environment such that the learners can efficiently generate and test hypotheses through purposeful language use. In-class activities should emphasize contextually meaningful tasks and problems rather than pattern rehearsal, communication strategy rather than recitation.

6. Language learning is not best viewed as simply a linear, additive process with each well-defined learning task sequenced neatly from beginning to end in a planned syllabus. We should not attempt to hold the learner responsible for mastery of all the content of all the materials of the course—or even for a large portion of it. To do so will seriously compromise the richness of the learning environment.

7. Students should not be expected to learn simply by mass repetition; they will learn only what they are ready to learn. They will perceive only what they are ready to perceive. The central problem of training is not the arrangement of reinforcement contingencies. It is rather the identification and exploitation of learning hierarchies. (From Gagné.)

8. Cognitive understanding of structure may enhance the enjoyment as well as the success of language learning for many students. There is no reason to assume that language learning must be approached inductively. It doesn't

matter how a student comes up with a satisfactory response or with a hypothesis, whether by induction or by deduction. In learning a skill, conscious attention to its critical features and understanding of them will often facilitate learning.

9. Language learning is much more than the acquisition of a broad repertoire of psychomotor habits, but that aspect of language learning cannot be left out of account. Practice of patterns is necessary, but its place in the instructional process will be greatly changed. Pattern drill per se in the classroom is out.

10. Students will learn best by doing—but only if what they do has meaning and purpose for them. They will retain only what they experience meaningfully, what they perceive to be useful to them. Habit strength is a function not simply of how many responses are emitted, but of how many responses emitted contain reinforcement power for the student. (From Stevick.)

11. The performance criterion for pronunciation and grammatical accuracy should not be so high during the first weeks of training that students come to feel that "the only purpose of speaking is to avoid making mistakes," as Stevick puts it. Relaxing performance standards at first can buy time and the disposition for the students to use the language in motivated communication.

12. An instructional program should not attempt to teach everything. There is no end to the study of multiple word meaning, idiomatic usages, etc. Much will necessarily be left to the teacher and the students to fill in on their own as the need and occasion arise.

13. Recognizing the extreme discrepancy between proficient language learners and low-performance language learners, it may be wrong to attribute the discrepancy to differences in "language aptitude," "intelligence," or other supposedly unchangeable native endowments. The differences in performance may be due rather to one or more factors that are subject to change. It may be the case that more efficient language learners know something or do something or have acquired something that the less efficient do not know or do not do or have not acquired. Assuming this to be so, we should seek ways to help less proficient learners acquire some of whatever it is their more successful peers have in the way of cognitive knowledge, foundational skills, or strategies in language learning, positive attitude, etc.

14. There is already such an enormous accumulation of experimentation and experience in adult language training that, despite the claims of some, it appears unlikely that a methodological breakthrough is imminent such that the learning performance of all learners can be very substantially, consistently, and immediately increased through the introduction of methodological innovations. Rather it is more likely that significant improvements in language training will be incremental and will apply to only certain learner profiles. Posing researchable questions about certain learner problems, such as those of inept language learners, would seem a more promising activity at this point than searching for one eminently superior, universal methodology for all.

I did not expect these to become my articles of faith, and they did not. But they did contribute to my receptiveness of what was to come. I had by then come to believe that the search for ways to overcome language-learning deficiencies would become bogged down if it concentrated mainly on how languages work and how they can be described or presented so as to "expose their naked heart" to the learner. In short I had lost faith in the power of descriptive linguistics to provide much help to the average language learner. I felt strongly that progress in the language-teaching profession would come from a different source, primarily from language learners of different types and in various learning situations.

It was natural then that in the ensuing years I got into more "radical" ideas on language learning and teaching as I learned about the Silent Way, CLL (Community Language Learning), Suggestopedia, the Natural Approach, the Confluent Approach, and others and as I came to better understand the rationale of the comprehension approaches of Asher, Postovsky, and Burling, and the communication approaches of Lipson, Harvey, and Francis. The 1970s were to see the elaboration and refining of my earlier assumptions, a great deal more experimentation with various approaches, a solidifying of my faith that the efficiency of language instruction and language learning can be greatly increased as we learn more about it, and that continuing, open-minded questioning, experimentation, and research are the keys to progress.

I had learned of Dr. Caleb Gattegno's remarkable success in teaching children by the Silent Way from John Holt's book *Why Children Fail*. I later learned that Gattegno taught spoken language to adults using the Silent Way. How in the world can a spoken language be taught through silence? I asked. Curious, I read Gattegno's book *Teaching Foreign Languages the Silent Way*. It was obvious that the author was schooled in neither linguistics nor instructional psychology. Many of the things he had to say about language were not only quite remote from the mainstream of American linguistic thought but also counter to my own intuition and training. This disturbed me at first more than seeing that his approach to instructional psychology was equally remote from the stream of American psychological thought.

Worse than that, his writing struck me as being the work of a mystic. Except for copious testimonials provided by other users of the method, the reader was left to take the pronouncements of this man on faith. Fortunately I found enough fascination in the description of Silent Way techniques that I maintained interest and finally found my way to Dr. Gattegno's office in New York, where I had my first Silent Way language lesson. The language was Serbian and my teacher was Dr. Gattegno's associate, a native Yugoslav.

The effect of the lesson on me was electrifying. It was unforgettable, exciting, unlike anything I had ever experienced in learning before. And I immediately began to experiment with the Silent Way myself, first with my children, who loved it and wanted more, then with my students, who were not sure at first whether I was serious or not but soon were as caught up in it as I was.

I didn't use the Silent Way exclusively in my teaching. I never have. But I have used it in conjunction with Asher's Total Physical Response training, Alexander Lipson's techniques, mnemonics, and a rich composite of other things I enjoy doing in teaching a language. I discovered that with Silent Way techniques I could lead many students to perceive grammatical relationships and to master structural basics and details faster, more surely, and with higher retention and greater pleasure than I had seen before. I found in it a precision, a power of focus I had not seen before. I found many of my students as excited about learning this way as I was.

Also I experienced renewed joy in creatively working with my students at their level of perception. And interesting in an incidental way, I found that I could read Gattegno's books without cringing. In fact I found them to be more and more rewarding. Before long his writing had had a profound effect on my own thinking about learning and instruction in general and about language teaching in particular. I am glad my initial prejudice did not keep me from investigating the Silent Way.

I continue to use Silent Way techniques in both beginning and advanced language teaching—not exclusively, but in combination with other things. And I continue to read and ponder the thinking of Dr. Gattegno, an original thinker whose work should have permanent effect on American education.

Within a year after my initiation into Gattegno's approach to instruction, I discovered another, equally profound, equally radical thinker and experimenter in language learning and teaching: Charles A. Curran, author of an approach called Community Language Learning. Not a language expert, not read at all in language pedagogy, not trained in instuctional psychology, not even a practiced language teacher, but simply a brilliant Roman Catholic priest who was a student and colleague of Carl Rogers in counseling psychology, Curran argued that both stimulus-response psychology and cognitive psychology are incapable of explaining learning or providing a worthy model for instruction.

Curran's eminently humanistic approach to learning and instruction is what he calls a "whole person" approach. It takes into account dimensions of both psychological and social phenomena that characterize human behavior and social interaction in learning and instruction. These were crucial dimensions of language learning I had never thought of. Nor, of course, had I thought of how to deal with them. Curran had. And deeply.

As I studied Curran's book and then attended a counsel-learning workshop I was not just excited, I was moved. My mind resonated with his. I was aware that others had found his writing and his lectures as mystical as I had found Gattegno's. But to me Curran was addressing key questions I had about learning, as well as giving me a whole new domain of questions I had never thought of. I was ready for it. I found it tremendously stimulating and fruitful. And it didn't take long for me to begin to experiment with his ideas on language instruction and to incorporate them into my own expanding philosophy of language learning and instruction.

At that point I could see that my 1970 assumptions were seriously deficient in that they were based on acceptance of a dichotomy between habit-reinforcement theory (stimulus-response psychology) and cognitive-code theory, one or the other or both together held by most experts to be sufficient to account for language learning and to provide a principled basis for language instruction. On reading Curran, I was persuaded that neither the one nor the other nor both together were sufficient. In fact, the reduction of language learning or instruction to these two dimensions had blinded us to a third and crucially important dimension that Curran calls the "whole person."

I currently use CLL. Not exclusively, but I find I cannot be as effective a language teacher without it as with it. I find Curran's humanistic philosophy of education, his "whole person" approach, consonant with my own, and it is as natural for me to use a CLL approach in my language teaching as to use a fork in my eating.

In 1975, I learned of yet another "radical" approach to language instruction. The course of this one was as unlikely as for the previous two. The approach was being kept a secret in Bulgaria but was brought to light in a best-seller paperback entitled *Psychic Phenomena behind the Iron Curtain*. The report told of Dr. Georgi Lozanov, a medical doctor specializing in psycho-therapy, who became interested in the phenomenon of hypermnesia: mem-orizing large amounts of material in a short period of time. He had researched this interesting phenomenon in India among yogis who do indeed perform prodigious feats of text memorization. In Bulgaria, Lozanov began to experiment with intensive language learning and reported that subjects in his experiments learned to speak and understand a language with considerable fluency in an incredibly short time.

When reports of this experimentation reached the American public, there was, naturally, general skepticism. Lozanov used the term suggestopedia for his training approach. Was it hypnosis? There was enough mystery about it all to spark considerable interest among the public. Of course the language professionals were properly skeptical. I certainly was. But not uninterested.

Between 1975 and 1977, Robert Bushman, a graduate student in linguistics and educational psychology at BYU, did a dissertation on suggestopedia, going first to Canada to learn how it was done there; then, although not fully trained in the approach, he and I cooperated on two experiments in language learning using an improved version of the method. We taught two Russian courses and two Finnish courses, comparing the results of groups taught with an audiolingual method against groups taught with a suggestopedic method. The fact that the data Bushman collected for the dissertation significantly favored the suggestopedic groups was less important to me than the feeling I got from teaching with suggestopedia and from the feedback from students in the course.

One of the prominent features of Lozanov's approach is the input of massive amounts of material—many times more than with traditional methods. In the first class (preferably 2 or more hours in length) 15 or 20 pages of text material containing hundreds of words as well as grammar of considerable complexity is introduced through dramatic readings against a background of classical music. This performance is called a "concert." One of the principal aims of suggestopedia is to produce the "spa effect," the feeling of euphoria that can result from complete relaxation and enjoyment of a pleasant experience. Learning is incidental to the enjoyment. In later sessions the material of the text is elaborated through role-plays and other means, always without pressure or stress. Students' errors are not treated; what is monitored and supported is communication.

Since 1977, I have incorporated certain principles and procedures of suggestopedia into my own language teaching, and this has made an enormous change in my classes and in the results observed. I am very comfortable with a "materials-intensive" approach which introduces massive amounts of language content. I see this as a way of simulating a natural acquisition environment. I also see relaxation and the "spa effect" as contributing to the natural assimilation of a language, and I consider the strategy of monitoring and supporting communication in Lozanov's approach, without treating surface errors, as congruent with the implications of research on language acquisition.

Also since 1977, I have intensified my search for and experimentation with other innovative approaches to language teaching that are consistent with my developing understanding of the nature of language learning. It is impossible to list all the persons who have contributed to this thinking and experimentation, but prominent among them are the authors, selections of whose writings are included in this volume. To each I owe much for helping to shape my thinking about language learning and teaching and for fueling my quest with enthusiasm and hope.

What I have written here is largely autobiographical and by nature subjective. It may seem to some that my approach to theory and practice is unprincipled, that I am ready to believe anything and anyone with a kooky new idea. Let me state why I am ready to at least listen to whoever is probing the matters I am interested in, even if their perspective seems eccentric or questionable. It seems to me that in attempting to probe the nature of language learning and teaching, linguists and other language people have been like the famous blindmen of Hindustan attempting to discover the nature of elephants. After examining only the tail of one elephant, one of them reports that an elephant is like a rope; another, feeling only the trunk, responds that no, an elephant is more like a snake than a rope; a third, examining only a leg, insists that an elephant is rather like a tree; the fourth, feeling only the elephant's side, argues confidently that in fact an elephant is quite like a wall.

We may be mystified at how four men can fool themselves about something so finite, concrete, and knowable as an elephant. After all, all they needed to do to learn what an elephant is really like was to be more thorough and more discriminating in their investigation.

It is easier to understand how language professionals can be fooled about language and how learning psychologists and others can be fooled about learning and teaching, since language and learning are not finite, concrete things, fully accessible to empirical investigation. Language is incredibly complex, intangible stuff. Its "substance" is of the brain and the psyche; at the same time language is a social thing shared with a community of users, each differing from the others in linguistic and other ways. Like the stars, the essence of language may be forever beyond our reach. We probe it only indirectly and tentatively with crude instruments—much like astronomers dealing with light emanations from stars. And if language is complex and intangible and inaccessible, so is learning and instruction. We may approach the study of learning and instruction through scientific methods, but it seems doubtful that they will ever be reduced to laws or formulas that will render them predictable.

Indeed I fear that many of us language professionals have been like the blindmen of Hindustan, drawing conclusions based on insufficient evidence, taking the obvious for granted. We have quit investigating, ceased experimenting, limited our questions too narrowly. We have, I fear, become doctrinaire, caught up in an unquestioning faith in one or another system, caught up even in an unquestioning faith that empirical science and its proven methods and procedures are sufficient to provide the ultimate answers about teaching and learning.

Perhaps many of us feel that what we already know and can do, what we have paid a great price to learn, is sufficient for the present. We cannot be forever experimenting. We are too tired, too overworked, too old and set in our perceptions and our ways. And after all, there is not much encouragement in the "system" for trying out new things.

Even if after centuries of searching the sure answer has not been found, the search must go on. I am satisfied that we can theorize, investigate, experiment, and learn more about language and the language-learning process without supposing we will arrive at ultimate truth. But I am not satisfied that we can sit back and accept present theory and practice as good enough for the 1980s and beyond. I believe that our traditional assumptions and our traditional methods don't work well enough. I am forced therefore to look for alternatives—even radical alternatives. And I cannot allow blind bias or traditional preference to get in the way. I may want to be theoretically pure and rigorous, but I'm forced to be pragmatic. That is why I experiment with new alternatives, if they make sense. But I find I cannot always trust myself to discern at first what makes sense. What makes sense may depend on what questions I am asking. I cannot afford to reason that a more thorough examination of the elephant's tail will reveal the nature of the animal.

In his address to the Northeast Language Teachers' Association 15 years ago, Chomsky said:

All we can suggest is that a teaching program be designed in such a way as to give free play to those creative principles that humans bring to the process of language learning. I think we should probably try to create a rich linguistic environment for the intuitive heuristics that the normal human automatically possesses.

Although Chomsky has made no claim to expertise in the field of language instruction, and in fact seemed to view academic language instruction with considerable cynicism, his statement suggested two questions I wrestle with continuously: what consistitutes a "linguistic environment" optimally rich for a variety of language learners, and how can such an environment be created in or out of our classrooms? Asking this question, I have found in each of the approaches presented in this book an attempted answer.

My search continues. I have not found the ultimate answer. I don't believe anyone has. Nor is it likely to be found in the near future, I have concluded. But I feel we are getting closer.

THEORY VERSUS PRACTICE IN LANGUAGE TRAINING

Stephen Krashen

EDITOR'S NOTE ABOUT STEPHEN KRASHEN

Stephen Krashen is a highly esteemed scholar in the field of second language acquisition. His publications are numerous and impressive in their clarity and reach. His distinction between second language "learning" and second language "acquisition" in his widely discussed "Monitor Model" of second language learning provides a key to understanding the rationale that separates the new from the old ways of approaching language instruction.

The paper by Krashen included here (a lecture given at Brigham Young University on October 25, 1979) was chosen because it provides an up-to-date, authoritative, and comprehensive perspective available on essential issues of language acquisition theory and language instruction.

The lecture is an example of Krashen's inimitable style of informal, casual lecturing without notes in which the ideas and the expression are fresh and compelling. This lecture impacted on the audience with powerful and prolonged effect. One senior language professor remarked after the lecture: "If what Krashen just said is correct, we had better rethink our language program." Here is the slightly retouched transcription of the lecture, preserving the vigorous spoken style of the author.

Given two methods of language teaching, method A and method B, suppose we want to know which is the more effective method. I will approach this question of "best method" in several ways. To give the punch line in advance, what I will conclude is that revolutions in language teaching will not be new ways of analyzing grammar, expensive laboratories, exotic methods, or the like, but the proper utilization of what we already have: speakers of the language. I will also suggest that the better methods are also the ones that are the most pleasant. (The converse is of course not necessarily true: just because a method is pleasant does not mean it is effective.)

I will begin by describing three areas that can influence us in our quest for the best method, suggesting how these areas can influence and help each other, and then what each of them has to say about method. The areas are: theory, applied linguistic research, and intuition. My contention is that each of the three ways we will consider arrives at basically the same conclusions.

Area 1: Theory of Second Language Acquisition. This consists of a set of related hypotheses put forth to account for observed phenomena in second language acquisition. Its generalizations are supported by empirical evidence, experiments, research done with theory in mind. They cannot be proved or definitively verified, but they are subject to disconfirmation. They can be disproved by counterexamples, unless some deeper generalization or better theory emerges that can account for the counterexamples. At the moment each of the hypotheses I will give you is without serious counterexample. Moreover they are interrelated; evidence for one will count as evidence for another. Let me add that theory is not intended to be practical or even applied to anything, but in the long run there may be nothing more practical than sound theory.

Area 2: Applied Linguistics Research. Applied linguistics research may or may not be done with theory in mind. It is aimed at problem solving. For example, applied linguistics research may engage in comparing language-teaching methods, or research the question whether bilingual education is beneficial or harmful to the full development of L1.

Area 3: Intuition. This is the world of intuitions that do not belong to any theory but come from experience, reflection, introspection, informal observations. It is ideas that work in the classroom, practice not derived from theory.

The three different areas can and should influence teaching practice, all three at once, and they should influence each other. That is, theoretical researchers should be students of applied research, and vice versa. Knowing theory will give applied linguistics researchers some idea of where to look, even if they are not interested in testing a given theory. Similarly applied linguistics researchers as well as theoretical researchers would benefit by experience in area 3, by teaching a language in the classroom and/or attempting to acquire second languages.

In reality, there is very little interaction among the three domains. And the consequences of this are evident. We have seen theory appealed to in the past all by itself. But theory by itself is inadequate. [This is what happened with audiolingualism. We had basically a theory (behaviorist psychology)—not about language acquisition, but about something else—applied whole-hog to the language classroom.] Transformational-generative grammar was tried, but all it did was make teachers feel bad they did not know Chomsky's theory very well. (Neither behaviorist psychology nor grammar theories are theories of language acquisition. Both are based on analysis of product, not of process.)

As a result of the failure of interaction among the three domains, the third domain, that of intuition and ideas, is currently the primary input into practice. This is due to the failure of linguistic theory and the lack of substantial applied linguistic research. What we see now are texts and materials based pretty much on classroom experience alone.

How are we to know what direction to go in? I think we can safely adopt an approach when all three sources of knowledge support it.

THEORY

First, then, I will present a theory, a set of hypotheses about adult second language acquisition. I will say here again that these hypotheses are supported by empirical evidence and by research done with theory in mind. The hypotheses are interrelated and they are without significant counterexample. I will conclude by looking at pedagogical implications of these hypotheses and show that these implications are consistent in all cases with applied linguistic research and with our intuitions about language acquisition.

Let me now go through the hypotheses. I will try to give you a feeling for what the evidence is for each of them. I will give you nine of them:

1. The acquisition-learning distinction hypothesis
2. The natural order of acquisition hypothesis
3. The monitor hypothesis
4. The input hypothesis
5. The affective hypothesis
6. The aptitude hypothesis
7. The filter hypothesis
8. The L1 hypothesis
9. Individual variation in monitor use

Hypothesis 1: The Acquisition-Learning Distinction

The first is the most central and has been the most useful to me in understanding the literature and understanding second language acquisition. We think that for adults approaching a second language with the intent to "learn" it there are two ways: (1) they can "acquire," which is the way children "get" their first language, subconsciously, through informal, implicit learning. Once you have acquired something you're not always aware you have done it. It just feels natural; it feels as if it has always been there. Quite distinct from acquisition is (2) conscious language learning. This is knowing about language, explicit, formal linguistic knowledge of the language. We generally see this in language classrooms.

To make a long story short, our conclusion after a few years of research is that the first way, acquisition, is central, far more important than we ever thought it was, and that the second one, learning, is in fact peripheral.

Hypothesis 2: The Natural Order of Acquisition Hypothesis

Two years ago this was the central concern of our research. It is still quite interesting, but other things now are more exciting. What this says is that in acquisition people acquire items in a predictable order. Certain things come first, certain things come in the middle, certain things come late. Given the average language acquirer, we can make a pretty safe bet as to what will come first and what will come later. If we do correlation statistics, we get orders that nearly always come out significant. (This applies to acquisition, of course, not necessarily to learning.)

The main research here was begun by Roger Brown in first language acquisition and carried on by Dulay and Burt and others in second language acquisition. And what has been found applies to a fairly wide variety of phenomena. Let me take a moment here to illustrate this.

With English as a first language and English as a second language some morphemes come early. The progressive marker and the plural marker are very early for some reason. (The order of acquisition of some morphemes is not the same in first and second language acquisition; these happen to be the same; so it is a good example.) Others are late. The third person singular on verbs: (*He goes to the store*) is late. Also the possessive marker in English, *John's hat*, is late. In first language acquisition you might see from 6 months to a year separating those two groups of markers. In adult second language acquisition, you might see 10 years. Or you might not see the later ones come at all.

Some children will have plural before *-ing*, some will have *-ing* before plural. The same goes for second language acquisition. But you can talk about a statistical average. Practically no one is going to have plural way at the end. Practically no one is going to have third person singular at the very beginning.

Hypothesis 3: The Monitor Hypothesis   *Rules + grammar*

This hypothesis tells us what the interrelationship is between the conscious and the subconscious processes. What it says is this: when we get our fluency in a second language, when we can use it easily for communication, it comes from acquisition, not from learning. That is very important. Let me illustrate it with a diagram.

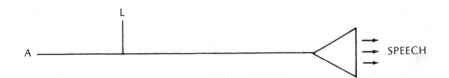

The L stands for conscious learning. The A stands for acquisition. When we talk, the speech is initiated or "driven" by the acquired system. In other words, your fluency in Spanish or French comes from what you have acquired, not from what you have learned. All those grammatical rules you have do not make you fluent. I did not believe this years ago, unfortunately, when I studied French, but the data have borne it out, linguistic research supports it, and what is going on today in teaching backs it up.

Learning, we think, has a limited function in language performance. It can only function as a monitor, as an editor. We apply learning after the utterance has already been generated, or sometimes after we say it, by way of self-correction. So we use learning to make corrections, in fact only to make small corrections. We can use learning only for very simple rules, the ones that are easy to teach, easy to remember. Also we hypothesize that the things we can consciously monitor are not very important for communication. They are the fine tuning, the things that give speech a more finished look. We apply learning to our output, sometimes before we speak, sometimes after we speak. It is only a corrector. It does not make things go. It is an afterthought, a polisher, an autocorrector. Learning then plays a fairly limited function here.

This brings us to the subject of error correction. People ask me whether error correction is good. As a first attempt at trying to answer that question, I give a subhypothesis of the acquisition-learning hypothesis: error correction is aimed at learning. When you make a mistake, if your teacher corrects it, what he is trying to get you to do is change or recall your conscious mental representation of the rule.

An ESL student says: "I goes to school every day," and the teacher says: "No, I go to school every day." The student is supposed to think, Oh yes, that-s is third person, not first person. That is what is supposed to happen. So theoretically, error correction is aimed at learning, not at acquisition.

So conscious learning (L) does have some function, but it turns out to be quite a small function, relatively small with respect to acquisition. As our research proceeds, that function seems to be getting smaller and smaller.

We now hypothesize, and this is a subhypothesis of the monitor hypothesis, that if you want to monitor successfully, many conditions have to be met, and these are necessary conditions.

1. Time. You have to have time if you want to use conscious rules. If you are involved in a conversation, you do not have time to think of the rule for the subjunctive. It's your turn to talk. You'd better come out with a sentence.

Do you know what I do in the languages I'm intermediate at? I plan my next sentence. Do you do this? I note whether the verb is subjunctive or not, whether I've got the subject-verb agreement and whether I've done all the contractions. But while I'm doing all this, my conversational partner is not waiting. He is talking. I'm not listening. I'm busy planning. So I rapidly lose touch with the conversation. That is what happens when you overuse the monitor in conversation. You get in trouble. So you have to have time.

2. Focus on form. You have to be thinking about rules if you are going to monitor. You have to be thinking about correctness. But if what you are talking or writing about is very interesting, even if you have all the time in the world you may not think about conscious rules. You're in a conversation in your second language and you are talking about things that are very dear to your heart. You do not care about subject-verb agreement any more. You do not care if you have the relative clause just right. You're thinking about what you are saying, not how you are saying it.

3. Knowing the rule. You have to know the rule if you want to monitor. Do this. Draw a circle about the size of a quarter. The circle represents all the rules of a language, let's say English. Now draw a proper subset, a circle within that circle, that represents all the rules of English you think the best linguists have actually described, let's say all the rules that Chomsky knows.

Now think of what the best applied linguists know. Represent the rules that these people know by a circle within the other circles.

Now take all the rules that the best teachers have learned. Then all the rules presented in class. Then all the rules that the best students actually learn. Then all the rules that the best students remember. Then all the rules that the best students carry around in their heads as mental baggage that they can apply to their output. That is what the monitor can do. No more.

I have not told you why we think the monitor hypothesis is valid. I'll just tell you this in a nutshell. We find that second language performers, when we put them in positions where they cannot monitor, display the same error patterns that children make. I'm oversimplifying it grossly, but that is the thrust. Under these conditions we see the acquisition laid bare. We see the same natural order in adults as in children.

In a test we have given to ESL students on several occasions where time was not allowed for them to use the monitor, we have found that they have the same order children do when they learn English as a second language: *-ing* and the plural will be up there; third person and possessive will be way down. Take the same subjects and give them a paper and pencil grammar test and you no longer see the same error pattern that children have. It changes. We get an unnatural order. What is happening? They are bringing in the conscious grammar. This is the intrusion of the monitor. In adults that third person singular jumps up. It is an easy rule to learn.

My study of German with its complicated case endings is a good example. We used to bring our monitors to class with us. Remember your German tests? As you are walking up the stairs to class you're thinking: der die das, des, der des, dem, den, dem. . . . And then you sit down and you immediately write those at the side of the page! No one acquires the morphology of German articles in first year German. But that is a major focus of the course, right?

Hypothesis 4: The Input Hypothesis   *Comprehensive input*

This hypothesis is, in my opinion, the most interesting in second language research today. To my mind it is crucially important because it attempts to answer a question of great theoretical and practical importance: How do people acquire language? It states simply that the way we acquire language (not learn it) is through comprehensible input: focus on the message, not the form. The input hypothesis goes for child language acquisition as well as for adult language acquisition. It claims that listening comprehension is of primary importance in language acquisition, and that speaking will emerge with time.

Let me say it a little more formally for you. Acquisition is brought about when you talk to acquirers so that they understand the message, and when the input includes a little language that is somewhat beyond them. So if you want to teach someone to talk, do not teach them to talk, give them comprehensible input! That is what research is saying to us now. Their ability to talk will emerge with time. It is not my idea, but this is screaming out from all I have seen. This is where our research is going.

Let me expand on that a bit. The input hypothesis says that if a student is at a certain stage in language acquisition (i.e., some stage along the natural acquisition order) and he understands something which includes a structure at the next stage, this helps him acquire that structure. Let's say you are at stage 3; the question becomes how do you move to stage 4? More technically, you are at stage i and you want to move to the next stage, $i + 1$. You want to pick up the next structure or group of structures.

But how do you understand something beyond you? The answer is probably context—extralinguistic information. When caretakers talk to very young children, they talk so that the children will understand. Caretaker speech, which we used to call "motherese," is not designed to teach language. It winds up doing so, but that is not what it is meant for. It is designed to communicate. Caretakers speak in a simplified register or code to get children to understand. They talk about the "here and now." They talk about what is going on in the room at the moment in front of the child. They do not say, "what do you think happened upstairs yesterday?" They talk about the "here and now," because that is the sphere of mutual interest. But look what that does to comprehension. Look how it makes it possible for the child to figure out subconsciously what the linguistic system is.

As the child gets older and grows more linguistically mature, the input from the caretakers will get a little more complicated. If you look at the correlation coefficients between complexity of input and linguistic maturity, however, you will find that they are not really high. It is *not* the case that the caretaker exactly tunes the input to the child. The input is not finely tuned; it is roughly tuned. Caretaker speech contains input that covers the $i + 1$.

What I think is going on is this: the child talks, and from that output the caretaker gets a rough idea of how to talk to the child so it will understand. In doing this the caretaker will generally include structures that are next up in the child's built-in syllabus for language acquisition. The caretaker does not *exclusively* provide those structures, however. That makes sense. It would really be unusual if it were any different. Caretakers would have to be incredibly sensitive to language to finely tune input.

Think about this. Think about how in some ways fine tuning is less practical than rough tuning. If we did finely tune, we would have to make a guess as to where the child is in his acquisition syllabus—which we might miss. And if we have more than one child in the room, one child might be getting good input, but the others aren't. In rough tuning a whole day-care class can be covered!

After reading Snow and Ferguson, Roger Brown stated that he finally knew what to say to mothers when they ask how to get their child to acquire language faster. (This is what Piaget calls the American disease: we always want to get there fast. Formal operations by age eight!) Brown's advice is simply this: Talk to your child so that he understands what you are saying. Bear in mind that he can understand more than he can say. Don't worry about consciously trying to do anything. There are more things you will subconsciously build in than you could possibly program for comprehensible input.

So children get simplified codes, speech in a reduced register, where the focus is on communication roughly tuned to their level, and they get comprehension help from extralinguistic context.

The next question is whether adults have the same simple codes available to them. I think they do. And I think that these simple codes are in fact not just helpful for language acquisition; practically, they are probably the way nearly all second language users make progress.

There are three potential simple codes we can talk about: "foreigner talk," "teacher talk," and "interlanguage talk." Foreigner talk is defined here as the adjustments native speakers make in talking to less competent speakers. Foreigner talk in the classroom is "teacher talk." This is the language of explanation in second language classes. When you take roll or explain how many points the midterm is worth or how an exercise works, that is teacher talk. And finally "interlanguage talk" is the speech of second language acquirers to each other.

Available studies tell us that foreigner talk is roughly tuned. So is teacher talk. All studies confirm that teacher talk is simpler than what goes on in the outside world. (Usually you find that more advanced students get somewhat more complicated input language.) All this, foreigner talk, teacher talk, and interlanguage talk is for communication. The goal is the message, not the form. It may be the case that these kinds of simple codes are analogous to caretaker speech in child language acquisition.

In a French IV class I was in last year the teacher walked into the class the first day and said in French: "I couldn't find a parking space, I'm sorry I'm late, this is such a complicated campus, I'm really sorry, this won't happen again." Then she switched into English and announced how many points the midterm was worth and how many points quizzes were worth. What a mistake! Nobody cared where she parked her car. Everybody was thrilled that she was late. But everybody wanted to know how many points were on the midterm. If that had been in French, that would have been real input. That is where she made the mistake.

In another French class I took two summers ago my teacher was trying to explain some phrase to us and none of us had any idea what she was talking about. This was a direct method class where the teacher used absolutely no English in class. She tried to explain with one anecdote that took about three minutes, and came to the last sentence, where she brilliantly used the phrase in a contextualized situation, thinking we could figure it out. Do you understand? she said. None of us did. So then she told another story, a longer one, and in the conclusion she used the phrase again, expectantly. Still no one understood. She thought she had blown ten minutes of class. Not true. We had ten minutes of comprehensible input where we were hanging on every word.

When foreign students speak to each other in ESL situations you get a great cohesive peer group built up, and this language is real communication. The focus is on the message. When I first went to Austria, I was terrified of native speakers. I had had three semesters of college German, but I could not understand a word. When I went to a German class for foreign students I heard teacher talk, which I understood. And when I met my fellow students from other countries in class, German became our lingua franca. And as time went on and I grew in competence I could then relate to native speakers who would talk down to me. (In the beginning even that was too much.) This, I think, was the bridge to real competence in the language.

There are problems with this. Teacher talk will take you only so far, because of the limited discourse domain of the classroom. After a while it won't include much of the $i + 1$. I could go to a French III class the rest of my life, even if they were all in French, and they wouldn't give me the input I need now.

Let's look now at the advantages and disadvantages of fine tuning versus rough tuning. Fine tuning is what is known as the lockstep approach. Today we do the present progressive; tomorrow we are going to do the future. And suddenly all the characters in this book switch tenses. Each structure gets five class periods, and if you haven't gotten it, too bad! Except that the second year you review it all over again. That is what they do in foreign language courses: the first year we go through the whole grammar and nobody has come close to mastering it; so the second year we review it all over again. What we are doing here is guessing at what our students' $i + 1$ is. We are guessing as to what comes next in the natural order. And we are also guessing that we know how much to give them. And that we know how to present it. Unfortunately, we usually guess wrong on all these things.

If we give people natural communication, there's no problem: if you don't get the future tense today, you are going to hear it again. And again. And again. Because natural communicative language is a rich source of grammar. All the structures are there. Especially all the frequent ones, all the ones you're going to need. So there is no guesswork as to where a structure is on the natural order. There is no guesswork as to how much. Comprehensible input at the $i + 1$ level has built-in review, built-in recycling all the time. And it handles individual variation. It is certainly the case in any class that the students are going to be at slightly different stages. So $i + 1$ for Johnny is not the same as $i + 1$ for Betty. With natural input everybody is covered as long as there is comprehension.

What this means is that the good teacher is the one who speaks so that all the students understand, not necessarily the teacher who presents things in a structured syllabus. The best syllabus may simply be the natural communication situation, simply talking to someone so that they understand.

Comprehensible input.

How do good language teachers help someone understand something that contains grammar that is beyond them? Context. Situational context. They use things like pictures, visual aids, algebricks. It is good pedagogy. I did not understand why pictures and realia were important before, but I do now.

This to me then is the single most exciting subhypothesis of the single most exciting hypothesis in second language acquisition theory and practice today: that the language acquirer has a built-in syllabus in his head. So if I can talk to you and make you understand what I'm saying in a second language, I'm doing better than the best-planned syllabus in the world. It is that simple. The best input is the input we naturally give people when we talk to them so they understand.

I have referred to rough tuning in technical papers as the "net" which is cast by communication: when someone talks to you in another language so that you understand most of what is said, the speaker casts a net of structure around your current level; this net will usually include lots of instances of what is next for you, your $i + 1$. This means that when we talk to our students in the target language and they understand what we are saying, we are not only giving a language lesson, we might be giving the best possible language lesson. All we are trying to do in our teaching is aim a net at $i + 1$. It may be the most efficient thing we can do. (You could draw analogies to a fishing-line versus a net if you wanted, or to single-vitamin therapy and a well-balanced diet.)

How do students understand something that is beyond them? The answer, which is something all teachers know, is context, extralinguistic context. In other words, first we understand the message and that "teaches" us grammar, not vice versa. We do not get grammar first and then use grammar to understand. First we understand, and that helps us acquire.

How do we teach production then? We don't. Production will emerge over time. The best way to teach talking is to give people input. Talking will come all by itself.

I think that the input hypothesis is a very conservative theory. It is the most conservative one I can think of. And according to the way we do science, because this is the most parsimonious, this is the theory we should prefer. We should not add to it unless we have to—unless there is counterevidence. The input hypothesis happens to fit with everything we know about the reality of subconscious language acquisition.

Hypothesis 5: The Attitude Hypothesis

What the attitude hypothesis says is that people with certain personalities and certain motivations perform better in second language acquisition, and also that certain situations are more conducive to second language acquisition.

It comes as no surprise to us today to discover that low-anxiety situations are more conducive to language acquisition than high-anxiety situations, and that people with high self-confidence and self-esteem acquire faster than those without these characteristics.

stress

Hypothesis 6: The Aptitude Hypothesis

There's also something called language aptitude, and we'll simply define it as how well you do on the Modern Language Aptitude Test. What is interesting is that the literature has said for many years that both attitude and aptitude are positively correlated with second language achievement, but they are not correlated with each other. You could be good in one, good in both, bad in one, bad in both. They're independent.

My interpretation of the literature is that attitude relates directly to acquisition, for the most part, and that aptitude relates directly to conscious learning. We think that aptitude relates to conscious learning for the following reasons. If you look at an aptitude test, you will see that the tasks are learning tasks. They involve conscious linguistic knowledge, induction of rules. In fact one of the authors of the MLAT, John Carroll, points out explicitly that this is what the test does.

Second, we see high correlations between how well people do on aptitude tests and how well they do in foreign language classes in grammar tests. Aptitude measures how fast you learn; so it probably relates to learning and not acquisition.

Hypothesis 7: The Filter Hypothesis   *Barrier.*

Dulay and Burt suggested that a filter, an affective filter, can keep input from getting in. We used to speak of a mental block, a block against language learning. Filter is another word for mental block. You have to let the input in. There can't be a filter keeping the input out, which is what we think the effect of attitude motivation is. With acquirers who do not have self-confidence, where the situation is tense, where (in Stevick's terms) they are on the defensive, the filter goes up. Even when the input is there, even when it is understood, they do not acquire with full efficiency.

What the filter hypothesis says about pedagogy is that the more we do to lower the filter, i.e., the more our classes are low-anxiety, the better off our students will be.

So input is necessary but not sufficient. What you also need is a low filter. You need comprehensible input, a low filter, a low-anxiety situation where people can focus on the message and not on the form.

The newer methods, the more successful ones, are the ones that encourage a low filter. They provide a relaxed classroom where the student is not on the defensive. So good methods concentrate generally on getting comprehensible input in and/or getting the filter down. When we do both we're going to have real success.

Hypothesis 8: The L1 Hypothesis

The L1 hypothesis says that the first language is used as a substitute utterance initiator in situations where L2 acquired competence is not available.

In picking up a second language, a child may have a prolonged silent period while he or she acquires by input. An adult, on the other hand, often initiates speaking very early, using his L1 as a substitute generator for L2 and repairing the product with his monitor, his conscious knowledge of L2.

In terms of the Monitor Model it looks like this. We substitute first language competence for second language competence because we have not acquired the second language yet. Let's say it is the first day of a German class. The students have been exposed to 15 to 20 vocabulary words and a couple of rules. Now what? It is time to talk German. They expect to talk the first day. They want to go home speaking German. What can they possibly do? The only thing they can do is to use English sentences, plug in German words, and use their monitor to make as many repairs as they can think of.

What we often do in second language classrooms is force people into using this mode. It is in fact a very limited mode. It will get you a short distance into the language quickly, but it won't take you very far. The reason it won't is that you are at the mercy of your monitor. You must have it turned on all the time. And what it does is correct the places where the first language does not fit with the second. You have to watch your sentence the whole way. You are about to make an adjective come before a word and you remember that in this language it is different, so you have to switch it around as you go. That is no way to speak a language, but that is what we do when we make people talk too soon. We get performance without competence.

Note how a method that pushes production early goes against the input hypothesis. If instead of pushing production we give them listening comprehension and interesting reading, the acquisition will come by itself.

What happens to children in second language situations at the beginning? What do they do? Do they talk very much? No they don't. Take an immigrant child six or seven years old, put her in the middle of an American community, and see what happens. Put her in a kindergarten . . . hardly a word for three or four or five months in many cases, except for a few memorized expressions.

What these children are doing during this silent period is building up acquired competence the natural way. When they're ready to talk they'll talk. One mistake adults make (because we push them into it) is to use the first language as the generating device for producing utterances in the second language. In fact we do not have to force people to use this mode. To do so is counterproductive, we now think. If you want to beat the system, to produce in a language right away, you can do it with L1 plus Monitor Mode. You can use conscious learning plus the surface structure of the first language, and you can talk right away. And that is what a lot of adults do. But this mode has limitations.

Hypothesis 9 (Individual Variation in Monitor Use)

This is a very illuminating one for me. This says that we can predict at least one kind of individual variation by how people monitor. Some people monitor a lot, some people monitor not at all, and some people do it just right.

Monitor overusers are people like you and me who do not trust acquisition but who are constantly thinking of rules. Every time you utter a sentence, you are checking it with that grammar up there to make sure you got it right.

What happens to an overuser? Hesitancy. Disability in following and participating in conversations. Pathological language output. And we help bring it about with the way we teach languages. We focus you on form, we focus you on correctness.

There are interesting case histories in the literature on overusers, people who are so concerned with grammar they can hardly get a word out. And I'm sure that at universities you see more overusers than anything else.

Another type that you see in adult education programs in ESL, but only occasionally in a college language class, are underusers. These are people who, for some reason or another, have no conscious grammar to speak of. These are people who rely totally on their acquired competence. What is very interesting about these people is that they often do quite well with the language. They often acquire substantial amounts of English syntax—not all of it, but a lot of it. If you think conscious learning has to come first, please explain those people to me. These are people who don't know a prepositional phrase from their elbow.

I think our pedagogical goal should be to produce optimal users. These are people who monitor, but it does not get in the way of communication, people who refer to conscious rules when they can, but do not get hung up on them. They use them in written language and in prepared speech. But in normal day-to-day conversation they may use them very little.

APPLIED LINGUISTIC RESEARCH

I think I have given you enough theory so we can talk about some of the implications, but let me give you a little evidence now from the area of applied linguistic research. If you look at the history of method comparison, comparing method A with method B, you will find that the results are rather striking in that there are very few differences between methods. The classic experiment is something like this: five classes are audiolingual or inductive method with pattern practice; five classes are grammar-translation or deductive method. It usually turns out that at the end of two years one method proves a little better than the other. The results generally show that with adults the deductive ones are slightly better. It is usually statistically significant, but not by a large margin. On a 60-point test maybe the deductive people will score 38 and the inductive people will score 33. The inductive ones still acquired language, they got something out of the course, and they weren't much worse than the deductive students.

So what is going on?

This question prompted Earl Stevick to ask his "riddle": if method A is based on one theory of the brain (that we are stimulus-response organisms), and method B is based on a totally different theory of the brain (that we are cognitive thinkers) and yet both methods give approximately the same results, how can this be accounted for? How can both theories of the brain coexist? My answer is that neither of these systems is much good; neither is really getting much comprehensible input. And the only reason either of them works is by accident: they happen to provide people with some comprehensible input, despite their best efforts to keep comprehensible language use away from the students. We will do much better, theory predicts, if we have methods that focus on the input.

There is a variety of new methods which we might call "input" methods. These are methods with the following things in common: (a) Focus on communicative input in the classroom—not listening-comprehension for form but listening for meaning—where the student is actively attending to the message. (b) There is very little emphasis on output. Output is allowed to develop on its own. (c) Something is usually done to keep the affect as good as possible.

One example, which has not received the attention it deserves, is Asher's approach called Total Physical Response. In Asher's system the instructor gives commands to the students such as stand up or sit down, and the students follow the commands as the instructor demonstrates the expected action. Not only are students who have been trained through total physical response better, they are apparently a lot better. In one study they did in 32 hours what the standard students did in 150 hours—that is, five times faster. They do about equally well in reading, writing, and speaking, and far better in listening comprehension. That is not just one study; many studies scattered through various journals report this since the mid-sixties.

INTUITION

We move to the third way of determining what kind of method we should have: anecdotal evidence, intuition, observations, what teachers are doing. This kind of evidence is difficult to gather and difficult to evaluate; so I will rely on my own biased observations of what I see going on.

If you go to ESL conferences and foreign language conferences, what you see is interesting. What kinds of papers are teachers presenting to each other? You no longer find people giving presentations of new pattern practice techniques, a new analysis of the relative clause using stratificational grammar, or the like. Instead what they talk about is: using the newspaper in the language class, how to get your students to understand TV, role-playing, socio-drama, etc. I see them focusing on what works, on affect, getting the students to get to know each other, and getting concrete spoken language input, real language use, helping them to survive on the outside so they get more language use.

Another source of evidence we can bring to bear on this is from language learning in other cultures. There is an interesting piece of reporting from Arthur Sorenson, who observed apparently successful language acquisition in adulthood among certain Indian tribes in the Amazon Basin in South America. He reports that about two dozen languages are spoken among these people. No member of any tribal group is allowed to marry anyone who speaks the language of his or her own group. (That would be incestuous.) You can only marry someone who speaks a different language. These people are constantly learning languages from the time they are little kids to the time they are old.

How do they do it? According to Sorenson, the Indians do not practice speaking a language they do not know well yet. Instead they passively learn words and phrases in it and familiarize themselves with its sounds. They may occasionally attempt to speak a new language in an appropriate situation, but if it does not come easily they do not force it. Input lets speaking emerge.

Let me tell you now about a method that takes into account all the theory we have talked about. It is not the only possible manifestation of it, but I think it is a good one, and it is one we're trying out at USC with some success. The method is called the Natural Method. Its inventor is Tracy Terrell of the Spanish Department of the University of California at Irvine, and this approach has been used there in teaching Spanish and German.

The classroom is for acquisition. Learning is done somewhere else. The function of the classroom is to provide students with comprehensible input. No grammar is presented in the classroom ever. The teacher uses the second language exclusively. His goal is to make students understand. The student can respond either in his L1 or in the L2. (This is not new. No single idea in the Natural Approach is new, but put together like this the approach is novel and it works.) If they choose to respond in the second language, the errors are not corrected unless there is a breakdown in communication.

The idea is that talk helps us get more input. That is it: get input. Comprehensible input. This allows speaking to emerge. Homework is grammar: standard, old-fashioned, discrete-point grammar to be used in monitoring. And it is given so that it can be used under appropriate conditions: when you have time, when you have the rule and occasions when the focus is on form.

The results of this approach have been quite encouraging. People understand fairly complex things right away. It handles individual variation. In a college class you may have a lot of homework. In adult education or a class for children you may not have any. In junior high school you may have some. In any case acquisition is central in the classroom and conscious learning is not the goal.

Children do this in picking up a second language. They are quiet for about three or four months before they say a word. They are building competence through listening. The new pedagogical strategy is to allow adult learners to have a silent period. Give them comprehensible input, and natural language will emerge on its own.

SOME PROBLEMS

Now let me list a few problems with all this.

1. Acquisition is slow and learning is fast. Using discrete-point grammar testing, learning appears to produce quick results. If you give a grammar test to

the people who have been having acquisition only, they may not do well. Take a group of linguists and we can conquer the grammatical structure of a language very rapidly. We can do well in a discrete-point grammar test, yet not be able to speak a word of the language. On the other hand acquisition is applicable to any situation. It is slow, however, and needs time to emerge.

2. Learning feels good. Especially to monitor users like myself. Every time I use the subjunctive correctly in French I rekindle the thrill of having conquered it.

3. Who has control of the language teaching profession? People interested in the structure of language. Monitor overusers, many of us crazy about grammar. And we think our students are going to be just as crazy about it as we are.

So that leads us to problems of implementation if all this is correct. The students think that language is grammar. They have expectations of getting grammar. Administrators think that language is grammar.

SOLUTIONS

I can think of two solutions to this. In the long run we will have to educate the administrators and the masses. In the short run we can practice a little useful deception. We can teach vocabulary, situational routines, grammar, whatever we like, and as long as we fill it with acquisition opportunities, as long as we keep providing comprehensible input, we are contributing to natural language acquisition.

2

THE EVOLUTION OF THE COMPREHENSION APPROACH

INTRODUCTION

At the present time in America the dominant model of language instruction gives primary attention during the first year (the initial 90 to 150 hours of class sessions) to developing speaking and listening skills. Whether "cognitive," "behavioral," or "eclectic" in orientation, language teachers using an audiolingual approach (defined here as any approach aimed at teaching both listening and speaking skills simultaneously) devote considerable time to modeling and stimulating the production of L2 sentences and providing feedback on student performance. Variations within the model are many, of course, but the results of training under any of the successful variants of the model are not consistently different enough to have proved one variant better than another. Under none of them do many students achieve comfortable fluency within a year, or even within two or three years.

Given the nature and size of the task of mastering a language, it may be that this is all that can reasonably be expected. The audiolingual model together with all its derivative methods has after all been tested and researched in countless ways. Materials of every description have been developed in scores of languages, advanced technologies have been harnessed to aid in the instruction, and tens of thousands of "man-years" have accumulated in applying the model. And although its theoretical and practical variations are legion, its essential logic is compelling: language is speech and speech is acquired through practice—lots of practice over a long period of time.

That logic is in fact so compelling, so natural, so intuitively satisfying, that as with the propeller airplane before the jet age it seemed inconceivable to most people that there could be any sensible alternative. But progress belongs to the dissatisfied. While recognizing the DC-6 as a great aircraft in its day, someone had to be sufficiently dissatisfied with its performance to question basic principles of its design. Similarly, unless we can accept the performance limitations of the current model of language instruction, we must question its basic principles, its underlying assumptions, its essential logic. That is what the authors in this volume have done. Each one independently has questioned the

33

logic of traditional assumptions about language teaching, and each has contributed to the formulation of an alternative model or models.

The idea of language instruction beginning with a long period of training in comprehension prior to oral production is not a new one. The idea was clearly and forcefully advocated by Palmer at the time of World War I (Palmer, 1917), but for some reason the idea did not "sell." (Listening before speaking was also advocated by Charles Fries, Nelson Brooks, and other early designers of audiolingual approaches, but the idea of an extended period exclusively for comprehension training ahead of production training was apparently given little serious attention before the mid-1960s.)

Some interesting anecdotal evidence now gives credence to the idea. In an interesting account about language learning (in Winitz, 1981), Leonard Newmark tells of a four-month period he spent in Holland during which his four-year-old son, a monolingual English speaker, and a Japanese monolingual child were enrolled in a preschool nursery. Both children began with no knowledge of Dutch and both acquired considerable facility with the language in the course of four months. Newmark observed that the two children said little or nothing in the language for some three weeks, then began to use only a small stock of set expressions such as yes and no, until finally, once they understood the Dutch spoken around them quite well, they began to create whole sentences.

The teacher reported that she had had many foreign children in the nursery in past years, but that she never attempted to teach them Dutch; she simply treated them with the same love and attention accorded the Dutch children. Typically they went through a silent period before attempting to say anything, but speech emerged on its own, and within a year she usually could not detect differences between the speech of the foreign children and that of the native Dutch. (The similar experience of my own six-year-old Carolyn acquiring fluent Chinese during our eleven-month stay in China in 1980–81 convinced me that Newmark's observation is valid.) Newmark argues convincingly that a prespeech phase for adults, following the strategy used by children in a second language acquisition environment, during which a foundation of comprehension skills is built up, could equip adults for a more efficient acquisition of production skills.

Another anecdote is told in an unpublished paper by Albert Storm, former linguist at the Foreign Service Institute. Albert Storm was one of the younger of several children of Norwegian immigrants to the United States. The older children were bilingual, but the younger children, though they understood Norwegian, spoke only English. From the age of about seven until the age of almost thirty Albert was in a monolingual English-speaking environment, completely out of contact with Norwegian. At that time he married a girl of Norwegian birth and they went to Norway to spend three months at the home of her monolingual parents in Oslo. Even though some two dozen years now separated him from contact with Norwegian, in those three months during which he was "bathed continually" in the language in the warm and accepting atmosphere of his bride's home he developed the ability not only to understand Norwegian again, but now also to speak it with some fluency. The language just seemed to emerge by itself, without formal study. One thing he did in Norway to entertain himself while increasing his feeling for Norwegian was to read several "cowboy novels" in Norwegian translation.

With this personal experience with natural language acquisition he was one of the first to emphasize the significance of building strong foundational skills in listening and reading comprehension ahead of production skills. In a stimulating discussion in 1968, he communicated clearly and forcefully this point of view, which now at last is being recognized as an important contribution to language teaching.

More anecdotal evidence comes from the Defense Language Institute (DLI), where need was seen in the 1960s to train military personnel for tasks requiring only receptive skills (such as monitoring Russian radio broadcasts). For this purpose special courses known as aural-comprehension courses (ACC) were developed. These provided several months of full-time, intensive training in listening skills, but none at all in speaking skills.

It came as a surprise when it was found that after several months of study ACC students could be transferred to the standard (audiolingual) course and compete favorably with men who had been trained for an equal time in speaking Russian.

The report by Arthur Sorenson (1967) on language acquisition among the Tukano tribes of South America adds additional evidence of the effectiveness of an approach in which adults pick up several languages in a lifetime, learning to understand each language before attempting to speak it much.

Parallel to Sorenson's report of language acquisition among Indian tribes are reports conveyed by Eugene A. Nida and others about people in certain multilingual areas of Africa where monolingualism is an oddity and even bilingualism is atypical: most people there (and these are members of illiterate societies) reportedly acquire three or more languages, and think nothing of it. Multilingualism is the norm.

From these and many other examples it is clear that in natural language acquisition environments an incredibly complex learning task is successfully and often rapidly accomplished by ordinary people without conscious study, without guidance, instruction, syllabus, or materials of any kind, without behavioral objectives, tests, or grades. Although these situations deserve more careful study, there seems to be a common thread in the way people in these societies acquire so many languages so well: they learn to comprehend the spoken language well before attempting to speak it much.

Another kind of anecdotal evidence is also of interest here. Reports of American soldiers based in rural areas of England tell of how they initially encountered extreme difficulty in understanding the folk speech of the local population. In many cases at first they were unable to understand anything; the speech of the natives sounded like a foreign language. But in time an amazing thing happened for most of them: without the help of a dictionary, without a grammar book of the dialect, without audiotapes, workbook, or tutor, even without ever seeing the dialect written, in fact without any conscious effort, but only with intensive and continual interaction with the natives over a few hours' or days' or weeks' time, most Americans were able to acquire the ability to understand the strange dialect. They went all the way from near zero to near total comprehension without much trouble. It was like going from night to day, from initial discomfort in the presence of alien speech to comfort in the presence of friends.

This rapid transition may not seem remarkable. It is so normal that it is expected. It is a natural phenomenon that requires no special endowment of intelligence or language ability. Both children and adults do it with little fuss or bother. All they need do, it seems, is find friends and spend time talking with them. It all seems quite unremarkable because, after all, Americans and British regard each other as speakers of English. So we count it no great thing that we readily acquire the ability to understand dialectal English; we sense that all forms of English are based on a single underlying form, a common deep structure. We feel that picking up comprehension ability in any dialect of English is like learning a simple code, like acquiring pig Latin, perhaps. No one needs a dictionary or audiotapes or grammar or teacher or even basic literacy to learn pig Latin. And no one lists pig Latin or an acquired dialect of his native language among the languages he or she knows. Ah, but learning a new dialect is not the same as acquiring a foreign language, someone says. But maybe it is. At least it is illuminating and instructive to consider how this rapid and very natural transition from little understanding to almost full understanding of speech takes place. It is illuminative of the process of natural language learning and instructive of how, by simulating it, we might be able to improve language teaching and language learning.

We have already noted that our Americans in England do not consciously study the dialect, in fact have no books, teacher, or course to aid them, yet even without these fully expect to learn to understand the dialect. What is equally notable is that they do not attempt to speak the dialect. They do not intend to learn to speak it. They feel no need to speak it. They only need to learn to understand it. They sense that if they do not struggle against it, if they just give in to it, surrender themselves to it, with patience they will sooner or later acquire understanding. And they do. In talking with the British, Americans do not appreciably alter their own speech, unless it is to use a few new words acquired from the natives, and even those words they will give an American pronunciation. They discover ways of using their native speech in special registers (akin to "foreign talk") which serve as a means to handle their side of communication. And the natives reciprocally adjust their speech register at first and use extralinguistic context helpfully in talking to the Americans to facilitate understanding.

Very soon the Americans discover that they can use speech as a tool to get lots of focused, comprehensible input from the natives and to get clarification of portions they are interested in but not satisfied that they understand. Meaning is what they are after, and they apply their natural learning strategies, their natural faculties of analogizing, inferencing, and hypothesizing, to the task of figuring out the meaning of the speech of the natives.

Reflection on the aims, modes, strategies, and results of learning a second language or dialect in these natural acquisition environments leads to the question of what is relevant here for language instruction. In Part 2 key pieces are reprinted from the writings of five authors who grasped the significance of this question. The answer of each of them is now seen as a seminal contribution to the development of a comprehension model of language learning.

1. Harold E. Palmer. Although most language teachers may not have heard of him, without doubt Harold E. Palmer ranks at or near the top of the list of people whose ideas have most influenced language teaching in the twentieth century. His monumental book, *The Scientific Study and Teaching of Languages*, contains the essentials of what came to be known in America forty years later as the audiolingual method. But the two ideas that may bring him greater appreciation in the 1980s are : (a) introducing into beginning language classes massive amounts of spoken and written material that exploits textual and extralinguistic redundancies, and (b) giving initial priority to listening over oral production. In this latter view Palmer anticipated Asher and Postovsky by half a century.

2. Eugene A. Nida. It is quite possible that Eugene Nida has been in intimate contact with and has seriously studied more languages than anyone who has ever lived. As secretary of the American Bible Society, he has worked for over thirty years with Bible translations in many languages. His publications on translation, semantics, linguistics, applied anthropology, language learning, and Bible exegesis are prodigious. His book, *Learning a Foreign Language*, first published in 1954 and reprinted many times since then, contains a view of language acquisition that was years ahead of its time. Chapter Three of that book is reprinted here.

3. James J. Asher. In the mid-1960s James J. Asher, an American experimental psychologist, proposed a radical alternative for language training.* He argued persuasively (though few saw the point at that time) for taking as the exclusive aim of the first weeks or even months of language course the building of listening-comprehension skills. He reported experiments using what he called Total Physical Response (TPR) training, an approach based on giving commands calling for overt, physical response chains that can be monitored visually by the teacher. Asher showed that auditory training of this kind can lead readily to parallel training in responding to written commands, so that both the receptive skills, listening and reading, can be taught exclusively and extensively

---

*Coincidentally, at Indiana University, H. Robert Cook (1965) wrote a dissertation on the effectiveness of prespeech training in language teaching. His work spurred experimentation which led to the development of course materials based on this model. (See also Carleton T. Hodge, 1968, 1973.)

before the productive skills of speaking and writing are engaged. Clearly Asher's proposals and experiments were revolutionary, but they were ahead of their time. Now at least they are being understood and seen by increasing numbers of linguists and language teachers as truly significant contributions.

4. Valerian A. Postovsky. In the 1960s, Valerian A. Postovsky, one of the ACC (Audio Comprehension Course) developers at the Defense Language Institute at Monterey, became interested in the discovery that with students in the ACC Russian program comprehension skills significantly facilitated their acquisition of speaking skill. He grasped the fact that comprehension implies competence, and that the ability to understand spoken and written language constitutes a very important and valuable aspect of language competence in itself and, more than that, may constitute an ideal latency from which speech production can emerge on its own.

His approach, as implied in its name, Delayed Oral Practice, was designed to foster the rapid acquisition of all the linguistic systems except speech production. He saw speech as being dependent on the same grammar as comprehension, but requiring in addition the retrieval of grammatical forms and therefore imposing a much heavier load on the memory system as well as engaging very complex psychomotor skills.

His 1970 dissertation at UC/Berkeley, entitled *The Effects of Delay in Oral Practice at the Beginning of Second Language Teaching,* and his articles in language journals describe his comprehension approach and argue powerfully for consideration of this revolutionary model of language instruction.

His untimely death in 1977 cut short a notable career, but his name will always be associated with the concept of comprehension training. The direct heirs of his work, now extending and refining the model, are Harris Winitz and James Reeds at the University of Missouri at Kansas City and James Nord at Michigan State University. Winitz and Reeds state the input hypothesis in its strong form: that oral production cannot be taught directly, i.e., that language training "techniques which focus on speech output (imitation, prompting, and expansion) are valueless as training devices." They go on to explain the function of speech in the language acquisition process:

Speech is used to solve or to demonstrate the comprehension of increasingly difficult syntactic problems. What does this position have to say for language training programs? The answer is simple. Teach comprehension only, but teach it as a problem-solving task. . . . Do not discourage speech; let speech enter the problem-solving task.

5. Robbins Burling. At the University of Michigan during the past several years, Robbins Burling has experimented with teaching French through reading. That is nothing new, of course, but Burling has approached the task with extraordinary perspicacity and creativity. In contrast to traditional language instruction practices in which small increments of carefully sequenced data are given and the learner is held accountable for mastery of it all, Burling hypothesized that for optimally efficient language acquisition it is necessary to provide learners with language material that is from the first massive, engaging,

and comprehensible. Of course, there is no problem achieving one or even two of these; the trick is in putting the three together, providing input that is truly massive, engaging, and comprehensible.

This is what Burling has attempted to achieve in his French reading course. He has taken a large, popular French novel and provided means that enable a beginning student to read it rapidly and with a minimum of bother, facility in reading French emerging as a by-product of a pleasurable experience in reading a good novel. French is approached as if it were a progressively changing dialect of English, one which starts out very close to normal English and then gradually shades into French. At any point along the continuum of change the students are helped to infer meaning by what they have already learned. The situation of the students is similar to that of the Americans in contact with the folk speech of rural England and interested primarily in understanding it, not analyzing it. Burling's French reading materials thus constitute an innovative and interesting attempt to simulate elements of a rich environment of natural language acquisition.

THE PRESPEECH PHASE
IN LANGUAGE LEARNING*

Harold E. Palmer

During the course of the last twenty or thirty years many systems of language teaching have been designed, the object of which is to cause the language to be assimilated by processes similar to those by which each of us has learned his mother tongue. In setting forth the manifest advantages of this over the purely artificial type of method, it has been rightly observed that the degree of success attained by adults in their efforts to acquire a foreign language is always in direct ratio to the degree in which they observe the natural laws of language study. It has been pointed out repeatedly that most persons taking up their residence abroad acquire with remarkable rapidity and fidelity the speech of those by whom they are surrounded, *provided that they observe certain conditions.* These conditions are generally assumed to consist of the exercising of their powers of observation and imitation, unaided by such artificial processes as translation, etymological analysis and synthesis, or the mental conversion of written into spoken forms.

In support of this theory it has been pointed out that the illiterate often seem to succeed where the educated fail; that, other things being equal, the scholar will be handicapped by his developed intellect and the peasant will profit by his ignorance and unformed mental capacities.

A family of French people takes up its residence in England. A year later the younger children may be speaking to each other in idiomatic and fluent English; the older children also speak, but less in conformity with English habits of thought and articulation; the parents, if they speak at all, produce the usual French variety of broken English.

In view of the vast amount of cumulative evidence tending to prove this thesis, the compilers of methods appear to be justified in their efforts to organize programs of study in accordance with it. One factor, however, seems to have been overlooked, a factor which in the opinion of the writer is the most essential of all, and the neglect of which constitutes an omission of the most serious kind.

---

*From *The Scientific Study and Teaching of Languages (1917).*

It is the undoubted fact that the *active* use of speech under natural conditions is invariably preceded by a period during which a certain proficiency is attained in its *passive* aspect. The faculty of recognizing and of understanding the units of speech is probably always developed by the child long before he ever reproduces them in order to make himself understood.

From a most illuminating work by M. Jules Ronjat, entitled *Le Développement du Langage Observé chez un Enfant Bilingue* (published by Champion, Paris, 1913), we may note the following passage:

Preverbal children show evidence of a kind of storing up and incubation of language. They assimilate vocabulary and pronunciation so that from the very first day they can speak they have a vocabulary of twenty, thirty or forty words. A French girl had an Italian nanny who spoke French with a strong Italian accent. One month after the departure of the nanny, the child began to speak French with the vocabulary of her parents and with the accent of her nanny, the person with whom she had closest contact during the first year of her life. . . . A German girl spent the first eighteen months of her life in Silesia and there acquired a patently Silesian vocabulary. She subsequently went to Berlin, where she acquired the standard vocabulary, at about age three. Then, at about the age of five her speech occasionally reverted to Silesian, which she hadn't had occasion to hear for three and a half years; the only explanation for this behavior is the persistence of the latent impressions stored during the first three years of her life when for all intents and purposes she could not speak.

During this *incubation period* it would seem that a vast number of units are "cognized" in all their aspects: sounds, combinations and successions of sounds, metamorphism, and the semantic values represented by all of these. We suggest that success in the production on a wholesale scale of linguistic matter (either in its spoken or in its written form) can be attained only as the result of the previous inculcation of such matter by way of passive impressions received repeatedly over a period the length of which has been adequate to ensure its gradual and effective assimilation.

Passive work is not necessarily subconscious work, any more than active work is necessarily conscious. Passive work means listening and reading; active work is speaking and writing. We may listen and read consciously and subconsciously; we may speak and write consciously and subconsciously. In the case of our mother tongue the probability is that there is a vast preponderance of subconscious work, both active and passive; when the average person studies a foreign language, the contrary is usually the case.

We would suggest that one of the essential principles of all methods designed on the "natural" basis should be never to encourage or expect the active production of any linguistic material until the pupil has had many opportunities of cognizing it passively. If this principle is valid, most of the teaching of the present day violates a natural law!

LEARNING BY LISTENING

Eugene A. Nida

Perhaps there is no place in the world where so many people speak more than one language than in Africa. Tens of thousands of Africans speak a trade language or a colonial language as well as their own tribal tongue. Thousands more speak two or more tribal tongues. In learning various African languages, these people have never enjoyed the presumed benefits of printed grammars, a study of phonetics, or instruction in how to learn other languages, but they master diverse tongues with apparent ease. I have personally inquired of a number of African polyglots just how they learned the languages of neighboring tribes. Almost without exception the story is the same: they want to live in a neighboring village, or on some plantation, or in the mines, where they were working with people who spoke another language. But instead of trying hard to learn the language, they seemed to just take it for granted that after listening to the language long enough, they would find that they could "hear" it. "We just live there and listen, and before we know it, we can hear what they say. Then we can talk," one African explained. This does not mean that he expected to be able to understand (i.e., "hear") everything in the language before he said anything, but his whole attitude was one of passive absorption, confident that his ears and brain would take in the language and that, without particular worry or concern on his part, he would be able to understand and to speak sooner than even he imagined.

This African way of language learning is ultimately the best way to acquire a foreign tongue, for it is the natural way—the way children learn. Children do not worry about genders, declensions, conjugations, and subjunctives. They just listen, repeat, and put together words which they have heard (often with mistakes, but these are corrected by later hearing). Listening is the basis of this learning process, repeating is the inevitable response to listening, and putting words together in different combinations is the natural outgrowth of anyone's desire to communicate his desires and observations. The initial step in this process of language learning we can call "passive listening."

42

PASSIVE LISTENING

The seemingly effortless way in which children and many indigenous people learn foreign language can be designated as "passive listening," though in a sense it would be quite wrong to imagine that our brains are idle—by no means. What we mean by passive listening is the absorption of a language without the conscious effort which usually characterizes our attempts at boning, cramming, memorizing, drilling, and mastering a language. Our brains are amazingly active in registering noises, smells, and sights, even when we seem to have directed our attention to something else or are even sleeping.

The capacity for the brain to assimilate, sort, and store information is strikingly illustrated by what happened to a missionary's child in Thailand. This small girl did not leave Thailand until she was about one year of age. Up to that time she had not spoken any Thai or English, though she had heard Thai constantly from her nursemaid and from the other children. She had heard some English from her parents, but not much. About two months after returning to the States, she began to speak, but the language she used was Thai, not English. Naturally the vocabulary was restricted, as is the vocabulary of any small child, but the sounds (including the complicated tones) and the order of the words were a baby's close approximation to correct Thai usage and were far better than the usage of many foreign adults. Precisely how the brain can assimilate and store up such information we do not know, but we are sufficiently aware of the end results of such unbelievable capacities of our brains that we need to be more alert to the possibilities of better use of these latent abilities.

The fact that our brains work for us even when we are not conscious of such activity is recognized by anyone who has gone to live in a foreign community. At first all the people seem to look alike. For example, we can't seem to tell one Korean from another, and we are quite unable to distinguish Koreans from Chinese or Japanese, even though we soon discover that the Koreans themselves can almost always tell the national origin of any Oriental-looking person. After a few weeks or months we begin to discover that all Koreans do not look alike and that we ourselves can distinguish Koreans from other Orientals. What has happened to us? Must we study a book on physical anthropology or anthropometry in order to make such judgments? Of course not! What has happened is that our brains have been registering thousands of impressions and without our realizing it the brain has sorted, classified, and stored such impressions. We could not define precisely what are the distinguishing characteristics of different Oriental types, but we can make the distinction, nevertheless.

What our eyes help our brains do with visual images, our ears help our brains do with acoustic impressions. When we first arrive in any place where a foreign language is being spoken, we are usually impressed by the speed with which everyone seems to talk. But if we stay around a while, we begin to think that people are speaking quite a bit slower, even though we may not understand a word of what they say. Of course, people are not speaking any slower; it is just that our brains have been assimilating those sounds—even when we were not conscious of the process—and have begun the process of identifying and sorting them. Since the sounds are more familiar and hence more quickly recognized (even though imperfectly), the rate of speech seems to be slower.

Even a person who makes a "flying trip around Europe," spending no more than a few days in each capital (in order to "do the place"), discovers that he has learned a great deal about the language of which he has been totally ignorant. If before going on this trip he ever listened to short-wave radio, he probably could not tell French from Italian, German from Dutch, or Spanish from Greek. But after the trip something happened. He finds that he can recognize certain language. He usually does not know quite how, but he is able to distinguish between them, although he did not pay the slightest attention to the foreign languages while dashing about Europe with English-speaking guides. His brain was working all the time, taking in sounds and registering their peculiarities, while he went merrily on, convinced that languages "were not for him."

Since even without conscious effort our brains can do a great deal for us in mastering a foreign language, we might as well take full advantage of this hidden resource. We should give our brains every opportunity to work at full efficiency. To do this we need to employ certain helpful techniques:

1. *Provide the brain with plenty to listen to.* The big advantage which Africans have in learning another indigenous tongue is that African community life is characteristically very talkative. In the average African village there are few hours in the day or night when one cannot hear from any point in the village at least five different conversations. If we cannot duplicate the ideal conditions of an African village, we can nevertheless provide by means of radio programs, recordings, and listening to lectures sufficient raw material for the brain's use in assimilating, sorting, and storing of important data on the language.

2. *Be relaxed.* Anxieties, even about learning the language, seem to short-circuit the efforts of our brains to do their work.

3. *Do not erect barriers to sounds.* People who live near a noisy railroad tend to protect themselves by a mentally erected "sound screen," so that they rarely hear the train when it passes. Some people tend to erect sound barriers to foreign languages, and as a result they do not assimilate the language in such a way that it ever seems to be of much help to them on a conscious level. In some instances, however, these people, when they are drunk or mentally deranged, have been known to use the foreign language with considerable fluency.

4. *Give the brain enough time.* By the end of a week most people think they should be starting to speak a foreign language. Of course, they can no doubt use a few expressions, but for the full benefits of "passive listening" one must let the brain go about its work for several months.

5. *Let the brain work while you are doing something else.* It is a very good technique to put on a recording in a language while one is shaving, eating, reading the evening newspaper, or even playing with the children. One does not have to pay attention all the time. All this may seem quite ridiculous, if one does not take into consideration that this is precisely the manner in which many

people become familiar with pieces of music. Even without paying attention to the music, one may become thoroughly acquainted with even the most complicated musical numbers by the process of passive listening. Many of us have had the experience of learning a song (often one we didn't even care to know) simply by hearing it over and over again on some neighbor's radio or from the drugstore jukebox. What applies to this inadvertent learning of music is also applicable to learning a foreign language.

It is even possible to learn a great deal while one is asleep. Believe it or not, one can assimilate an incredible amount of information in one's sleep. Perhaps some professors who have worried about students sleeping in their classes can have some consolation, for now they are assured by psychologists that even when students are sleeping they are learning—particularly if the information is repeated frequently (and fortunately for the sleep listeners most lectures are highly repetitious). Some people have taken advantage of this "learning while sleeping" to have recordings played during their sleep. Others have discovered that sleeping in the noisy hubbub of conversation has certain compensating advantages as far as language learning is concerned.

Regardless, however, of whether we do our passive listening while awake or asleep, we should make certain that we fully exploit the often unrecognized capacities of our brains. Even if we are convinced that our brains are not good for much, they are good for passive listening. They have already demonstrated this fact, for it was largely by this process that we learned our first language. Why should we not use this procedure more in learning another?

SELECTIVE LISTENING

As effective as passive listening is and can be, it is usually regarded as sufficient. Our characteristic activism would not let us be content to employ such a passive technique even if we had ideal conditions and were convinced that it would work. In addition, however, to the psychological problems posed by our activism, there are two valid reasons why we need to supplement passive listening with selective listening: (1) we rarely have an opportunity to participate completely in a foreign culture, and hence our dual lives greatly impair our capacity to absorb, and (2) our present speech habits tend to make us reinterpret the acoustic stimuli which our ears relay to our brains, and accordingly we get a skewed impression of the foreign tongue.

Selective listening, however, should not supplant passive listening, but should be supplemental to it. We should attempt to employ both techniques and by this means compensate for our cultural isolation from the foreign language society and our tendency to reinterpret all that we hear in terms of the language we already know.

When we first try to listen to a language, we are usually completely bewildered, for it sounds like a chaotic jumble. We cannot make head or tails out of it. Even if we are given a relatively short phrase and asked to pay strict attention to it, we usually get hopelessly lost in the multiplicity of unfamiliar sounds. We no sooner think that we have grasped one part of a phrase than we realize that we have blanked out as far as the succeeding syllables are concerned. At this point most students despair of trying to learn by an oral approach. They would rather retreat to an old-fashioned textbook—regardless of how inefficient it may be—for there the syllables and words remain in the same spot on the page. They can be looked at time and time again. Never do they disappear into thin air as does the fleeting pronunciation of a native speaker. Our inability to seize with our ears the whole phrase or sentence tends to discourage us. What we need to realize is that we should not be expected to grasp the entire acoustic phrase. It comes too fast (at an average rate in most language of between three and five syllables a second). The only possible way in which we can become familiar with the acoustic form of language is to listen selectively first to one feature and then to another. In the same way as we examine written words from many standpoints—sometimes in terms of the shapes of letters, their order, ways in which they combine into syllables—so also we need to examine the acoustic forms of language from many perspectives by listening first to one and then to another feature. Only in this way can we hope to hear the language properly.

If, however, we are to listen intelligently to the various features of language, we need to follow an order which will help us to find our way in the maze of seemingly unordered elements. Some languages require certain adaptations to the following suggested order of procedures, but for the most part these successive features of languages should be listened to selectively in the order given here:

Tone of the Voice. The tone of the voice, whether it goes up or down or remains level, is apparently one of the first things which a child notices about a new language, but it is usually the last thing an adult learns. A child almost inevitably uses the right intonation, even when babbling with badly distorted consonants and vowels. But an adult seems to be almost incapable of learning the intonation of a foreign language. In fact, he may speak a foreign tongue with absolutely correct grammatical forms, excellent choice of words, and almost impeccable pronunciation of consonants and vowels, but his faulty intonation usually betrays him as a stranger. It is highly possible that the completely unconscious manner in which he assimilated the intonation of his mother tongue makes him unaware of basic differences between languages. But be this as it may, selective listening to the intonation is exactly where everyone should start in listening to a foreign language.

Most people assume that they cannot listen to the tone of a language until they understand the words, but then it is too late. In order to hear the changes in the tone, we usually need to be able to blank out all the rest and hear only the tone. That is why listening to the tonal modifications should begin the very first day. One convenient device for noting tone is to draw the contours on a pad of paper. When the voice goes up, one can draw the line going up; if the voice goes down, the line goes down. If the voice gradually falls off in tone, the line can slope gradually, but if it pitches off precipitously, the line should reflect this abrupt drop.

Some people have assumed that they could not do much about the differences of pitch used in speaking unless they had mastered the so-called tones of the language, e.g., as in Chinese, Thai, Vietnamese, Burmese, Zulu, Yoruba, or Navaho. But all this knowledge is not necessary before beginning to listen selectively for the contrasts in pitch. Of course, in a language such as English, German, Spanish, Swahili, Hindi, or Tagalog the variations in pitch are usually spread out over several syllables, while in the so-called tonal languages there are many abrupt shifts from one syllable to another and numerous glides on single vowels, even very short ones.

As a person first listens to a foreign language, he usually gets the impression that there is absolutely no limit to the variations in the pitch of the voice on various words, phrases, and sentences. But gradually, the more one listens to a language the more one becomes aware that there are some very strict limits to what the speakers do with their voice. For example, after comparing a number of contours drawn on a scratch pad, one may realize that there are only four or five principal patterns, with a number of relatively rare exceptions. In listening to some of the languages of West Africa one is impressed with how the speaker's voice jumps up and scoots down rapidly between three different levels. However, at the beginning of a sentence these modifications are in a relatively higher range than they are toward the end of the sentence. It is almost like a fast-moving roller coaster, shooting up and down, but constantly going toward a lower level.

As we shall see from later chapters, the detailed analysis of precisely what happens to the voice pitch in different languages may be very complex, and one may never succeed in fully analyzing it. But that is not actually necessary for one to learn to reproduce the total differences. If by listening sufficiently one becomes aware—consciously or unconsciously—of the meaningful distinctions, and is able to reproduce them, that is all that is required of the practical user of a language. Very few people understand the highly complex structure of English intonation, but all of us as native speakers and all others who have learned English so well as to imitate our intonation can use this intricate system even though we are incapable of analyzing it or even explaining it to others.

Strange Sounds. As one is listening selectively to the tonal variations in a language (something which one should concentrate on for at least a week or more), certain strange sounds, either consonants or vowels, inevitably attract one's attention. Accordingly, the next features in the language to which we should listen selectively should be these unusual sounds. If a sound is quite frequent, it is a good policy to concentrate on only that one sound. Everything else should be erased from one's mind, while attention is concentrated on hearing each occurrence. Within a very short time it will be noticed that this sound is not always the same. There are slight differences, but enough of the basic characteristics are present so that one can recognize what seems to be really the same distinctive sound.

The identical process can then be followed in listening to other sounds which are strikingly different from those of English.

As anyone listens carefully to the sounds of a language, almost without exception he finds that he is moving his tongue, lips, and jaw in imitation of the sound in question. All this happens without any conscious effort to move the various parts of the speech mechanism. When one first hears a sound, there is often some confusion as to just how to reproduce it, but after listening carefully to such a sound for a number of times, it seems as though the various speech organs almost automatically move in the right directions and at the right time in order to reproduce the sound. We do not have to study phonetics to be able to make a "stab" at imitating a sound. In fact, we don't even know what parts of our mouths have moved. All of this highly organized activity is taken care of by our brains, which we may say are already "wired" for just such corresponding signals between acoustic impressions and the motor mechanisms involved in reproducing the sounds.

This almost automatic relationship between acoustic impression and the mechanism for reproduction explains how children learn language in the first place and how adults may learn foreign languages without knowing a thing about the intricate mechanisms and fine adjustments in position and timing which are necessary for the production of speech sounds. These built-in neural connections between hearing and speaking are one of the principal reasons why we insist upon the priority of listening in the process of language learning. Reading, on the other hand, presents quite a different situation. There is absolutely no relationship between the graphic forms of symbols used to represent a sound and the way in which it is reproduced in speech. No amount of mere looking at the Hindi or Arabic alphabet could tell one how to pronounce the sounds which are represented by the different symbols. We have to hear the sounds or have them described in terms of other sounds with which we are familiar. There is no built-in "wiring" between the graphic impression signaled to our brains by the eyes and the motor mechanisms which have to be employed in reproducing the sound. Accordingly, we may be able to read a language well and not be able to say a thing, while anyone who can understand anything which he hears in a language can always say something, and with some practice can become quite a fluent speaker. All this means that listening and speaking are very closely related processes, but reading is far removed from the central function of language—hearing and speaking.

Similar Sounds. After listening selectively to strange sounds, we should begin to direct our attention to sets of similar sounds. We do not refer here to the similarity of such sounds to English, but to the similarities between the sounds in the foreign language. For example, one may hear what seem to be several sounds, some like English *p*, others like *b*, and still others which appear to be halfway between English *p* and *b*. Careful attention to this grouping of sounds will make it possible to isolate first the *p* like English (one which usually has a puff of air after—compare *pea* with *bee*) and the *b*. The intermediate sound, which sometimes seems to be like *p* and at other times like *b*, may very well turn out to be a *p* without any puff of air. It does not matter, however, whether we can make a proper scientific description of each sound. What we are more concerned with is that we can detect these sounds accurately each time they occur. If we hear them correctly, we are likely to be able to reproduce them correctly. If it should happen that we have trouble because of our own English language habits, we can correct our faults by attention to some of the helps provided by the study of phonetics. But the practical purpose of phonetic study is primarily to help us hear and reproduce sounds correctly, that is, in terms of the similar and different sounds in the language in question. Whether they happen to be similar or different from those in other languages which we have studied is usually of very minor concern to us. What counts is how they work in the language which we are learning.

As we begin to distinguish between similar sounds, we soon discover that such similarities go in bunches. If, for instance, we find in a language an intermediate sound between *p* and *b*, we will probably also find a corresponding intermediate sound between *t* and *d*, and another between *k* and *g*. That is to say, the similarities and differences in languages are systematic. Languages are nothing more than very complex signaling systems, and they must be systems or we could never remember them.

As we continue listening for various sets of similar sounds—both consonants and vowels—we soon realize that instead of the language having what seemed to be an inexhaustible supply of sounds, there is actually a quite limited number of really distinctive sounds—in some languages only about a dozen and in others as many as sixty—but regardless of their number they are far less than what we at first imagined.

It may seem as though up to this time we are advocating that a person listen for sounds without paying the slightest attention to words and their meanings. In a sense this is what we would recommend, for this is almost precisely what a child does. Before being able to say anything in a language, a child usually learns to babble in a language, using most of the consonants and vowels with proper rising and falling of the pitch of the voice. Many small children acquire an almost complete inventory of the sounds of a language before beginning to talk. But no adult would wait so long. Furthermore, it is not necessary to do so. In the very process of listening for similar sounds we inevitably come across words which are almost identical, except for one difference in a similar sound. Sets of words such as *peak:beak, tick:dick,* and *kill:gill* we call minimal pairs, for there is just one significant difference in sound between them. As we learn to distinguish between the significant and meaningless differences between similar sounds, we inevitably refer back to such sets of minimal pairs. By listening to them again and again, we can sort out the distinguishing features. This does not mean that we can necessarily describe these differences to others, but if we hear these contrasts in enough places, e.g., *cab* vs. *cap, clabber* vs. *clapper, rumple* vs. *rumble,* etc., our brains sort out the differences in such a way that any new word which we hear having a *p-* or *b-*like sound is immediately classified as a *p* or a *b,* depending upon the "models" made familiar to us by these sets of minimal pairs. But even when we cannot find sets of minimal pairs, our brains are incredibly adept in classifying sounds if we give them only half a chance by listening selectively to sets of similiar sounds.

Words and Phrases. As we have already implied in our discussion of selective listening to similar sounds, anyone who is listening carefully to a foreign language will soon pick out recurring combinations of sounds. If one hears over and over again an identical combination of two or three syllables, this is very likely to be a word or stem. If one hears recurring combinations consisting of five or six syllables, these are likely to be phrases. But whether such recurring combinations are words or phrases does not really concern the language learner too much. Children certainly do not know the differences between words and phrases, and neither do we need to distinguish such units when we are beginning to speak. In fact, we are often better off if we do not know such grammatical details, for we are more likely to learn and use the combination as a unit—just as it is used in the language—rather than breaking it up by artificial pauses corresponding to what are sometimes arbitrary spaces written between so-called words.

One of the most important phases of listening selectively to words, phrases, or sentences is to try to figure out from the context what they mean. This is the way children learn, and we would do well to imitate them. The value of this procedure is that a combination of sounds which one can identify and to which one can assign meaning on the basis of the context has been learned in a manner ideally fitted for instant recall whenever a corresponding context requires. We sometimes think we cannot learn a language without a dictionary, but adults in aboriginal societies never heard of a dictionary. They never write down words and ask people what they mean. But they learn languages by recognizing words in context. From this they determine their meaning. A dictionary, however, can be of great value to a language learner, for, in a sense, a dictionary is a record of concentrated language experience. But a person must not "misuse" a dictionary, by thinking that it is complete in its description of the meanings of a word or that it is always right. The dictionary is only a set of helpful clues for one to follow in tracking down the full significance of a term, that is, what it signals in all the contexts in which it can be employed.

Selective listening to words usually begins by noting any recurring combination of sounds which seems to "stand out" in the flow of speech. If a person has the advantage of listening to a recording over and over again, he can perhaps spot two or three such expressions the first time through. With the help of a translation or a teacher, he can find out what these combinations mean. The next time he listens to the recording, he can spot a few more combinations, and some of these he can no doubt figure out from the context. Gradually, as he goes over and over the same recording, the number of recognized words and phrases increases and the number of unknown ones correspondingly diminishes.

At first one listens selectively to recurring sequences of which the meaning is quite unknown. Once these are identified, one needs to listen for such combinations in other recordings or in daily converation. As these words become thoroughly familiar, one continues to add other words that are newly learned, pushing out further and further the limits of one's receptive control of the language.

Grammatical Forms. In most languages what we call words do not always appear in the same forms. Sometimes an addition is tacked onto the word, e.g., *walked* vs. *walk* and *roses* vs. *rose.* In other instances something within the word itself is modified, e.g., *ran* vs. *run* and *feet* vs. *foot.* In still other cases, we find that we have to use utterly different words, e.g., *better* (not **gooder*) and *went* (not **go-ed*). But whatever the changes (the types are discussed in Chapter 6), we need to direct our attention to them by listening selectively to sets of modifications.

If we find, as in most of the so-called Bantu languages, that all the nouns, pronouns, adjectives, and verbs show by prefixes certain distinctions between singular and plural, then we need to listen selectively to these contrasts, while trying at the same time to erase everything else from our minds. The concords in Bantu languages are exceedingly important to anyone who wants to learn such a language. He will of course want to drill extensively on them, but as valuable as drilling is, it cannot substitute for nor should it precede selective listening. By the process of listening attentively to just this one type of contrast, we build up in our minds a mechanism by which the brain can begin to classify the respective parts of the complicated grammatical system.

Even without listening selectively our brains do perform part of this function. In many instances we may not be able to remember exactly what form should be used, but we have a "feeling" that one form is correct and another incorrect. Though we may confess that we are not certain, we nevertheless reflect part of the pattern formulated by our brains by saying that one form "sounds right" and another "sounds wrong."

As we learn more and more about the grammatical structure of a language, we should listen selectively to each type of grammatical feature, e.g., genders, tenses, moods, voice, cross reference of pronouns, order of words, phrases, and clauses, and dependence of clauses. Any and all features of grammar, especially those which may give the learner any special difficulty, should be listened to selectively.

One of the important advantages of selective listening to grammatical structures is that the patterns of structure absorbed by this process tend to make "ruts in our brains." Even after we have ceased to listen especially for such forms or arrangements of words, our brains continue the process of automatically classifying all that we hear. Accordingly, we can keep right on improving our knowledge of and facility in the language long after we have stopped studying grammar in a formal way.

In our description of selective listening we no doubt have given the impression that one should do nothing else than listen selectively to everything that is said. Of course, this is quite impossible, for by the time we are listening for grammar—a process which should occupy the better part of a year or more—we also need to be using a language in practical communication. We obviously cannot erase from our minds all that someone else may be saying to us in order to concentrate on the grammatical forms. Accordingly, we must often restrict our concentrated selective listening to those situations in which we need not reply or are not under special obligation to remember the content, e.g., political speeches, radio talks, recordings, and sermons. It will be amazing, however, to anyone who has tested the techniques of selective listening how easy it is to follow the meaning of what is said, even though we may concentrate on the grammatical forms. It is as though our brains were doing two things at once, classifying the grammatical forms while letting the meaning filter through. This is practically what happens in reverse when we listen to the meaning while the grammatical structure filters through.

There is one more aspect of language learning in which selective listening is important, namely, in listening to ourselves. Quite unconsciously we all listen to ourselves speak, that is, we "monitor" our own speech constantly. By this means we are able to speak as others do. The person who becomes deaf loses this power of monitoring, and his characteristic distortions of normal speech are soon recognized.

Though we are all quite proficient in monitoring ourselves when we speak our own mother tongue, we seem to be conspicuously bad in monitoring ourselves when we speak a foreign language. One of the reasons for this is that we have never heard the language "correctly." If, whenever we listen to the language, we unconsciously equate the different sounds with the closest corresponding English sounds, then in the monitoring of our speech we will automatically make the same erroneous adjustment. However, if by selective listening we are able to overcome this bad habit of equating sounds which are really quite different, we are then better prepared to correct our speech as we listen to ourselves. The monitoring is, however, twofold. First we monitor the muscular movements—this gives us constant control—and second we monitor the actual sounds as they come out, which gives us a delayed control. But if we are to learn to monitor ourselves properly in a foreign language, we must give some conscious effort to this process. That is to say, we need to listen selectively to ourselves, constantly comparing the acoustic impression which we receive with that which we have heard from others. At first this process of conscious monitoring of oneself is very distracting and confusing. We tend to get so absorbed in listening to what we are already saying that we lose the momentum to keep talking. However, with some practice we can achieve good results.

If we have special difficulty in conscious monitoring, it is helpful to make a recording of our speech and then to listen to ourselves. In this way we can identify ourselves with the speaker as well as be the hearer. By a careful comparison of our speech with the models to which we have been constantly listening we can make almost unbelievable improvements in a relatively short time.

It may be that we have difficulty remembering precisely how the foreign language should sound. In such instances it is advisable to make a recording of our own speech (a sentence at a time) followed by a native speaker correctly uttering the same expressions. By reversing the order, first the native speaker and then our own speech, we may monitor our speech in a situation in which we are consciously trying to imitate a native speaker.

Learning to speak a language is very largely a task of learning to hear it.

THE TOTAL
PHYSICAL RESPONSE APPROACH*

James J. Asher

THE FIRST CLASS

Motivation of students. One powerful way to motivate student interest is to show one or more of the documentary films which demonstrates what will be done and the language skills achieved by other students. Another excellent approach devised by Ramiro Garcia of San Jose, California, is to tell students attending their first class in Spanish: "When you leave here you will understand perfectly everything I am going to say next." Then Garcia would rapidly utter about ten commands in Spanish. The immediate reaction of students is keen interest and skepticism. Many say, "Who, me, understand everything you just said? After one session? Never!" Still a third way is to simply demonstrate the approach with a few students.

For English as a second language, Carol Adamski has found that at least a brief explanation of the theory, goal, and instructional format is most helpful in setting students at ease and quickly involving them in the action. Since a variety of languages are spoken in a beginning ESL class, an explanation is not always possible. However, beginning students often come to class with a relative or friend who speaks some English and can translate. And, often there is one student in the school who can act as a translator.

Orientation of students. If you would like to further orient your students with a detailed explanation of the theory behind this approach, the following rationale may be helpful:

The first step in learning another language is to internalize the code of that language. You will internalize the code in the same way you assimilated your native language, which was through commands. Like most of us, you probably have amnesia for your infancy, but research suggests that many of the utterances directed to you when you were a baby—perhaps half of what you heard—was in

---

*From *Learning Another Language through Actions: The Complete Teacher's Guidebook.*

54

the form of commands such as "Don't spit up on my blouse!" "Give mommy a big kiss!" "Hold daddy's hand!" or "Look at the bird on the branch of that oak tree!" So what I am saying is that, as an infant, you probably deciphered and internalized the code of your first language in a chain of situations in which people manipulated and directed your behavior through commands.

For hundreds of hours you were silent except for babbling, but during that time you were deciphering that important code. You were sorting out the patterns that would transform the noise coming from people's faces into information. It was only after many months of decoding that you began to speak, and even then your understanding was far in advance of your speaking skill and it remained that way for years. Well, that's the way you will enter this new language—through commands. I will utter a command and act along with you for several times. Then each of you will act alone when I give you a command. Gradually, the entire code of the new language will be visible to you, and spontaneously your tongue will produce utterances in the new language.

Let's begin. I need four volunteers. Using hand signals, motion four students to come up to the front of the classroom. Then gesture for two students to sit on either side of you facing the class. Other students in the class are often seated in a semicircle so that there is a rather large space for the action.

Then say, "Stand up!" and immediately stand up as you motion the students seated on either side of you to stand up. Next say, "Sit down!" and immediately sit down along with the four students. If any student tries to repeat what you have said, signal silence by touching your lips with your index finger. Then say, "Stand up!" and the group, including the instructor, should stand up; and then "Sit down!" and all sit down. Repeat the utterances "Stand up!" and "Sit down!" each followed by the appropriate action until all respond confidently, without hesitation.

Then the command is "Walk!" and all walk forward. The next commands are "Stop!" "Turn!" "Walk!" "Stop!" "Turn!" "Walk!" "Stop!" "Jump!" "Turn!" "Walk!" "Stop!" "Jump!" "Turn!" "Sit down!"

By observing the hesitation or nonhesitation of students, you can make decisions as to how many more times you should model with the students. For cues about student readiness to try it alone, after uttering a command, delay your own response slightly to give the students a chance to show they understand and to decrease their dependency on you.

When you think the students are ready to try it themselves, sit down and utter commands which the students as a group can act out. As you progress in a routine, it is important to vary the order of commands so that students do not memorize a fixed sequence.

By observing the group, you can decide when individuals are ready to try it alone. Certain students seem more confident and ready than others; so begin with those people. One by one, use gestures to invite each student to try it alone. Next, invite students from the audience to try. If you can memorize each student's first name in the beginning of the class while you take roll, you can then call out individuals from the audience with "Juan, stand up!" "Walk!" and so forth.

Of course, the concept of a command implies an authoritarian harshness, but this is not what is being advocated. The commands are given firmly but with gentleness and pleasantness. The kindness, compassion, and consideration of the instructor will be signaled in the tone of voice, posture, and facial expressions. You are the student's ally, and they will sense this in the way you direct their behavior.

Another hint is this: Students will be quite literal in their interpretation of what an utterance means. You must be careful to make "clean" responses that are uncluttered with extraneous movements or gestures. For example, one instructor would say "Turn!" then unconsciously move his head in either direction and then turn. Whenever the students heard "Turn!" they would swivel their heads from side to side and then turn. Remember, the students are watching every move you make and if you add irrelevant cues, they will internalize them as a false part of the meaning.

When the students can individually respond quickly and accurately to "Stand up!" "Sit down!" "Turn around!" "Walk!" "Stop!" and "Jump!" they are ready for an expansion of utterances that will move students to different locations in the room. With a few students, begin the expansion with:

Point to the door. (You and the students point to the door.) Point to the chair. (You and the students point to the chair.) Point to the table. (You and the students point to the table.)

After you have uttered the commands and pointed with the students, say: Point to the door. Walk to the door. (You and the students point to the door; then you all walk to the door.) Touch the door. (You all touch the door.)

Now try: Point to the chair. Walk to the chair. (You all point to the chair; then walk to the chair.) Touch the chair. (You all touch the chair.)

Next try: Point to the table. Walk to the table. (You all point to the table and then walk to the table.) Touch the table. (You all touch the table.)

At this point, say: Point to a chair. (Each student points to a chair.) Walk to a chair. (The students walk to their chairs.) Sit down. (The students sit down.)

You sit down also and direct individual students with commands such as: Maria, stand up. (Maria, who is sitting next to you, stands up.) Walk to the table. (Maria walks to the table.) Point to the door. (Maria points to the door.) Walk to the door and touch the door. (Maria walks to the door and touches the door.)

Novelty

Maria, point to a chair. (Maria points to a chair.) Jump to the chair. (You have now uttered a novel command—one Maria has not heard before.) She has heard "Jump" and "Walk to the chair," but not "Jump to the chair." Usually, Maria will delight you and the other students by responding correctly. If not, you demonstrate by uttering: Jump to the table. (Then you jump to the table.) Or perhaps you say, Juan, stand up. (Juan stands up.) Then you say, Juan, jump to the door. (Usually Juan will respond correctly by jumping to the door.) Then return to Maria with, Maria, jump to the chair.

Now try: Eduardo, stand up. (Eduardo, who was in the audience, stands up.) Eduardo, walk to the table. (He walks to the table.) Now point to the table. (He points to the table.) Now touch the table. (He touches the table.) Eduardo, point to a chair. (He points to a chair.) Walk to the chair and sit down. (He walks to a chair and sits down.)

Now try a novel command with Eduardo. He has been responding quickly and confidently to utterances he has heard you use to direct other students. Try a recombination of familiar constituents (i.e., a novel command). Try this: Eduardo, stand up. (He stands up.) Walk to the table. (He walks to the table.) Now sit on the table. Usually Eduardo will not disappoint you, but if he does not respond, do not press him by repeating the novel command. Rather say: Walk to the table (and you walk to the table). Sit on the table (and you sit on the table).

Or, illustrate with another student by saying: Maria, sit on the chair. (Maria sits on the chair.) Maria, stand up. (She stands up.) Maria, sit on the chair. (She sits down on the chair.) Maria, stand up and walk to the table. (She walks to the table.) Maria, sit on the table.

With practice you will become extremely skilled at recombining utterances to produce novel commands which students respond to correctly. Novelty is not meant to trick the students. We expect a successful response to each novel utterance. The intent is first to encourage flexibility in understanding the target language in the richness of recombinations. Second, novelty is a keen motivator. The surprises will delight both you and the students. And third, student self-confidence is enhanced because they are aware that they instantly understood an unfamiliar utterance—one they had never heard before in training.

Introduce more vocabulary. After individual students are responding rapidly and confidently, add new vocabulary such as window, light, ceiling, floor, clock, wall, and chalkboard. As a rule of thumb, be sure students are responding confidently to three new items before you try the next set of three. Too many items at one time is confusing and merely slows down the learning process. Since there is continual interaction with the students, you will have abundant cues from their behavior that will tell you when they are ready to continue with something new.

You are constantly monitoring their progress. You are able to "read" where each student is at all times. Relax! Don't be too ambitious and rush ahead so fast that the students experience failure. Each move—familiar or novel—should be a success for the student. Enjoy the adventure with them. Keep the action moving briskly. As a hint, the pace is fast-moving because students assimilate the target language through their bodies very rapidly. Therefore, have an outline or script because the movement of the learning experience tends to be faster than the instructor is able to think spontaneously.

Sample Lessons

The content of the following lessons is based on a training log used by one instructor to teach English as a second language. Each class was a 3-hour session with adults from ages 18 to 69. The nationalities of the students were Japanese, Chinese, Greek, Russian, Korean, and Latin American. The class size was approximately 25 students, which varied from day to day as new students continued to join the group throughout the year. The daily 3-hour classes were held 5 days a week.

The content of the following material is flexible and can be shifted around without negative consequences. The criterion for including a vocabulary item or grammatical feature at a particular point in training is ease of assimilation by students. If an item is not learned rapidly, this means the students are not ready for that item. Withdraw it and try again at a future time in the training program. The guideline for inclusion is this: If students do not assimilate an item in a few trials—preferably the first trial—they are not ready. Delay the introduction of that item until a future time.

THE SECOND CLASS

Review. The instructor selected a small group from the audience and spoke English to move them, beginning with:

Stand up.	Stop.
Sit down.	Turn.
Stand up.	Jump.
Walk.	Sit down.

Then she expanded to:

Walk to the window.
Touch the window.
Walk to the table.
Touch the table.
Walk to the door.
Touch the door.
Walk to the chair.
Touch the chair.

After a small group performed, the instructor manipulated the behavior of individual students selected at random. She said:

Juan, stand up and walk to the door.
Maria, stand up and walk to the window.
Jaime, walk to the table and sit on the table.

Notice that the instructor is the director of a stage play in which the students are the actors. You can "feel" the pace that is optimal for your students. The objective is to move students as rapidly as they are able to respond successfully. Remember, your intent is not to trick the students with complexity beyond their development. Your goal is continuous student success. Therefore, you should move students in a logical progression.

New commands. In the semicircle, the instructor had a table on which were pencils, books, and papers. She said, "Juan, stand up and walk to the table!" When he had responded, she led him around the table so that both the instructor and the student faced the class with the table in front of them. Then she said:

Touch the pencil. (She and the student touched a pencil.)
Pick up the pencil. (She picked up a pencil and gestured for Juan to pick up a pencil, which he did.)
Put down the pencil. (They both put their pencils on the desk.)
Touch a book. (They both touched a book.)
Pick up a book. (They both picked up a book.)
Put down the book. (Juan put down the book before the instructor could move, which indicated that assimilation was occurring.)
Touch the paper. (Now she delayed her response slightly to let Juan demonstrate his understanding.)
Pick up the paper. (Again she delayed a moment or so to let Juan make the correct action, which he did.)
Put down the paper. (Immediately Juan put the paper on the desk.)
Once Juan was responding quickly and accurately, the instructor called two other students to the table and moved them through the routine of:

Touch the book.
Touch the paper.
Touch the pencil.
Pick up the book.
Pick up the paper.
Pick up the pencil.
Put down the paper.
Put down the book.

Then the series was varied with commands such as:

Pick up the paper and the pencil.
Put down the paper only.
Now put down the pencil.
Pick up the pencil and the book.
Put down the book but do not put down the pencil.
Pick up the paper.
Do not put down the paper.
Now, put down the paper.

Notice that such "small" words as "now," "only," and "not" were presented in context and seemed to be assimilated easily.

Next, two other students were moved rapidly with the routine, which was expanded to include:

Open the book. (The instructor did it with the students the first time.)
Close the book. (She closed the book and the students closed their books.)

Novel commands. When students selected at random were able to perform quickly and confidently, familiar utterances were recombined to produce commands the students had never heard before but could instantly understand. Examples would be:

Jaime, stand up. Walk to the table. Pick up the pencil and paper. Walk to the window and put the pencil on the floor. Put the paper on your chair.
Maria, stand up. Pick up the pencil from Jaime's chair and put the pencil on the table.
Eduardo, pick up the book and put it on Juan.

To maintain the pace, it is wise to have a long list of novel commands (i.e., recombinations of familiar utterances) which you have prepared ahead of time. If a student is baffled, do not press; but simply try the same command with another student or act it out yourself.

New material. At this point in the 3-hour class, the instructor introduced the following lexical items:

Name	I will write my name on the board.
	Juan, run to the chalkboard and write your name.
	Jaime, go to the chalkboard and write your name.
	Everyone, write your name on your paper.
Address	I will write my address on the board.
	Delores, write your name and your address on the chalkboard.
	Write your address on your paper.
On	Maria, pick up the book ... (The instructor and Maria pick up a book)
	and put it on the chair. (They put their books on the chair.)
	Maria, put the book on the table.
	Put the book on your head.
Under	Jaime, pick up the pencil. (The instructor and Jaime pick up a pencil) and put the pencil under a chair. (They put their pencils under a chair.)
	Jaime, pick up your pencil and put it under the table.
	Now put the pencil under the book.
Numbers from 1 to 10	I will write the number 1 on the board.
	I will write number 2.
	I will write 3. (This continued through the number 10.)

	Rita, write the numbers 1 and 2 on the board.
	Miako, write 3.
	Jeffe, write 4 and 5.
Head	Pablo, touch your head (The instructor touched her head while Pablo touched his.)
	Everyone, touch your head.
	Wing, touch Ramiro's head.
Mouth	Carlos, touch your mouth (and the instructor touched her mouth while Carlos touched his.)
	Everyone, touch your mouth.
	Lauro, touch your head. Touch your mouth.
Ear(s)	Jose, touch your ears. (The instructor touched her ears while Jose touched his.)
	Wing, touch one ear. Now touch both your ears.
	Miguel, touch Ana's ears.
Eye(s)	Eduardo, touch your eyes. (The instructor touched her eyes while Eduardo touched his.)
	Everyone, touch your eyes.
	Elaine, touch just one of your eyes. Now touch both eyes.
Hand(s)	I will touch Ramiro's hands.
	Juan, touch my hands.
	Delores, touch one of my hands.
	Rita, put your hand on the table.
	Pablo, put your hands on Ana's head.
Arm(s)	I will touch Rita on the arm.
	I will touch Jeffe on both arms.
	Ramiro, touch both of Antonio's arms.
	Elaine, touch one of my arms.
Leg(s)	I will touch my legs.
	I will touch one leg.
	Carlos, touch your legs.
	Everyone, touch one leg.
	Touch both legs.

Remember not to introduce too much new material at one time. As a hint, try working with only three new items. When students are responding confidently to those items, try three more.

Review of new material. The instructor uttered one command at a time, then two in a row to move people all over the room. The object always was maximum involvement, which can be achieved by continual activity from each student. Do not work with one student too long. Keep an interesting pace by continually calling upon different students. Keep them moving and they will be happy and learning. Incidentally, at this point, the instructor reported that she felt her students were ready to respond to four or five commands in a row.

A final note on novelty. You probably noticed that novelty was integrated into both the review and the introduction of new material. Now, you have an abundant content to generate fascinating recombinations that will delight your students and at the same time increase their linguistic flexibility, which is critical for the achievement of listening fluency.

Again, as a hint, it is wise to write out the exact utterances you will be using and especially the novel commands, because the action is so fast-moving, there is usually no time for you to create spontaneously. Here are more examples of novel utterances used in this unit:

Pick up number 3 and number 7 (each of which was printed on large flash cards) and put "3" on your head.

Put number 10 under your chair.

Pick up the book, put the number 5 in the book, and put the book under your arm.

Touch your nose with the pencil.

THE THIRD CLASS

Review. This was a fast-moving review with individuals, small groups, and the entire class. Some of the commands were "Stand up!" "Jump!" "Turn around!" "Pick up the chair and put the chair on the table!" The instructor used two, three, and even four commands in rapid succession.

New commands. Notice that new vocabulary was integrated with familiar material.

Hit	your arm.
	the table.
	Juan.
	me on the hand.
Throw	the paper on the floor.
	the pencil to me.
	the book to Maria.
Give	the book to me.
	the pencil to me.
	the paper to Delores.
Take	the book from me.
	the pencil from me.
	the paper from Delores.
Turn on	the light.
Turn off	the light.

(Note that "Turn on" and "Turn off" were not optimal at this point in training because the expansion is limited to one possibility, which was "Turn on the light!" or "Turn off the light!")

In addition to verbs, the following nouns were introduced through the imperative:

Flower(s)	Pick up the flower and put it under the book.
	Throw the flower to me.
	Hit Jaime with the flower.
Magazine(s)	Take the magazine from Maria and give it to me.
	Put the magazine on the flower.
	Give Shirou the magazine.
	Pick up the magazines from the floor and give them to Rita.
Chalk	Walk to the chalkboard, pick up the chalk, and give it to Pablo.
	Pablo, put the chalk on your head.
	Maria, take the chalk from Pablo's head and write your name on the chalkboard.
Colors	Jaime, touch the red book.
	Maria, pick up the blue pencil and throw it to Juan.
	Juan, give me the pink paper and the yellow chalk.
Numbers	(Each number from 1 through 15 was on a large flashcard which students manipulated.)
	Rita, pick up 11 and 12 and throw them to Jaime.
	Juan, put 12 and 15 on your chair.
	Shirou, point to 14.

Hint: As a reminder, the pace is usually so fast-moving that you will not have time to "think on your feet." It is most helpful to write up the network of commands you intend to use, especially the recombinations. Again, we encourage novel commands that are playful, silly, crazy, bizarre, and zany. The element of surprise is exciting for the instructor and the students.

THE FOURTH CLASS

Review. All the commands in this review were novel, since they were recombinations of familiar constituents. The students usually understood, even though they had never heard the exact utterances spoken by the instructor. Examples would be:

Consuelo, pick up the book from the table and put it on Ramiro's nose.

Ramiro, throw the book to me, hit Consuelo on the arm, and draw a funny picture of Consuelo on the chalkboard.

Jaime, walk with Juan to the table. Now, put Juan on the table.

Most students could respond immediately with the appropriate action. If someone did not, the instructor would repeat the utterance and call upon another student to perform it, or she would carry out the action herself.

New commands. Notice that there was no drill in the sense of tedious repetition of the same sentence over and over and over. Rather, new items were constantly recombined with familiar elements so that students heard "fresh" sentences—ones they had never heard before, but the novel sentences were so thoughtfully recombined that almost every new command was perfectly understood by the students.

Here are the new verbs:

Draw	a circle around your name.
	a funny face on the chalkboard and write Miguel's name under it.
	a table on your paper.
Laugh	at the funny face on the chalkboard.
	at Juan who is on the table.
	when I call out your name.
Cut	the paper on the table.
	around the table which you drew on your paper.
	your paper in half.
Run	to the window.
	to the door.
	to the chalkboard.
Show	Juan your hands.
	your paper to Jose.
	the book to Maria.
Push	the table.
	the chair.
	Jaime into his chair.
Pull	the chair back from the table.
	the door open.
	my arm.
Scream	when you look at the funny picture Shirou drew on the chalkboard.
	when Carlos hits you on the arm.
	when I call your name.

The verbs were combined with these lexical items:

Straight line	Run to the chalkboard and draw a straight line.
	Use your finger to draw a straight line in the air.
	Jose, Jaime, and Carlos—walk to the table in a straight line.
Crooked line	Maria, run to the chalkboard and draw a crooked line next to the straight line.
	Miguel, walk to the table in a crooked line.
	Delores, use your finger to draw a crooked line in the air.
Circle	Write the number 13 on the chalkboard and draw a circle around it.

	Shirou, run to the chalkboard and draw a circle.
	Then write your name in the circle.
	Draw a circle on your paper.
Square	Write the number 11 on the chalkboard and then draw a square around it.
	María, write your name on the board; then draw a square around it.
	On your paper, draw a square. In the square draw a circle.
Cat	Pick up the cat and give it to Wing.
	Wing, give the cat to Miako.
	Eduardo, run to the board and draw a picture of the cat.
Shoulder(s)	Touch Miako's shoulders.
	Miako, scream and hit Jaime on the shoulder.
	Touch your shoulders.
Knee(s)	Touch your knees with a pencil.
	Miguel, run to the table and put your knee on the table.
	Put your hands on your knees and laugh.
Foot (feet)	Put the book on your feet.
	Drop the chalk on Jose's foot.
	On your paper, write the number of feet that Jaime has.
Hair	If Jaime has black hair, laugh at him.
	If Miako has blonde hair, hit her on the arm.
	Pull your hair and scream.
Wrist	Put the chalk on your wrist.
	Touch your wrist with two fingers.
	Touch the book with your wrist.
Wristwatch	Give me your wristwatch.
	Put your wristwatch to your ear.
	Put your wristwatch under your chair.
Between	Draw a straight line between the numbers 11 and 12.
	Wing, walk between Delores and Jose.
	Maria, put your chair between the table and me.
Next to	Write the number 15 next to the circle.
	Juan, stand next to Wing.
	Elaine, put your book next to Ramiro's shoulder.
Around	Draw a circle around your name.
	Walk around the table and scream.
	With your finger, draw a circle around your ear.

Reading. After the first week of training (12 classroom hours), the instructor distributed the first handout (Exhibit 1), which had all the vocabulary and grammatical structures which the students now understood when they were uttered by the instructor. It took 15 minutes for the instructor to read and act out each item on the page. The students did not read aloud or repeat each utterance.

EXHIBIT I

Verbs		Other Vocabulary	
1 stand	table	head	my
2 sit	chair	mouth	your
3 turn around	window	eye(s)	on
4 walk	door	nose	under
5 stop	light	ear(s)	in
6 jump	ceiling	arm(s)	between
7 point to	floor	leg(s)	next to
8 touch	clock	shoulder(s)	around
9 pick up	wall	knee(s)	
10 put down	chalkboard	foot-feet	
11 write	paper	hair	
12 open	pencil	wrist	
13 close	address	hand(s)	
14 hit	name	red	
15 throw	flower	pink	
16 turn on	magazine	yellow	
17 turn off	chalk	green	
18 give	cat	blue	
19 take	book	straight line	
20 draw	wristwatch	crooked line	
21 laugh		circle	
22 cut		square	
23 run			
24 show			
25 push			
26 scream			

DELAYED ORAL PRACTICE

Valerian A. Postovsky

It is generally believed that the initial phase of instruction in foreign language should be based on intensive oral practice. The more vocally active the student is from the very beginning, the faster, it is assumed, he learns the foreign language.

In this study I wish to challenge this assumption and to suggest a different approach to the initial phase of instruction. The rationale on which this hypothesis is based suggests that intensive pronunciation practice is not the logical starting point. It is proposed that the motor skill involved in production of speech output is an end result of complex and mostly covert processes which constitute linguistic competence.

It is further proposed that the linguistic competence includes at least two reciprocally correlated events: capacity to *process* auditory input and capacity to *generate* speech output, and that the former is concerned with decoding capability while the latter is concerned with encoding.

Clearly, decoding capability requires development of *recognition* knowledge, while encoding capability requires development of *retrieval* knowledge. Given this difference between the two events, it would appear to be logical to assume that in the natural learning process, development of recognition knowledge would precede, not follow, the development of retrieval knowledge.

When the student is tasked with production of a foreign sentence, he has to *retrieve* linguistic information stored in his long-term memory and control his speech on phonological, syntactic, and semantic levels simultaneously and with the speed of speech output. When he is tasked with comprehension of a foreign sentence, he has to *store* linguistic information in his auditory short-term memory for a brief period of time until it is further processed and matched with the information stored in his long-term memory. I suggest the latter process is more productive in the initial phase of instruction and that development of recognition knowledge is in fact prerequisite for the development of retrieval knowledge.

Priority of aural comprehension in the first language acquisition process is clearly evident. Children demonstrate comprehension of many utterances before they develop the ability to produce any intelligible speech. Empirical evidence to substantiate this commonsense notion has been provided by several excellent studies of child language.

Although there are significant differences between the process by which a child acquires his native language and that of an adult student learning a second language, the principle concerning priority of aural comprehension in the language acquisition process appears to be valid for both conditions. Indeed, it is implicit in the very name of the "audiolingual" method. The method, however, as it has developed in recent years, places much greater emphasis on the "lingual" part of the training. In the contemporary methodology of foreign language teaching in general, this principle has received only a very superficial interpretation. Usually, it is applied in reference to a single utterance or a short passage; i.e., comprehension of a particular segment of speech is believed to be necessary before production of that same segment. Needless to say, development of recognition knowledge prior to the development of retrieval knowledge, as is understood within the context of this article, implies that comprehension involves acquisition of an integrated linguistic system rather than acquisition of a single segment of speech.

In recent years interest in the dynamics of aural comprehension has been steadily increasing. Some 10 or 15 years ago, Robert Gauthier in Canada introduced the so-called "Tan-Gau" method for teaching French to English-speaking students. The method attempts to develop aural comprehension by the process of bilingual communication: the teacher speaks French, and the students respond in English until such time as each student individually approaches the state of "speaking readiness" (Gauther, 1963).

In 1965, Simon Belasco referred to aural comprehension as "the most underestimated and least understood aspect of foreign language learning" (Belasco, 1965). At about the same time Asher conducted his first experiments in "the strategy of the total physical response" (Asher, 1965, 1969), attempting to develop aural comprehension by requiring students to act out situations in response to commands in a foreign language. More recently Winitz and Reeds (1973) have developed a totally comprehension-oriented program in German in which meaning of utterances in the foreign language is conveyed by pictorial events. The method, called Optimized Habit Reinforcement, is described in a paper entitled "Rapid Acquisition of a Foreign Language (German) by the Avoidance of Speaking."

In this article I wish to report an experiment on effects of delay in oral practice at the beginning of second language learning (Postovsky, 1970) conducted for a doctoral dissertation during the academic year 1969-70.

The principal problem addressed in this study may be formulated as follows: If processing of auditory input is essential and intrinsic to the nature of the language acquisition process, then the linguistic properties of that input are crucial if it is true, as I propose, that the student learns essentially what he hears. But in the audiolingual class where each student is vocally active, students hear themselves more than they hear the teacher. The auditory input which they are processing, then, is not the authentic language, but the classroom dialect rich with all the distortions that are peculiar to the beginning students' speech output. It is not surprising, therefore, that after extensive study of a foreign language students still experience marked difficulty in understanding a native speaker, while displaying considerable fluency in communicating among themselves.

Based on the above reasoning we may tentatively propose that intensive oral practice is not productive in the initial phase of instruction and should be delayed until the student is better prepared for the task, that is, until he has learned to understand the spoken language. Recognition knowledge is prerequisite for the development of retrieval knowledge.

This theoretical orientation gives a new dimension to the old problem of negative transfer or interference in second language learning. In the production-oriented "audiolingual" approach, contextual meaning of a foreign utterance is viewed as a source of interference in the initial phrase of instruction because it tends to divert the student's attention from the phonological features presented and thus adversely affect his pronunciation. In the comprehension-oriented approach, contextual meaning becomes indispensable because the goal of instruction is to develop processing strategies for decoding of auditory input.

Similarly, in the audiolingual approach, writing is delayed at the beginning of the course for fear of graphic interference. In the comprehension-oriented approach, the argument may be reversed. Conceivably, one may argue that it is just as logical to present written forms prior to intensive pronunciation practice. In a classroom environment written forms are not normally presented in isolation; the student *hears* a foreign utterance and *sees* its transcription simultaneously. By training the student to write a foreign word in the presence of an auditory stimulus we are creating desirable associations, and possibly reinforcing his perception of auditory input.

The problem of interference is not limited to the phonological level alone, as Politzer (1965, pp. 1–10) clearly demonstrates. It extends to the morphological, syntactical, and semantic levels. On these levels a written form appears to be an asset rather than a liability.

Thus, by not requiring students to produce vocal output at the beginning of second language learning, we may reduce interference from the habits of the native language because the motor side of the student's linguistic behavior during the comprehension training will be minimal.

On the basis of the above argument, it is suggested that delaying oral practice at the beginning of the course will significantly enhance the development of language proficiency and will enable the student to develop better pronunciation and control of grammar than is presently possible with the audiolingual approach. It is emphasized that the goal of instruction remains the development of communicative competence and oral fluency. Intensive pronunciation practice is merely shifted to the second phase of instruction, when the student is better prepared for the task and, consequently, has less chance of developing poor habits in oral production.

Operationally, this system implies that the student will be able to write before he speaks. The writing system will be introduced on the first day of instruction and all students' responses during the prevocal training will be in writing. It is assumed that the dynamics of contextual meaning and the facilitation of the student's meaningful response will by far outweigh the problem of graphic interference.

DESCRIPTION OF THE EXPERIMENT

Objectives. Although the basic tenet, central to this study, is that in the second language learning situation aural comprehension must be developed ahead of production, the present experiment was not designed to test this tenet specifically. Rather, it was limited to testing the effects of delay in oral practice at the beginning of second language learning. And, since the delay in oral practice in the experimental condition was achieved by requiring students to respond in writing, the second objective of this study was to investigate the effectiveness of oral versus writing practice.

For this purpose a carefully controlled experimental investigation was conducted, comparing an experimental condition, a 4-week delay in oral practice, with a control condition, no delay in oral practice. Evaluation was carried out for all four language skills—listening, speaking, reading, and writing.

Learning Environment. The experiment was conducted at the Russian Department, Defense Language Institute, West Coast Branch (DLIWC), Presidio of Monterey, California. DLIWC offers a unique learning environment and an exceptionally favorable experimental setting. The Russian course is an intensive 6-hour-a-day program; four of these hours are conducted in small classes of nine or ten students, and two in a conventional language laboratory.

Subjects. The subjects used in the study were selected from military personnel who volunteered for language training and were assigned to learn Russian at the DLIWC. All native speakers of English, they came from different geographic areas of the continental United States. Most of them were between 18 and 24 years of age. Their education ranged from high school to 6 years of college. On the average they had approximately 2.75 years of college. They represented the same socioeconomic stratum, that of a middle-class American family.

Experimental Procedure. In order to ensure internal validity of the experimental procedure and to increase the size of the sample, two consecutive experiments were conducted. The first experiment started on September 9, 1969, and was completed on November 28, 1969. The second experiment—an exact replication of the first—was carried out in the period between January 9 and April 3, 1970.

Each of the two classes participating in the study was divided into the Experimental and Control conditions. Subjects in the Experimental condition were individually matched with subjects in the Control condition. The September class contained 73 students; of these, 11 were disqualified as experimental subjects because of prior exposure to Slavic languages. The remaining 61 students were grouped into 31 matched pairs and randomly divided between the Experimental and Control conditions. In the January class, following the same criteria for selection, 30 matched pairs were formed out of 78 students, thus bringing the total size of the sample to 61 matched pairs. That is, counting both classes, there were 61 subjects in the Experimental group (Es) who were individually matched with 61 subjects in the Control group (Cs). The experimental design followed by each of the two classes is graphically presented in Figure 1.

	Treatment	
Week	Experimental	Control
	6-Week Comprehensive Test	
1 2	No oral practice	Intensive oral practice
3 4	Equal emphasis on aural comprehension	
5	Transition ⟶	
6	Integration ⟶	Regular Russian program
	12-Week Comprehensive Test	
7 8	Regular	Regular
9 10	Russian	Russian
11 12	program	program

Figure 1   Experimental design. Effects of delay.

Note that the duration of each experiment was 12 weeks, but subjects were exposed to the experimental treatment only during the initial 4 weeks of instruction. Both the Es and the Cs were exposed to the same instructors throughout the experiment, and both followed the same daily cycle of instruction and had exactly the same number of contact hours per day, the only difference being in the methodology of instruction.

Upon completion of the prevocal phase of instruction, the Es were merged with the Cs in the regular Russian program. Common examinations were administered at the end of the sixth week and again at the end of the twelfth week of instruction. The test scores on all four language skills (listening, speaking, reading, and writing) were statistically treated.

Methodology. The delay in oral practice in the Experimental conditions was achieved by requiring students to respond in writing. The development of writing skill from the very beginning of the course in the Experimental condition was considered important for two reasons. First, it provided students with a meaningful mode of response during the prevocal phase of instruction; and second, it was believed that there is a high degree of positive transfer from writing to speaking, since both skills are productive. Hence, the Es were introduced to the conventional writing system (Cyrillic alphabet) from the very first day of instruction. To establish association between Russian sounds and symbols, the students were given some pronunciation practice along with the alphabet during the initial 3 days of instruction, but immediately thereafter and until the end of the fourth week, all students' responses were in writing. That is, dictation practice was substituted for oral imitation drill, writing practice of pattern-drill responses for pattern drills, and writing out dialogues from memory for recitation of dialogues.

The Cs from the beginning followed the regular DLIWC Russian program with great emphasis on habit-forming drills and oral practice. It was basically the audiolingual approach. However, short explanations of grammar were given *before* pattern-drill sessions, and the Cyrillic alphabet was withheld only for the first 3 days of instruction. Thus, the Cs had an intensive oral practice from the beginning of the course, while the Es had a delay in oral practice during the initial 4 weeks of instruction.

In an attempt to reduce the difference between conditions to the mode of student response, equal emphasis was made in both groups on development of aural comprehension. Covering identical teaching materials, both groups were exposed to exactly the same vocabulary, grammar, and lesson content. The same dialogues were first presented in both groups as comprehension exercises by the teachers. The oral repetition practice in the Control condition and dictation practice in the Experimental condition started only after comprehension of the dialogue was achieved.

Achievement Tests and Testing Procedure. The two comprehensive tests especially developed for this experiment were similar in format to the MLA-Cooperative Foreign Language Tests. These tests were designed to provide separate measures of listening, speaking, reading, and writing skills at two levels of achievement—the 6-week and the 12-week grading periods in the DLIWC Russian program. Administering and scoring of the tests followed the procedure recommended for MLA Tests by the Educational Testing Service (1964).

The test validity was established by computing the Pearson Product-Moment correlation coefficients between the scores obtained by the students on the tests and their classroom performance grades. The correlation coefficients for the oral part of the test were .72 at the 6-week level and .83 at the 12-week level. For the written part of the test, they were .84 and .87, respectively.

The test reliability measure was obtained by computing odd and even item correlation and applying the Spearman-Brown correction. The results are given in Table 1.

Table 1   Test Reliability

Variables	6-weeks R	12-weeks R
Listening	.76	.89
Speaking	.88	.91
Reading	.78	.68
Writing	.90	.90

The tests were administered to both the Es and Cs assembled together in a single language laboratory. All students' responses during the Speaking Test were recorded on tape. To enhance reliability of the Speaking Test, three raters were used to score each individual student tape. The raters were senior instructors, native speakers of the Russian language, who were skilled in scoring this type of test. They were not members of the Project Class faculty and did not know the students. Furthermore, students were identified on tape by code number only, and the order of listening to tapes was randomized.

ANALYSIS AND RESULTS

The data collected on each pair of subjects in this study represent several interdependent dimensions—listening, speaking, reading, and writing scores. Therefore, the principal statistical procedure used in the analysis of the data was to employ the Multivariate Matched Pair T Test. The Hotelling T_2 statistic appeared to be the most appropriate instrument, one of the most conservative statistical procedures available for an experiment in foreign language teaching methodology, because in testing for variance between the Experimental and Control conditions, it simultaneously accounts for covariance in all four related language skills.

As may be recalled, two consecutive experiments were conducted in which students' performance was measured at two different levels of achievement: (1) at the end of the 6 weeks of instruction, and (2) at the end of the 12 weeks of instruction. Mean scores obtained by each project class at each of the two levels of achievement are reported in Tables 2 and 3.

Table 2   Mean Scores Obtained on the 6-Week Test

Class	Condition	Listening	Speaking	Reading	Writing
September	Experimental	28.78	48.64	35.89	87.03
N = 28	Control	28.50	44.92	34.32	81.07
January	Experimental	31.33	47.15	36.37	87.37
N = 27	Control	29.96	45.33	35.15	82.67

Table 3   Mean Scores Obtained on the 12-Week Test

Class	Condition	Listening	Speaking	Reading	Writing
September	Experimental	24.64	48.56	31.92	81.20
N = 25	Control	23.20	44.84	31.68	77.44
January	Experimental	26.66	49.92	33.08	79.92
N = 24	Control	23.66	43.38	32.79	78.67

In order to ensure that the two groups represented the same population of students, the September and January classes were tested for equality, and when no significant difference was found between the groups ($p = .62$ at the 6-week level, and $p = .58$ at the 12-week level), the data obtained from both project classes were merged to form a larger sample. In a matched-pair design, the data obtained from the Experimental and Control conditions may be reduced to the difference in observed values for the paired members and subjected to statistical analysis as a one-sample problem. Thus, if we take the difference [Experimental (E)—Control (C)] for each matched pair in our combined sample, the data may be summarized as in the following diagram:

6-week level	12-week level
E – C	E – C
N = 55	N = 49

For easy visual comparison, mean scores for the Es and Cs on listening (L), speaking (S), reading (R), and writing (W) were transformed to the common scale and presented in a profile plot below.

Although one might begin with investigation of the difference between the 6- and 12-week levels, it was of interest in this study to determine first whether or not there was any difference between the Experimental and Control conditions at each of the two levels of achievement.

The analyses of the data were accomplished on the C.D.C. 6400 computer at the University of California Computer Center, Berkeley. The program utilized was that of Dr. Jeremy Finn, State University of New York, Buffalo.

From Figure 2 it can be seen that the difference between groups favored the Experimental condition on all criterion measures, but the statistically significant difference at $p < .01$ level was observed only at the 6-week level of achievement. At the 12-week level, when all language skills were considered simultaneously, a similar trend was observed—the direction of the difference on all criterion measures was in favor of the Es, but at a less than statistical level of significance. However, further analysis of the data (confidence intervals) revealed that the Es at the 12-week level were significantly superior to the Cs in listening comprehension ($p < .008$), while at the 6-week level, the most significant differences between groups was in speaking, reading, and writing skills.

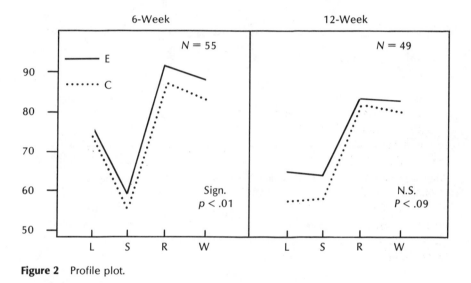

Figure 2 Profile plot.

The observed difference in reading and writing skills was not surprising. The Es received more practice in these skills; therefore, their superiority on these criterion measures was anticipated. Of more interest was the difference in speaking. For this reason the speaking score for each subject was broken into its component parts (see MLA Scoring Form for Speaking Test) and subjected to further analysis with the aim of determining which specific element(s) contributed to the observed difference.

The seven components of the speaking score are: (1) Mimicry (Mim.); (2)Reading aloud (Read.); (3) Answering questions (Q.A.); (4) Free narration (Nar.); (5) Control of grammar (Gram.); (6) Control of vocabulary (Vocab.); (7) Fluency (Fl.). Mean scores for the Es and the Cs on each of these variables were transformed to the common scale and plotted on the profile graph which is presented in Figure 3.

It must be noted that the difference between groups on these criterion measures was found to be significant at the .0001 level of confidence. The two variables that contributed most to this outcome were *control of grammar* and *reading aloud.* For a more detailed treatment of data the reader is referred to the original dissertation (Postovsky, 1970).

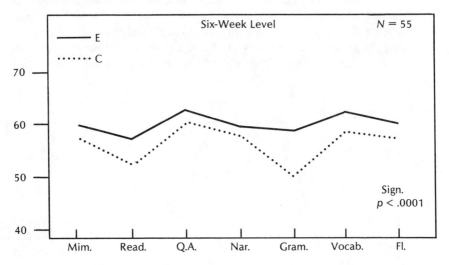

Figure 3   Components of the speaking score, six-week level of achievement.

AN INTRODUCTORY COURSE
IN READING FRENCH

Robbins Burling

In the following pages I will describe an unconventional method that I have been using to help people learn to read French. I begin by offering students a reading passage that is an almost literal word-for-word translation from French into English. It has English words in French word order. A text of this sort quickly conveys a sense of the overall patterns of French sentences. In subsequent passages the most common French words are introduced into the reading materials, where they take the place of their English equivalents. Step by step an ever larger proportion of French words appears in the reading passages and the text turns progressively into French. Starting with a text that a monolingual English speaker can understand with no more than a minimum of explanation, the student is led, by gradual steps, to a text that is written in French.

My method is strange enough that many teachers of foreign language may feel that it passes beyond the bounds of unconventionality and reaches the bizarre. It requires a text that is written in a mixed language, and at first sight, this may appear to be more ludicrous than useful. Students spend their time practicing with a text that is neither fish nor fowl but that fluctuates uncertainly between the two.

The final judgment about any method of language instruction must, however, be the pragmatic one: can students use the method to learn the language? Once I have explained the rationale for my suggestions, given concrete examples of the stages through which I have been guiding students, and pointed to the considerable advantages of the method, I hope that many readers will agree that I am offering a technique that deserves a serious trial, and I even hope that a few will be stimulated to try similar experiments.

POPULAR BUT DUBIOUS ASSUMPTIONS
ABOUT LANGUAGE PEDAGOGY

Language pedagogy seems to have drawn to itself more than its share of hoary assumptions. Some of these assumptions claim such nearly universal acceptance that no one bothers to make them explicit. They may be barely even recognized. I want to point out a few of the assumptions about language teaching that seemed pervasive in the 1970s, for I believe there is good reason to doubt them. Once the assumptions are questioned, my pedagogical proposals may seem more plausible than they appear on first sight.

I will consider four assumptions that appear to be widely, if not quite universally, held by teachers of foreign languages. I feel there are good reasons for doubting all four.

1. The Primacy of Oral over Written Language. It is obvious that children learn to speak before they learn to read and write. Linguists take spoken language to be the subject of most of their investigations, and they see writing as derivative, as a form that is secondary to the spoken language. My fellow linguists seem to have convinced most teachers of elementary languages that it must follow from these facts that spoken language should also have priority in second language instruction. Such a conclusion, however, should not pass unquestioned. In real life people do learn to read, for pleasure and for profit, in languages in which their control of the spoken language is minimal. For many students learning to read is a practical goal, a goal for which they can envision a realistic use. Learning to speak is a more remote possibility, one that is less likely to seem within useful reach. Students who want to learn to read but who would like to avoid the difficulties posed by the spoken language deserve to be taken seriously.

2. The Integral Unity of a Language. Most linguists (and, I suspect, most language teachers) seem to assume that the various aspects of a language are all rather tightly interdependent. Pronunciation is related to grammar and grammar to vocabulary. The noun phrase cannnot be fully understood without understanding the verb phrase. Case suffixes relate to everything, and so it goes. In some abstract sense statements of this sort are surely correct, but in the practical world where students live, the parts of a language are not always so tightly joined. When we hear someone speak grammatically fluent English with a strong foreign accent, we should realize that we have found a person who has learned some aspects of our language (grammar, vocabulary) but who has failed to learn another (pronunciation). Total control of a language requires a knowledge of all its aspects, but beginning students cannot possibly have total control. Our feelings about the unity of a language lead us to hope that our students can develop skills in all areas from the very beginning. We drill them on pronunciation, we teach them vocabulary, and we give them bits and pieces of grammar so that they can produce and understand whole sentences. They might make more satisfying progress if we could devise a means by which they could take up these topics one by one.

3. Inviolable Boundaries Separate Different Languages from One Another. This is really the obverse of the last assumption, for just as we take each language to have an internal unity, we also imagine the boundaries between different languages to be sharp and unbridgeable. Here again, however, practical experience shows our implicit assumption to be false. The person who speaks with a strong foreign accent not only demonstrates the lack of unity of a single language but also demonstrates the ease with which languages can be mixed. He communicates with the grammar and vocabulary of one language but with the phonology of another. Speakers of languages such as Hindi and Burmese who have a substantial knowledge of English feel free to use any English word that they think will be understood. The ease with which vocabulary flows across the language boundary is strikingly evident when scientific or technical matters are discussed in these languages, but the same processes can be observed in many other areas. Many Indians and Burmese speak a language that is Hindi or Burmese in grammar and phonology but that draws, almost at will, upon the English lexicon. We can hear the same sort of language among immigrants to the United States. They may use the syntax and phonology of their native language, but they also draw freely upon English vocabulary when referring to things American.

Every schoolchild who ever studied a foreign language must have made up sentences of mixed antecedents: Scramez-vous; What mangez-vous for dinner ce soir? He has away ge-gone. We do not usually take such linguistic antics seriously. We regard them, rather, as the frivolous games of schoolchildren. But the games do demonstrate the ease with which all of us can mix our languages, and they demonstrate the permeable nature of the boundaries between languages. Perhaps we should take our skill at mixing languages more seriously, for we might be able to build upon this skill when we try to help our students learn a new language.

4. Language Production Goes Hand in Hand with Comprehension. It is obvious that, at any given stage of his development, a small child's receptive ability in his first language outstrips his productive ability. In foreign language programs, however, we almost always expect a student to be able to say just about anything that he can understand.

Of all the assumptions about foreign language learning, it is this that I find most dubious. One reason for insisting upon production, I fear, is that it is easier than reception to test. When we ask our students to speak or to write, their mistakes show up immediately. It is easy to decide who merits an A and who must be content with a C. Testing comprehension is not quite so easy. Questions must be phrased a bit more carefully. The answers to be sought are a shade more subtle.

Ease of testing hardly offers legitimate grounds for deciding what to teach, but there are other, superficially more plausible, reasons for feeling that production should go along with reception. Perhaps it is felt that a "mere" receptive ability will not get anyone very far when he needs directions in Paris. Even more important, it may be supposed that language is a kind of "behavior" and that learning a new behavior requires practice and drill.

I find neither of these arguments persuasive. Most students will never get to Paris, but all will have the opportunity to read, and I argue at some length below that a focus upon receptive skills would cut through many of the most serious problems associated with introductory language instruction. The concept of language as a form of "behavior" for which mechanical practice is necessary seems to me to constitute the most serious of misunderstandings. There is ample evidence that it is possible to learn to understand oral language without being able to speak it, and many people have learned to read without gaining any confidence in their ability to write. Production is inhibiting because mistakes show up so quickly. Concentration upon reception allows the student to focus upon meaning—the area of language that is important to everyone except the linguist—and to let the mechanics of the language recede to the background. A strong and, to me, entirely convincing argument for postponing deliberate instruction in production has been made in a number of places by Valerian A. Postovsky.

If we remember the way in which children learn their first language, we may come to feel that emphasizing receptive skills would be a promising way to teach a foreign language.

THE EXAMPLE OF FIRST LANGUAGE LEARNING

Those who propose techniques of language pedagogy are continually tempted to justify their suggestions by reference to the way in which a child learns his first language. Proponents of different methods refer to different facets of the child's learning process, however, and few would argue that adults should follow the child's patterns in every respect. We should hope that an adult's broader experience will give him some advantages over a child. We ought to ask which aspects of second language learning can best follow the example of first language learning, and which other aspects can be made easier for adults by deviating from the methods of small children. I suggest that we should draw two lessons from the example of children.

First, I believe we would make more rapid progress if the initial stages of language instruction would emphasize comprehension and minimize attention to production. By concentrating upon comprehension we would avoid several problems. A student would not face the embarrassment of his inevitable mistakes. He would not be subjected to the terrible examples of his classmates' feeble efforts. He would not have to focus upon retrieving difficult new words from memory but could concentrate upon the far less difficult task of recognizing words. The learner, moreover, could almost entirely avoid conscious attention to some annoying details. When learning a second language such as French or German by conventional methods, for instance, gender is a constant headache and a constant source of error. If comprehension were emphasized, gender would pose few problems. The student would, to be sure, need to know that gender exists. When studying French, he would need to know that *le* is used with some words and *la* with others, but he would not need to struggle to memorize which form of the article goes with which word. The passive learner could allow many other fussy and irregular aspects of the language to slip by just as lightly.

This brings me to the second way in which second language learning ought to profit from the example of children. Children learn the fussy details through long exposure. By the time they are getting these details right most of the time, they have had years of passive experience. This allows them to sense that some phrasings do not "sound right." They can monitor their own speech and they need expend little conscious effort in mastering all these details. Second language learners ought to be able to learn the fussy details with no more struggle than children.

In some other ways, however, adult learners have advantages over children, and we ought to capitalize upon these advantages. The primary adult advantage would seem to lie in the ability to see the large picture. Broad patterns can be explained to adults and they can quickly grasp generalizations that might take long hours to induce from examples. The English-speaking student of French can be told that adjectives follow nouns and that pronoun objects precede verbs, and in this way he will avoid a good deal of puzzlement that might arise if he had to discover these generalizations, as a child must, by inducing them from examples. The nature of the gender system can be explained, but the details of which nouns are masculine and which are feminine can be left for slow, childlike, absorption. The nature of the tense system can be explained, but the multiplicity of irregular details in a language such as French can be left to a much more extended learning process.

SEQUENCING

I believe we should think harder than we have in the recent past about how to help those students whose primary goal is reading. I suggest that we could lighten the task of language learning if we would not require a student to produce the foreign language but let him concentrate, instead, on the easier tasks of recognition and comprehension. We could release the student who wants to read from the struggles with pronunciation that anyone who tries to talk must face.

I also feel that we could capitalize upon our ability to mix languages. We could start with the student's familiar native language and systematically introduce aspects of the new language into this familiar context. This would allow the student, at every stage, to practice with fully adult material. Whatever materials students find interesting can be adapted to this method. No one should ever be reduced to the level of Dick and Jane. If materials of high intrinsic interest were used, students would be motivated to continue not only from a long-term desire to learn the language but also from a short-term eagerness to find out what is happening in the book or story that they are reading. Concentrating upon only one aspect of the language at a time would allow rapid progress, so that students could have a real sense of accomplishment.

My proposals also allow a radical reordering of the sequence of topics that is presented to the student. It becomes possible, in particular, to present grammatical materials more systematically and more usefully than in conventional language courses. In the next section I give a detailed outline of the sequence that I have developed for teaching French, but the major point is that the method allows the most general and pervasive features of the language to be presented first while the fussy irregularities can be postponed until later. In a conventional course, when the students are expected to speak from the start, the very first lesson must touch upon everything. It must include something about pronunciation; it must introduce words of several grammatical categories; it must at least hint at a few rules of grammar so that the words can be joined together into meaningful phrases and sentences. When so many topics must be touched upon, no one of them can be dealt with in any depth. Each topic of grammar (pronouns, tenses, the gender system, etc.) comes typically to be spread across many lessons, and the student has trouble gaining any overall perspective of the linguistic processes involved. He is told about a thousand little details, details that he needs if he is to avoid mistakes in production; but at the same time he is likely to miss any general feeling for how the language is put together. His conscious attention is focused upon precisely the wrong part of the language. Details that should be left for slow, even unconscious, absorption become a constant conscious headache. The general, more pervasive, aspects of language can only be dimly perceived.

With the method I propose here it becomes possible to present a general description of a linguistic process, introduce the major features of that process into the text as a block, and then leave the irregularities and details to be gradually absorbed through long exposure. In French, for instance, gender and number work together in an interrelated system that is expressed through articles, adjectives, and nouns. This system can be explained in a few paragraphs, and the French forms of the articles and of the adjective suffixes can then be introduced into a practice text. The context into which these new forms are introduced can be entirely familiar, and this allows the learner to focus his attention upon what is new. The overall principles of the system can be learned quite easily in this way, while its irregularities (such as the irregular feminine and plural forms of many French adjectives) will be learned more slowly. When active production is required, these processes take much longer to learn, but if the principles of the system are clear and if active production is not needed, the irregularities can gradually fall into place without much difficulty. Many other aspects of the language can be introduced in the same way as the gender-number system.

THE LESSONS

In order to give a concrete idea of the program that I have developed, this section gives a lesson-by-lesson outline of the sequence through which I have been leading students. Short passages adapted from *La Dernière Classe* by Alphonse Daudet illustrate some of the levels through which students move. I will explain a number of special conventions as they arise.

1. Word Order. The first and most pervasive aspect of French to which students must grow accustomed is word order. Where French word order is like English nothing needs to be said, but I do explain that (1) object pronouns precede verbs, (2) adjectives often follow nouns, (3) negatives come in two parts that surround the verb, (4) subjects and verbs are more regularly exchanged to form questions than in English, and (5) the definite article is sometimes used in French where it would not appear in English. The only French words that I use at this stage are the most common words for negation—*ne . . . pas.* English equivalents for these could be found, but they would be so artificial that the simpler solution seems to be to introduce this single French form from the very beginning. Many details of French word order can be passed over in silence. Even where the order differs slightly from English, the meaning will often emerge quite easily and students will soon become accustomed to the French pattern through the examples in their reading. I use French pronunciation from the start. With this as a background, students have no trouble with passages such as this:

That morning-there I was very late for to go to the school, and I had great fear of to be scolded, all the more that Mr. Hamel us had told that he us would question on the participles, and I *ne* of them knew *pas* the first word. A moment the idea came to miss the class and to take my course across fields.

2. Gender and Number. As noted earlier, gender and number unite French articles, adjectives, and nouns into a single system. I describe the system in a few pages. The masculine, feminine, and plural articles are given (*un, une, le, la, les*) as are the regular adjective suffixes for gender and number (*-e, -s, -es*). Since the prepositions *à* and *de* form common contractions with the articles, it is convenient to describe them at the same time and to introduce both their free forms and their contractions with the articles (*du, aux,* etc.). All these French forms are then introduced into a reading passage. Students read a passage at the level of the sample given next and they quickly gain a feeling for the way in which these words are used in context. The French words are italicized as a means of keeping them distinct from the English. Occasionally where English speakers might be confused by the absence of a word from the French that would be required in English, an English word is supplied in brackets as a temporary crutch.

Le weather was so warm, so clear! One heard *les* blackbirds to whistle *à la* edge *du* forest, and *le* meadow [of] Rippert, behind *la* sawmill. All that *me* tempted much more than *la* rule *des* participles; but I had *la* strength *de* to resist, and I ran very quickly toward *la* school.

3. A, de, y, en. A and *de* are first introduced in lesson 2, but both are used in several quite varied ways and they deserve a fuller discussion than was possible when the focus was upon gender and number. The pronouns *y* and *en* are closely related to *à* and *de,* and these can be included in the discussion. *Y* and *en* are often quite difficult for English speakers, since English has nothing at all like them, but they must be easily understood if one is to read French with comfort. Their use can be learned relatively easily if they are introduced at the same time as the related *à* and *de,* and if they are first encountered in a text where the largest part of the vocabulary remains English.

This third lesson also includes a fairly detailed description of French verb sequences that correspond to such English phrases as "try to think," "help to swim," and "teach to count." In French many of these verb sequences require an *à* or *de*; so this is the natural place to introduce them. In order to prepare the student for having the French sign of the infinitive attached to the verb, the English word *to-* is joined to the English verb with a hyphen when infinitives appear in the reading passage for this lesson.

4. *The Infinitive, Past Participle, and Two Past Tenses.* The verb system poses greater difficulties than any other aspect of French grammar, and exposure to its complexities begins with this lesson. The lesson introduces only 14 new forms, the first conjugation suffixes for the infinitive, the past participle, the imperfect tense, and the past definite tense. These are used repeatedly in the reading passages that I have been giving to the students; so they soon learn to recognize them. In lesson 3 the student saw *to-* attached to the verb as if it were a prefix. Now he encounters *-er* attached to the end of English verbs, and the transition is not difficult. Nor is there difficulty in learning that *-é* is often the equivalent of English *-ed,* and the student will already have become familiar with feminine and plural suffixes that can turn *-é* into *-ée, -és,* or *-ées.* The difference in meaning between the imperfect and the past definite tenses is more subtle, but it is simplified by the fact that the student learns the endings for these tenses in a context of familiar words.

To start with, only the first conjugation endings are used. This limitation conforms to the principle that the first priority is to provide a feeling for the overall system of the language. Once the system is well understood, the student will be able to tackle the numerous irregularities with less difficulty. To simplify the student's task, even irregular verbs are translated as if they are regular. The French verb *faire* "do," for instance, is highly irregular, but it appears in the passages in such guises as *do-é.* This could stand in place of an original *fait* (the irregular past participle of *faire*), but the learner need never be concerned with whether the *do-é* that he encounters actually stands for the verb *faire* or for some other verb that is regular and that has a similar meaning. The actual forms of *faire* will not be introduced until much later when the student is ready to cope with the irregular forms. For now, forms such as *do-é* will help him to master the system. The next sample suggests the type of passage made possible by the materials of lessons 3 and 4.

In pass-*ant* in-front-of *la* town-hall, I see-*ai* that there was *du* crowd stop-*é* near *du* little screen *aux* posters. Since two years, it is *de* there that to-*us* are come-*ées* all *les* bad-*es* news, *les* battles lose-*ées,* *les* requisitions, *les* orders *de la* headquarters; and I think, without myself stop-*er.* What is-it that there is again?

5. *Some Relatives, Interrogatives, and Conjunctions.* This lesson introduces only four new words: *qui, que, où,* and *quand.* All four are difficult words,

for each is used in a number of distinct ways and they differ markedly from familiar English usage. A passage that incorporates these words in their varied uses allows sentences to approach the original French considerably more closely.

6. *Some Basic Vocabulary.* Next, a score of very common French words are introduced. These include such conjunctions, adverbs, adjectives, and prepositions as *et, mais, comme, très, autre, beaucoup, avec,* and *dans,* and three nouns: *jour, père,* and *chose.* These are words that appear constantly in the text. By turning them into French, the passage assumes a considerably more French appearance, and this gives the students a satisfying sense of progress. The words introduced in this lesson, unlike those introduced in lesson 5, are relatively straight equivalents of English words, and this makes them easier to learn. As always, of course, the reading passage for this lesson gives students additional practice with the materials introduced earlier.

From this point onward somewhat larger blocks of vocabulary are introduced with each lesson and, in the hope of blunting the student's temptation to resort to brute memory, a new convention is adopted. The first few times that a new word is used, an English translation is placed directly above it. The final appearance of the translation is signaled by an asterisk, and by this time it is hoped most students will have absorbed its meaning without a deliberate struggle to memorize it. The reading passage accompanying lesson 6, therefore, assumes the following form:

      as   with
Then, *comme* I cross-*ais la* square in run-*ant, le* blacksmith Wachter, *qui* was there *avec* his apprentice in process *de* read-*er le* poster, to me cry-*a:*

Ne yourself hurry *pas* so much, little one; you will-arrive anyway enough soon *à* your school!

                    all
I believe-*ai que* he himself tease-*ait de* me, and I enter-*ai tout* breathless in *la* little-*e* courtyard *de* Mr. Hamel.

7. *Pronouns.* The French pronoun system is considerably more complex than the English system, and since this lesson introduces all the personal pronouns of the language, the lesson is more demanding than any of its predecessors. By the time students get this far, however, they have grown accustomed to the method and my students have been able to manage the pronouns without undue difficulty. In spite of their large numbers, it is advantageous to introduce all the pronouns in a single block, for this allows a unified explanation of the system. A single chart can display the pronouns in a clear order and in a form that the student can easily consult.

The use of *on* and the difference between *tu* and *vous* require brief explanation, and a somewhat fuller explanation is needed for the distinction between direct and indirect object pronouns and for the reflexives. Learning the pronouns is made easier by the experience that the students have already had by the time they reach this lesson. They are no longer surprised to find object pronouns before the verb, and even the reflexive pronouns have appeared (translated as "myself," "yourself," etc.). This eases the transition to the French forms. This lesson does introduce more new words and more new grammatical materials than earlier lessons, however, and the reading passage is correspondingly longer.

I   my
Je count-*ais sur tout* this confusion *pour* reach-*er mon* bench *sans* be-*er* see-*é; mais* just that *jour*
                                                           I   my
-there *tout* was tranquil, *comme un* morning *de* Sunday. *Par la* window open-*e, je* see-*ais mes*
                            their   his
classmates already distribute-*és à leurs* places, *et* Mr. Hamel, *qui* pass-*ait et* repass-*ait avec sa*
terrible ruler *en* iron under *le* arm. It (was) necessary open-*er la* door *et* enter-*er au* middle *de* that
              You   I
great stillness. *Vous* imagine, if he was red *et* if *je* had fear!

8. Borrowed Vocabulary. The most obvious aspects of borrowing between French and English are now described, and hereafter, when French and English words are sufficiently similar the words are incorporated into the reading passages in their French form. This is a relatively easy lesson, and in addition to introducing some new material, it provides additional practice with the pronouns.

                        look
Eh well, no. Mr. Hamel *me regarda sans* anger *et me* say-*a très* softly: Go quickly *à ta* place, *mon* little Franz; *nous* (were going) *commencer sans toi. Je* leap-over-*ai le* bench *et je me* sit-*ai* quickly *à mon* desk. Then only, *un* bit relieve-*é de ma* fright, *je* notice-*ai que notre* teacher had *sa* handsome-*e* frock-coat green-*e, son* ruffled-shirt pleat-*é* finely *et la* skull-cap *de* silk black-*e* embroider-*ée qu'il ne* wear-*ait que les jours d'*inspection *ou de* distribution *de* prizes.

9. Demonstratives. As with personal pronouns, the characteristics of French demonstrative adjectives and demonstrative pronouns are described and gathered into a table, and they are then introduced into the text.

10. The Verb System: Infinitives, Participles, and the Seven Simple Tenses. By the time a student reaches this point he should feel quite comfortable with two tenses that English speakers usually find quite difficult, the imperfect and the past definite. He should have grown accustomed to finding tense markers suffixed to the verbs, and he will be familiar with subject-verb agreement. He will also be thoroughly familiar with the infinitive and the past participle. To these verb forms, this lesson adds the present participle (-*ant*) and the first conjugation suffixes for the four remaining simple tenses: the future, the conditional, the present subjunctive, and the imperfect subjunctive. The student must acquire a feeling for the semantic differences among the various tenses.

This lesson presents the heart of the verb system, and it is probably the most difficult single lesson of the entire series, but the burden on the student is lightened by continuing to use only first-conjugation endings. The vast complexities of the irregular verbs remain for the future. Two verbs, *être* and *avoir,* are so pervasively irregular and so uniquely idiomatic in their usage that little would be gained by giving them an artificially regularized conjugation. They continue, for the present, to be translated into English.

To help students untangle the complexities of the verb system, brief formulas are written over the new verb suffixes the first few times they appear. These formulas inform the student of the tense, person, and number of the suffix. As the suffixes grow familiar the formulas are gradually eliminated, and the student is then on his own. As in earlier lessons, the new French forms (in this instance the verb suffixes) can be tabulated on a single page. This gives the student an overall perspective of the system. Gradually, as he reads he will master the details.

Besides, *toute la classe* had some *chose d'extraordinaire et de* solemn. *Mais ce qui me surprise-a le plus, ce* was *de* see-*er au* back *de la* room, *sur les* benches *qui* stay-*aient* empty-*s* ordinarily, *des* people *du* village seat-*és et* silent *comme nous, le* old Hauser *avec son* three-cornered-hat, *le* former mayor, *le* former postman, *et* then *d'autres personnes* still. *Tout ce* people-*là* appear-*ait* sad-*e; et* Hauser had bring-*é un* old primer eat-*é aux* edges *qu'il* hold-*ait* wide open-*e sur ses* knees, *avec ses* big-*es* spectacles rest-*ées* across *des* pages.

11. Borrowed Vocabulary. Correspondences between English and French borrowed words are discussed in more detail here, so as to help students to recognize French words. Like lesson 8, this is intended as a relatively easy interlude between more difficult lessons. In addition to introducing a certain amount of new material, it provides more practice with the simple tenses.

12. The Seven Compound Tenses. This is the second of three central lessons on the French verb system. Along with lessons 10 and 14, it introduces the student to the core of the tense system. By the time a student reaches this lesson, he should be gaining some comfort with the simple tenses, and he will now learn that each simple tense has a corresponding compound tense. Since the compound tenses require *être* or *avoir* as auxiliary verbs, this is the most appropriate moment to introduce these two highly irregular verbs. Their full conjugations are tabulated, and thus the studens are able, at last, to face the irregularities of French verbs. These verbs, of course, are very common, and this means that students will soon have ample practice in recognizing their most common forms.

This is also a convenient place to describe passives, the reflexive verbs, and the set of intransitives that are conjugated with *être,* since all these matters are intimately involved with the auxiliary verbs and with the compound tenses.

By this time the reading passages have incorporated a great deal of French. Some sort of halfway point seems to have been reached, for at least half of the words are now French and the general structure of most sentences is essentially French. Beginning with this lesson, therefore, I italicize the English, rather than the French portions of the passage. This is a welcome signal to the students that a divide has been crossed. From now on an increasing part of the students' burden will be to clean up details and irregularities and to master more idioms and vocabulary. The more pervasive patterns of the language have already been presented.

The following passage, prepared at the level of lesson 12, includes a few of the notes by means of which I have indicated the tense, person, and number of some verbs. The meaning of these notes should require no explanation.

PqP 3-S
While, que je m'étonnais de tout cela, Mr. Hamel était *climb-*é dans sa chaire, et de la même *voice*
PqP 3-S
*soft-*e et *serious-*e *with which* il m'avait *receive-*é, il nous *say-*a: Mes *children,* c'est la *last-*e *time*
German
que je vous *do-*e la classe. L'ordre est *come-*é de Berlin de ne plus *teach-*er que l'allemand dans les *schools* de l'Alsace et de la Lorraine. . . . Le *new teacher will arrive tomorrow. Today* c'est votre *last-*e leçon de français. Je vous *ask-*e d'être *very* attentifs.

13. Negatives, Interrogatives, and Relatives. The overall plan of this series of lessons has been to start with the most pervasive patterns of the language and to move gradually inward toward its more idiosyncratic and irregular features. The assumption has been that the irregularities will pose fewer problems once the overall framework of the language is under control. The narrowing down to the more irregular aspects of the language is evident in this lesson. It introduces a larger number of lexical items than any earlier lesson—negatives, question words, and relative pronouns. Individually these cause few problems, but there are a large number of them and each has its idiosyncrasies.

14. Irregular Verbs and Idioms. This is the third of the central trio of lessons on the verb system. It proves to be quite natural to introduce the suffixes of the second and third "regular" conjugations and the most common suffixes of the irregular verbs at the same time. More often than not, these are similar if not identical. It is possible, in fact, to list the vast majority of irregular verb suffixes and second- and third-conjugation verb suffixes in a single table. Some of these are like the first-conjugation endings, and a few are like the endings of *avoir* or *être,* and this reduces the burden upon the student. So long as the student does not have to reproduce these endings, they pose no insuperable difficulties. Notes that identify the verb and its tense assist the student the first few times that a new form appears.

Up to this point, a general principle has been maintained: the French form of a verb is never introduced unless the proper French suffix is available. Regularization has been used only when an English verb is substituted for the French. With suffixes for second and third conjugations and for irregular verbs at last available, it becomes possible to introduce the French forms of a number of very common but irregular verbs.

This lesson also introduces the student to several common idioms that use verbs such as *aller, pouvoir,* and *falloir* in ways that differ markedly from English.

Ces quelques *words* me *overwhelm-*èrent. Ah! les miserables, voila ce qu'ils avaient *post-*é à la
savoir Impft
townhall. Ma *last-*e leçon de français! . . . Et moi qui savais à *scarcely write-*er! Je ne *learn-*erais
falloir Cond
therefore jamais! Il faudrait *therefore* en *stay-*er là! Comme je m'en *resent-*

ais *now* du *time lose*-è, des classes *miss*-èes à *chase*-ir les *birdnests* ou a faire des *sliding* sur la Saar! Mes *books* que *just now still* je trouvais si *tiresome*-s, si *heavy*-s à *carry*-er, ma

faire Cond

grammaire, mon histoire *sacred*-e me *seem*-aient à present de *old*-s amis qui me feraient beaucoup

aller Impft

de pain à quitter, c'est comme Mr. Hamel. L'idée qu'il allait partir, que je ne le verrais plus, me faire Impft

faisait *forget*-er les *punishments*, les *blows* de *ruler.*

Poor homme!

15. Adverbs and Adjectives. Except for the short list of adjectives and adverbs introduced in lesson 6 and those that are transparently similar to English, adverbs and adjectives have, up to this point, been translated into English. By now, however, the student should be thoroughly accustomed to number and gender agreement, and to finding adjectives after their nouns. This lesson introduces many of the most common French adjectives and adverbs, and since many of these are irregular it tabulates their various forms. The lesson describes comparison and introduces many comparatives and superlatives. Like lesson 13, it presents a considerable range of irregular details, but the student should now have a clear enough grasp of the system to allow him to see how the details fit into the larger picture. This should make these new forms relatively easy to recognize and, of course, he need not try to reproduce them.

16. Past Participles and Reflexives. This is the first of several lessons that spell out the details of particular tenses and verb forms. A considerable list of irregular past participles is given, tabulated according to the varieties of irregularity, and students should soon grow comfortable with these irregularities. This lesson also adds to the store of first-conjugation verbs that students should begin to recognize, and it discusses the reflexives in more detail than was possible earlier. Examples are given of the irregular relationship between some nonreflexive verbs and their corresponding reflexives.

17. Numbers and Prepositions. Until this point numbers have all been translated into English and only the short list of prepositions introduced in lesson 6 have been in French. The number system is now described and a considerable range of prepositions is added to the student's stock. The reading passage for each of the lessons in this part of the program is quite long, since many of the details now being introduced can no longer be expected to occur within the limits of a short passage. French has been accumulating steadily, however, and by the time students have reached this stage the reading passages are predominantly French.

last

C'est en l'honneur de cette dernière classe qu'il avait mis ses beaux *clothes* du *sunday,* et maintenant je comprenais pourquoi ces vieux du village étaient venus s'asseoir au *end* de la *room.* Cela semblait dire qu'ils regrettaient de ne pas y être venus plus souvent, à cette *school.* C'etait aussi

forty

comme un façon de *thank*-er notre *teacher* de ses quarante *years* de bon *service,* et de *pay*-er leurs *respects* à la *nation* qui s'en *disappear*-ait.

18. The Present Indicative and Idioms. The various kinds of irregularities of the most irregular of all the tenses are surveyed in this lesson, and a number of examples are given. The goal, as always, is not to have students memorize these irregularities but to get a feeling for the range of possibilities so that they will be able to recognize them when they encounter them in context. The lesson also describes a few very common idioms.

19. Nouns. Many French nouns are so transparently similar to their English equivalents that it has been possible to introduce a large number of them into the reading passages. Of all the grammatical elements of French, however, nouns are the last to receive explicit attention. In part, this is because nouns are relatively easy to learn. In part, however, it is because few individual nouns are very common, in spite of the fact that the language has more nouns than all other words combined. In the beginning little would have been gained by asking a student to remember many nouns, because each would have appeared so rarely in the text that he was reading.

This lesson concentrates upon the most common nouns. Some words for body parts, animals, people, the natural environment, and units of time are listed. A large proportion of these have given rise to related English words of more specialized meaning (*bras-bracelet, terre-terrestrial, homme-humanity,* etc.). Related English words are given with the French word wherever possible. This should help students remember particular words, but even more important it should give students the idea that it is reasonable to search their minds for such related English words as they encounter new French vocabulary.

20. Imperfect and Present Subjunctive. The irregularities of these two related tenses are discussed in lesson 18. The use of the subjunctive is described in more detail than was possible earlier, and some of the conjunctions and verbs that govern the French subjunctive are introduced.

21. Remaining Simple Tenses. The future, the conditional, the past definite, and the imperfect subjunctive are described and their irregularities are surveyed. By the time students reach this lesson, they are able to read passages that are in French in all essentials. Only certain less common items of vocabulary are translated into English.

J'en étais là de mes reflexions, quand j'entendis appeler mon nom. C'était mon tour de reciter. Que n'aurais-je pas donné pour pouvoir dire tout en *full* cette fameuse *rule* des *participles,* bien *loud,* bien clair, sans un faute; mais je me *blunder-*ai aux premiers *words,* et je restai *up* à me *sway-*er dans mon *bench,* le coeur gros, sans *dare-*er rais-er la tête.

22. Building Vocabulary. The final lesson of the series consists of some rather discursive suggestions about how to go about building vocabulary. The conventions of French dictionaries are described, but students are encouraged to read widely and to use a dictionary as little as possible. They are urged to try to absorb the meaning of words gradually as they are faced in context rather than by attempting to commit them to memory by brute force.

The reading passage for this final lesson is given in its full original French. The student is encouraged to look up as few words as possible and to try instead to gain practice at guessing the meaning of unfamiliar words. To help him when he gets stuck, footnotes translate those words that would have been given in English in earlier passages. By the time students have finished this lesson, they are ready for one of the many available reading books that are equipped with footnotes or a glossary. With the help of a dictionary they can work their way through unedited materials.

DISADVANTAGES AND ADVANTAGES

The disadvantages that are inherent in the method I have described must not be minimized. The mixed texts, for one thing, are unaesthetic. Those with a sensitive appreciation for the language may find the language salad that the method requires to be frivolous if not repellent. I would rather counter this criticism by pointing out that the childish materials that we give to beginning students in conventional French courses are even less aesthetically pleasing. If we are to worry about delicate sensitivities, it is surely the sensitivity of the students who must read the materials about whom we should be concerned. Those already skilled in the languages who find the mixed texts distasteful need not look at them. Students have no choice.

A more serious problem is posed by pronunciation. I have refrained from asking my students to pronounce anything at all in French, but now and then they mention French words and it is apparent that their ideas of the pronunciation are entirely eccentric. Some students seem willing to read in happy ignorance of the native pronunciation even while admitting that they cannot refrain from inventing their own pronunciations for their private use. Other students seem very much to need to know how the words are pronounced. They are bothered if they cannot subvocalize as they read. Some even want to be able to read aloud. I have offered two kinds of help to such students.

First, I have provided them with a description of French pronunciation. More accurately, I have given them description of how the letters of French are pronounced under varying circumstances. Students can refer to this when they feel they need help. The relationship between French pronunciation and orthography is so complex, however, that this is a much less than satisfactory solution. Students with no exposure to the spoken language find it difficult to use a written description.

My second method of helping students with pronunciation has been to record the text, French and English all mixed together, on tape. Students can then listen to the tapes as they follow the written text on paper. At first I thought of this as almost a joke, but it proved far easier and more natural to read the texts aloud than I had expected. One has a certain problem with articulatory acrobatics as one repeatedly jumps back and forth from French to English pronunciation, but the reasonable solution to this difficulty is to aim for accurate

French pronunciation and let the English words acquire a French quality if that makes the text easier to read. I asked a native French speaker to read some of the text for me, and I was amused to find that as he read and as he grew accustomed to his task, his pronunciation of English words became more and more accented. If the intention is to give students a feeling for French pronunciation, the distortion of the English words would seem to be of little consequence.

Reading the mixed texts aloud proved less artificial than I had anticipated. When first inspected, the texts certainly look artificial, but when working through them in sequence it proves quite natural to read them as a coherent language. They can easily be given a natural intonation and, while one must slip rapidly back and forth between words of English and French origins, these meld together into a single communication system that soon loses its initial look of implausibility. Students who have used the tapes have reported them to be quite helpful. Not only did the tapes give them a sense of what the language sounds like and a sense of how the letters are related to the sounds, but the rhythm and intonation of the sentences and the varying emphasis that readers give to different words made the passages easier to understand. The recordings helped students to gain a feeling for the structure of the sentences.

Some students have felt no need for help with pronunciation, and I have let them decide for themselves whether or not to spend time with the tapes. The tapes cannot solve all pronunciation problems, but for some students they seem to cut through the worst of their difficulties.

The final and most obvious disadvantage of my method, of course, is that when students have finished my materials they can neither write nor engage in conversation. For many students, I believe, the advantages of rapid progress in reading far outweigh the limitations on conversation, but other students would certainly prefer a course which promises progress in the spoken language as well. My method is not the right one for all students.

One question that must arise is whether a student who has learned to read with my materials will be handicapped if he later wants to add a conversational ability to his repertory of skills. I cannot yet give a confident answer to this question, but I expect few difficulties. It may be that a student who has invented his own pronunciations will need some corrective relearning, but the feeling for structure and the considerable stock of receptive vocabulary that my method provides should allow the student to make relatively rapid progress once he is motivated to work on the spoken language. On this, however, we need more experience.

The disadvantages of the method are counterbalanced by a number of striking advantages. Several of my students have told me that they became so caught up in the story they were reading, so eager to find out what was going to happen next, that they found it difficult to spend much time on the grammar as they felt they should. In response, I have always told them that what really mattered was their ability to understand. The grammatical notes were provided only as a means of helping them to find their way through the reading. If they could read with little attention to the notes, then so much the better. It is a rare language course that allows beginning students to become this engrossed in the content of their reading. A course that can motivate students to read in this way and that can spare the student the tedium of childish reading materials would deserve to be taken seriously even if it had little else to recommend it.

But the method has some other advantages too. It allows the student to focus his conscious attention upon the more pervasive characteristics of the language and to leave the eccentricities to sort themselves out gradually. Sooner or later the language learner must cope with the eccentricities, but learning to recognize them is far easier than learning to produce them. A beginning student who is asked to speak or write must, if he is to avoid multiple errors, keep a hundred details in his mind at the same time. With no need to produce the language, progress can be much more rapid, and if a student finally decides he wants to speak or write, his experience with hundreds of pages of mature French will have given him a sense of the language, and even some of its eccentricities will have come to seem natural—to "sound right"—with little explicit attention ever having been directed toward them.

The changing proportions of English and French in the text give the student a constant and visible measure of his progress. As the weeks go by he can watch the text shift inexorably toward French. At every point he can see just how far he still has to go.

Finally, the method focuses much of the student's conscious attention upon the area of language that is of greatest concern to the ordinary speaker: the meaning. Always he must read for understanding. the grammar is given only as a means to the end of extracting meaning. New words and new constructions are always learned in a familiar context. At every stage the student can bring to his task a full and mature language system. As each new element sinks back into semiconscious and then into unconscious familiarity, it becomes part of the context within which the next elements are learned. He never needs to be frustrated by the kind of fragmentary isolated knowledge that ordinarily limits elementary language students.

CONCLUSIONS

The early lessons in the sequence are shorter than those that come later. This is because the first language features covered are so common that a very few pages of text are enough to give adequate practice. Later lessons cover rarer aspects of the language, and some of these may not appear at all in a short passage. For this reason the later lessons have much longer passages, and to make such a long passage profitable, each of these lessons also introduces more material. At the start, therefore, my students cover three or even four lessons each week. Later, they work through no more than two. In the course of the term they read about 70,000 words of text. If only half these words are in French, they are still well ahead of first-term students in more conventional classes.

Students with no background in French have had no trouble working through my materials in a single 14–week term, and they report spending no more than 4 or 5 hours each week on the lessons, including 1 hour in class. Convincing comparisons with courses that use different techniques are difficult because of differences in course goals, and because of varying student background and motivation. My students may have been stimulated by the experimental nature of the situation. On the other hand, they were not taking the course officially and they had no need to cram for an examination or to worry about a grade. My preliminary estimates suggest that my students reach at least as far as the level of second-year high school French, and they do about as well as students who take one term of the special reading course offered by the Romance Languages Department of the University of Michigan. The latter students, however, have reported that they spent about twice as much time each week on their French as do my students, and all indications are that students in the conventional reading class find their French to be far less agreeable than do mine.

I have often been asked how I would handle languages, such as Russian, that do not use the Roman alphabet or, even worse, languages such as Arabic or Hebrew, in which the direction of writing is different from English. For Russian, I would be tempted to introduce the Cyrillic alphabet by first teaching students to read English that has been transcribed into Cyrillic. Once the alphabet is mastered, it would seem possible to proceed much as I have done with French. It might be possible to teach Arabic and Hebrew orthography in the same way, but mixing right-to-left Arabic or Hebrew into the same passage with left-to-right English might pose insuperable problems. Since we read with a series of discrete fixations and not with continuous sweep of our eyes, however, it might even be possible to mix together words of differing directions in the same passage. The possibilities for Chinese seem, at first sight, to be quite promising. Chinese characters could easily be sprinkled in among the English words in gradually increasing proportions. The reader might even vocalize the characters by means of English words. The method would make it difficult to capitalize upon the considerable phonetic component of the characters, however, and this might be a serious drawback. The problems posed by different writing systems, however, will only be clearly seen when experiments are made with practical lessons.

Preparing materials for a course such as I have described is a laborious process, but it can have a peculiar and rewarding fascination. It has liberated me from all sorts of notions about the purity of my language, and it has shown me how easy and natural the process of borrowing between languages can be. And, of course, I have also had the satisfaction of watching students avoid some of the agonies of language learning that I still remember so vividly from my own education. I would be endlessly pleased if others found the methods that I have proposed to be sufficiently intriguing to merit imitation.

3

APPROACHES TO A RICH ACQUISITION ENVIRONMENT

INTRODUCTION

Thanks to an enormous investment in language and learning research, the past two decades have been marked by a prodigious advance in understanding of first and second language acquisition, of learning psychology, and of language itself. However, the effects of this progress are not easy to find in language teaching observed generally in schools and colleges. In fact, the approaches to language training that currently predominate have not developed significantly beyond the notions and assumptions of the linguistics, psychology, and pedagogy of the forties and fifties. In spite of the admittedly high attrition rate and modest proficiency attainment of most students in language classes generally, most language courses still today differ little in design or content from their predecessors.

Perhaps this is to be expected. Language courses are generally the work of one of two writers, usually college or high school language teachers with confidence in their own intuitions drawn from years of training and experience in the classroom. Language teachers and textbook writers are discouraged by the "system" from plowing new ground: publishers are admittedly shy of radical change, budget-conscious administrators are resistant to sudden changes and are not easily swayed by enthusiasm or argumentation for new ideas, and even colleagues question "rocking the boat" with new departures. (How can the radical ideas of one's friend down the hall be that much better than those of the authors of the scores of existing French textbooks?) Thus change comes only gradually. The "system" is extremely conservative and the traditional model continues to carry the day.

In this model, to characterize it in general terms, teachers require their students to demonstrate their degree of mastery of all or nearly all the material of each lesson, and in drills and tests pay close attention to details of spelling, pronunciation, grammar, and word selection. It is form, more than content, that is monitored. Student performance is graded against an ideal norm of near-native performance. (It is felt by many teachers that tolerance of less than near-native performance within the scope of the current level of study will foster the development of "sloppy habits" which are difficult to eradicate later, so that imposing a "perfection criterion" from the first helps establish good habits and avoid the necessity of having to uproot bad habits. Obviously the authors under discussion question that view.)

Instructional materials for beginning language courses in this model present a set curriculum or syllabus within a textbook, a workbook, and nonprint media for home or laboratory use, all containing carefully selected and logically arranged content. Whether it is a grammatical syllabus or a functional (or "notional") one, vocabulary input is very limited, and lexical and grammatical complexity, irregularity, and foreignness are presented very gradually: simple sentences precede complex, regular word forms precede irregular, indicative mood comes far ahead of subjunctive, and so on. The learner is led step by step through a linear or hierarchical sequence of discrete learning tasks.

The "payoff," the purpose and ultimate aim of it all, is supposed to be "liberated communication"—actual flight. But it usually turns out that most of the time is spent, as it were, studying the theory of "flight," tuning up the engines, warming up and simulating takeoff, leaving very little time for actual flight. The danger of crashing is presumably too great to allow premature takeoff.

The approach is thus based on the assumption that we have the sophistication to program language instruction so as to consistently fulfill the conditions of learning suggested by Robert Gagne, author of *The Conditions of Learning*, phrased thus in a talk at Brigham Young University in 1969:

The most dependable condition for the insurance of learning is the prior learning of prerequisite capabilities. Some people would call these "the specific readinesses for learning." Others would call them the "enabling conditions." If one wants to insure that a student can learn some specific new activity, the very best guarantee is to be sure he has previously learned the prerequisite capabilities.

The logic of this consummate ideal of learning is so simple and so compelling that it has been uncritically accepted by many language professionals as being achievable or roughly achievable in prepackaged language instruction. Clearly implied in it was the principle of mastery learning, mastering each small step or level of instruction before proceeding to the next. What was not so clearly seen is the impossibility of determining for any one learner, much less for a classroom of learners, what those steps are that will provide the prerequisite capabilities, the enabling conditions at any point so as to ensure the ready acquisition of each next step and ultimately the acquisition of language. In a very real sense it is not possible to construct an ideal syllabus for bringing about the acquisition of a language.

Yet so convincing is the argument for the model and so powerful is the thrust of the traditional viewpoint that one can easily fail to make this one crucial observation: if the goal of language training is communicative competence, and that implies the freedom and ability of our students to choose to say what they wish to say and to understand fluent native speech at a high level, then the training model is not working well, at least not for the great majority. Few students acquire the ability to speak fluently or understand fluent native speech through classroom training of this kind in 1, 2 or even 3 years' time.

It was only in the past decade or so that a few independent pioneers were able to see clearly some basic fallacies in the traditional approaches to language teaching and perceive that a very different approach with a very different kind of curriculum might serve better. They began to see that the traditional model violates some of the conditions of learning found in natural language acquisition, conditions that are probably necessary for the efficient induction of language: sufficient opportunity for the creative and truly communicational use of the language, the provision of a "linguistically rich" learning environment in which the learner can work out intended meanings through contextual clues, the opportunity to remain silent and develop receptive skills in advance of speaking, etc. These people saw that "under-the-gun, total accountability" for everything presented in a course fails to take into account the limitations of memory, deprives the learners of the use of their natural strategies for language acquisition, and seriously compromises the richness of the learning environment. They also saw that the dream of programming language instruction on the ideal mastery learning model was a chimera.

But more than this, like Berlitz, de Sauzé, and other direct methodologists of years past, they saw that the way people learn languages naturally in nonacademic "real-world" situations suggested an alternative model for language instruction. This anticipated Krashen's distinction between language *acquisition*, the natural, unconscious process observed in children as well as adults in informal learning environments, and language *learning*, the conscious process of language learning observed under conditions of formal instruction. In acquisition environments the input data are not preselected, graded, sequenced, or presented in small, discrete doses and in well-edited form, nor are they practiced in artificial ways. The input is massive and unorganized, leaving to the learner the task of extracting from it what he will in formulating the generalizations he needs in order to become a proficient user of the language.

As noted above, they saw that in language acquisition environments an incredibly complex learning task is successfully and often rapidly accomplished by ordinary people, without guidance, instruction, or materials of any kind, without the specification of behavioral objectives, without a planned syllabus or learning schedule, without requirement for oral response to the situation, even without mastery tests of grades, and that often the product of this unacademic kind of language acquisition is more respectable than the product of formal language training.

In effect the question they posed was: Can the efficiency of classroom language learning for some or all students be increased by introducing into formal language learning environments any of the features found in informal language learning environments? Can classroom language training be designed to open up to students new possibilities for employing strategies used successfully by adult language "acquirers"? And if so, how? What would be the curriculum for such a course?

These questions had been posed before, of course, and had led to various methodological innovations, though none as successful as hoped for. In asking these questions again, the modern innovators had much more information about the acquisition process to go on than the direct methodologists of yesteryear, so their accommodation of features of informal language acquisition into formal learning situations was, I think, more successful.

The six authors presented below took a radically different view of language training than their predecessors. They created successful systems of language instruction based on the view that language acquisition can thrive in the classroom if an environment is provided there that is rich in diverse and contextually clear communication rather than having limited and narrowly focused input aimed at building hierarchies of learning structure that satisfy ideal conditions for learning.

Leonard Newmark. Most college language departments are administered by scholars who have come up through the ranks. Mostly these are specialists in literature; only a few are professionally committed primarily to linguistic studies with major interest in language instruction. One of the rare ones, however, is Leonard Newmark. In 1963, he left his position as chairman of the Linguistics Department at Indiana University to accept the position of chairman of the Linguistics Department at the newly opening University of California at San Diego. The "plum" that enticed him there was the promise of complete liberty to develop and administer language training programs in the standard languages.

What Leonard Newmark did with that assignment was interesting, though at the time it seemed both unacademic and radical. He did not hire professional language teachers, literature specialists, or language majors to teach languages. He hired native speakers and trained them to teach their language in a natural way, the way he describes in the paper reprinted below. As to the success of the students in learning languages in that very different kind of language program there is no question. But in terms of the methodological doctrines and commonly held notions about language learning then prevailing, it was not easy to account for such success at the time. Now, however, in the light of the progress in understanding the dynamics of learning in general and of language learning in particular their success is easier to account for. Newmark's model was far in advance of its time, and today it still stands as an interesting paradigm of language pedagogy.

Earl W. Stevick. If asked to name the persons who have contributed the most to the development of language training methodology congruent with current views of instructional psychology and language acquisition, without hesitation I would put the name of Earl W. Stevick at the top. From his earliest publication on language teaching in the 1950s to his most recent in 1980 it has seemed to this reader that Stevick has consistently penetrated core issues of language teaching methodology deeper and with more elucidation than anyone else. He is a masterful teacher of language himself and open to new ideas. His informal experimentation with various innovative approaches to language instruction and his insightful probings into what makes them tick, published in many articles and books, have earned him the high regard of the profession. Language teachers who are not well read in Stevick are missing out on some profound and enlightening insights and ideas on teaching and learning.

The article chosen for inclusion here, published in a relatively obscure linguistics journal, is not one of his better-known pieces and has not been read by many language teachers, but its argument for a learner-created curriculum is up to date, and its insight into the dynamics of language learning is remarkable for its time. Appearing at the time I was engaged in designing and developing intensive language training materials, this article for me marked a watershed in my thinking about language training and prepared me to see later in Community Language Learning a rational, principled, and powerful model.

Charles A. Curran, Georgi Lozanov, Tracy D. Terrell, and Beverly Galyean. Traditional wisdom recommends as a sensible, gentle way to introduce a language that a course give at first only a small handful of easy words plus two or three rules of syntax to work with, and add new words and rules very gradually, lest the learners drown or their memory systems collapse from the overload. This slow and carefully controlled entry could be called the "milk before meat" or the "crawl before walk" approach.

In a lecture on language instruction models (1974), Karl C. Sandberg argues that while it is wise to be concerned with overloading the learning system, it is not wise to leave out of account the ability of the mind to select from a rich environment those elements that have particular relevance to its current interests. He suggested that a thin, weak, and overly limited progression in the volume of language input in beginning classes creates a deficient learning environment, providing little for the student to select from in his attempts to acquire the language or to communicate. He called this the "empty bin" approach.

Sandberg contrasts an "empty bin" approach with a "full bin" approach in which a great volume of material is introduced and opportunity is given for the learner to select from it what he finds meaningful and useful. Clearly this is the essence of a student-centered curriculum.

In another view the contrast between the two widely different approaches can be seen as two ways of working a gem mine. In the one way a new worker is introduced to a mine glittering with gems jutting out of the clay wall and ceiling and strewn along the floor of the tunnel. He is given the freedom to gather up whatever he can carry, whatever gems catch his interest. The mind of this worker is awake and alert as he makes his selections. With such an exciting task to perform, he doesn't tire early but handpicks cartloads of precious gems. In the other way a new worker is introduced to the same mine glittering with gems, but he is instructed to take a pick and pick away at the next square meter portion of the carefully mapped out clay wall down to a depth of half a meter in order to extract any gems buried there. He is not to pay any attention to the glittering attractions farther down the shaft but must exploit the mine methodically and mindlessly by picking at the clay according to the boss's preset plan.

To language teachers who have not experienced the approaches of Curran, Lozanov, Terrell, or Galyean, it may be that only a systematically mapped out course, a methodical approach that takes the learner step by step through the language, makes sense. The suggestion that an "unsystematic" approach which encourages learners to gather their own "gems" from a rich learning environment may seem at first indefensible. But to those who have experienced such a "full-bin" or "gem gathering" approach, the arguments in its favor are compelling.

Like all enlightened teachers, Curran, Lozanov, Terrell, and Galyean see the learner rather than the subject matter as central to the learning process, and the teacher and materials serving mainly to help activate this process. They view the learner not as a disembodied brain or acquisition device, but as a whole person, body and soul, a unique, enormously complex and delicate composite of past successes and failures, likes and dislikes, hurts, fears, beliefs, doubts, tolerances, preferences, etc. They see the ego-involvement in the dynamic and delicate teacher-learner relationship as a primary force for or against learning. They see the acquisition of skill or knowledge as resulting not simply from the injection of subject-matter data reinforced by drill (no matter how carefully programmed) but as requiring receptive readiness before it can be assimilated and become functional. In effect, then, Curran, Lozanov, Terrell, and Galyean (together with Newmark and Stevick) reject as complete and adequate paradigms for language learning both the behavioral and the cognitive models of learning which focus more on the brain or the nervous system than on the whole person in a dynamic social matrix. Their approaches do not eclectically borrow parts of one and parts of the other but introduce and stress this other dimension, the dimension that takes into account and deals with intrapersonal and interpersonal aspects of the learning process.

In terms of Krashen's model of language acquisition, they are less concerned with the "input" and more concerned with the filter, the blockage of "intake." They see that a crucially important key to language acquisition lies in getting the learner to lower his filter (or, in Curran's terms, in "cultivating" the learner's receptiveness or emotional readiness to receive and "nourish" the intake). With the reduction or removal of the filter (the learner's mental blocks, self-doubts, inhibitions, etc.) more of the "input" can become "intake."

In various ways Curran, Lozanov, Terrell, and Galyean deal directly and effectively with this critical dimension of language teaching and learning. Each makes a unique and important contribution to the increased understanding of how languages can be taught and learned more efficiently with a "full bin" or "gem-gathering" approach if the filter is effectively dealt with.

If asked to name language teachers whose seminal contributions to language teaching in the past two decades have influenced current thinking and practice, I would include among them the counseling psychologist Father

Charles A. Curran, who brought from his collaborative work with Carl Rogers in counseling therapy a revolutionary view of education in general and of language teaching in particular, including an understanding of how to deal with the filter; the Bulgarian psychotherapist and learning experimentalist Georgi Lozanov, whose experiments with memory training have been directed to finding ways of tapping the reserves of the unconscious mind through suggestion and desuggestion; the linguist and language teacher, Tracy D. Terrell, who saw in the findings of language acquisition research startling implications for language teaching, and constructed a very different method of teaching languages that has proved to be effective; and the humanist-educator Beverly Galyean, who uses language teaching to enable learners to look within themselves and find meaning and values they can share.

What I have learned from these people in workshops, in talking with them and reading their writing and in my own informal experimentation with their ideas, has profoundly changed my approach to language training and increased my enjoyment and success in teaching.

In the remainder of this section I will introduce these four innovators who have made what I think are monumental contributions to language teaching and whose ideas cluster together—at least in regard to the need for massive input and for dealing with the filter.

Charles A. Curran's Community Language Learning. Many language teachers who have observed a typical beginning Community Language Learning session have remarked how utterly simple it is. There is no prepared text or syllabus to guide the class. A group of learners just sit in a circle and banter with each other about anything they like in their first language, and the teacher translates what each one says and then has him or her repeat it in the target language. A record of all that is said in the target language is kept, which may or may not be made available to the students in a "reflection session" that follows each banter session.

Seeing only these outward features and unaware of Curran's profound concepts of the dynamics of learning and of the learner-knower relationship, many language teachers have taken this piece of Community Language Learning as simply another activity they can introduce into their classrooms, a classroom enrichment or frivolous change-of-pace activity to be used perhaps at the end of a class or on Fridays when there is not time or motivation for more productive "core" learning activities.

In fact, though Curran's approach is beautifully simple when compared with traditional approaches—like a Piper Cub compared with a 747—still it does not "fly itself" but requires considerable understanding on the part of the pilot.

At Loyola University where Curran experimented for many years with counsel-learning/Community Language Learning, it is reported that with this approach students in a regular college class were able in one year to acquire impressive comprehension skills in two or three languages and speaking proficiency in one of those languages, in fact, a level of proficiency not ordinarily attained by students studying one language the traditional way. If this is so, then clearly the way such achievements were made is of high interest.

For a teacher to borrow only certain outward features of the approach without understanding what its real power is would be, it seems to me, like using an airplane only as a car or a sophisticated computer only as a typewriter.

The introduction to Community Language Learning as well as to all the other innovative approaches presented here is of course inadequate to fully inform the reader. Personally I have found that the more I use CLL the more I feel I have to learn about it and about the philosophy and psychology which underlie it. I go back frequently to the writings of Curran and others who have worked with this model, and I recommend the same to all language teachers.

The 1960 article is one of the earliest and most concise statements of the fundamentals of Curran's counseling-learning approach to education. The central focus in this article is on the counseling relationship between the "language counselor and the language client." His 1978 address, presented at the TESOL Convention in Mexico City, is based on the intervening years of study, during which he deepened the understanding of these basic ideas. A number of further clarifications emerged as the central focus of his research shifted to the learning experience. One of these clarifications which delineates more explicitly the conditions necessary to foster a creative learning experience is specifically treated in the TESOL address under the acronym SARD.

Note: Since Dr. Curran's death in 1978, Associates of Counseling-Learning Institutes (a not-for-profit educational organization founded by Charles A. Curran for the purpose of continuing his work) continue to use and develop this approach in a number of educational settings. Three books in particular by Curran are recommended for people interested in learning more about this approach. These are: *Counseling-Learning; A Whole-Person Model for Education,* 1977; *Counseling-Learning in Second Languages,* 1976; and *Understanding: An Essential Ingredient in Human Belonging,* 1978.

Georgi Lozanov's Suggestopedia. Since my first experimentation with Lozanov's ideas on language teaching in 1975, of particular interest to me have been two dimensions of his approach, the rate or amount of data input and the mode of input.

As to the rate or amount of data input, Lozanov gives learners a truly enormous amount of complex spoken and written materials, many times more than standard approaches provide. The script (a dialogue or narrative) presented the first day is over ten pages long and contains hundreds of words and a large variety of grammatical forms. But the approach does not aim for mastery of the materials. There are no mastery tests and no pressure for the students to learn any specific part of it. Clearly what the mass of material provides is an exceedingly rich source of language information, a "gem mine" from which the learner is allowed to mine what he finds functional and interesting to him. In effect the mass of material provided to the learner in this approach creates a learning environment that in certain regards comes close to simulating the "real-world" acquisition environment.

Commenting on this feature of his approach, Lozanov stated that to give only a little material and to expect mastery of it as traditional approaches do "suggests" to the learner that language learning must be very hard, for it is parceled out in very small doses. On the other hand, giving very large amounts of material "suggests" the opposite, that language learning is easy!

My own informal experimentation with this approach has convinced me of the value in language training of massive input of data. In a Maya course that met 5 hours a day for 6 consecutive days I introduced a truly massive amount of language data through four very long and complex narratives. Contrary to the expectations of common sense, what the learners achieved in listening comprehension and speaking proficiency in that brief course with that enormous mass of material was to me truly remarkable. Their achievement was not finely tuned mastery, of course. In fact it was what one might well call "quick and dirty." But it was, I believe, many times richer than they could have achieved if the approach had aimed only for the more usual refined but limited objectives.

In stocking the language learner's environment with enormous amounts of data (and providing the means to understanding the meaning), Lozanov has contributed a key notion to my thinking about language acquisition, the notion of a "critical mass." This notion suggests that the most efficient language learning takes place only where the learner is immersed in an environment in which he is actively receptive to rich, intensive, and prolonged bursts of "bombardment" of a stream of language which he has some way of decoding. The usual high school or college language class of 1 hour a day for 4 or 5 days a week is highly inefficient in that it fails to provide the amount (and usually the kind) of exposure to the language that is needed for effective language acquisition. An optimally rich language learning environment, I now presume, is not simply a saturated state; in order to achieve a state of "fission," the learner must have intensive and prolonged bursts of exposure to massive amounts of the language, most of which he can understand.

(This view of the need of a supersaturated learning environment and intensive exposure to it to create a "critical mass" necessary for "fission" to take place and Kenneth Pike's view of the need of a very restricted environment in which the focus is on the mastery of structural patterns necessary for "nucleation" to take place are apparently in mutual contradiction.)

The mode of input is the second dimension of interest to me in the Lozanov approach. Its most widely discussed feature is the dramatic reading of dialogue and narrative texts against a background of classical music while students listen in a relaxed state. These things have to do with the reduction of anxiety and the increase of pleasure in learning. Through these presentation modes and in the way he elaborates the method, clearly Lozanov is working on the filter, and seemingly with success.

Suggestopedia has been characterized by some as a "right-brain" approach to learning that slips information into the relaxed mind without conscious buffering or monitoring by the cognitive brain, the left hemisphere. Whether this characterization is scientifically valid or not I cannot say, but people who have experienced suggestopedic language training do apparently assimilate a large amount of material without conscious study or struggle and are able to demonstrate remarkable proficiency in both listening comprehension and speech after a relatively short training period.

Although I had used Lozanov's ideas since 1975, it was not until 1979 that I had the opportunity to attend a workshop on the method conducted by Lozanov and later that year to observe a beginning Spanish course at the Lozanov Learning Institute in San Diego conducted by a teacher certified in the methodology. Enrolled in the course were a dozen adults ranging in age from about 30 to 70, with an average age of about 45. They were in their sixth and last week of the course. The instructor spoke only Spanish. I observed the instruction from the sixtieth to the sixty-sixth hour and was given opportunity to interview the course participants and the teacher and institute director.

The students in the course were immersed during the 3-hour sessions in a steady stream of Spanish which provided an unusually rich source of comprehensible input. And they were given considerable opportunity to use the language in directed but open-ended conversation with each other and the teacher. At the beginning of the course each participant had assumed a new name and a pseudo-identity by which they were known to each other. This is standard procedure in the Lozanov approach and is seen as a contribution to the relaxation of self-conscious inhibitions that characteristically hamper adult language learners as they begin to speak their new language. Many of the participants appeared to be uninhibited, relaxed, and enjoying the class activities even when it was their turn to speak. Most of them apparently understood the elaborate Spanish that flowed in great volume from the instructor, and most of them succeeded impressively in their attempts to communicate in the language.

There were two or three who were less able or willing to attempt ambitious communication in the language, yet they did not evidence discomfort or anxiety with their obviously more limited achievement. For beginners in their sixth week of training most of them demonstrated an ability to communicate that was, I would have to say, phenomenal for its volume, ambitiousness, and fluency—if not always for its grammatical accuracy. For a class of mature adults just 60 hours into a language I would say that they were launched and sailing beautifully in Spanish.

Excellent though it was, I think that that course failed to achieve all its aims. One of the most striking aims of this approach, one which if not achieved reveals, according to Lozanov, that the real power of suggestopedia was not successfully tapped, is what I have referred to above as the "spa effect." Properly run, a suggestopedic language learning session is supposed to produce the same therapeutic effect as a visit to a health spa: a sense of euphoria, the feeling of being rested, refreshed, and recharged. Learning that is meaningful, relaxing, and relevant to one's interests, and does not load the learner with cognitive stuff or put him through meaningless drills must be, according to Lozanov, an exhilarating experience that conduces to health and vitality, not to fatigue and boredom. While none of the students in the San Diego class said they were bored, some did note that after three and a half hours they were a little fatigued!

At several places in the United States and Canada people have been or are working with a Lozanovian approach to language instruction. Primary among these, and the only one officially authorized by Lozanov to use his name and the registered trademark "Suggestopedia," is the Lozanov Learning Institute, Inc.

Tracy D. Terrell's Natural Approach. Of all the innovative approaches discussed in this book, the one which has been most clearly explained and placed against a background of current second language acquisition theory is Tracy D. Terrell's Natural Approach. Unlike Curran and Lozanov, strangers to the language profession and interested primarily in learning and instruction, Terrell was a trained linguist and seasoned language teacher when he developed the Natural Approach. The article included in this book was written in 1975 but not published until 2 years later. When it appeared in the *Modern Language Journal* probably most of its readers were not ready for it. Though it was by someone from within the profession, the article was for many just "too far out" to be taken seriously. Since then, however, the believability and reputation of the Natural Approach has greatly increased, partly because of the dissemination of information on its success at the University of California at Irvine. Also the professional workshops given by Dr. Terrell on the approach are extremely well received. In the years since 1975, of course, the approach has been greatly elaborated and enriched, but its tenets and procedure have remained basically unchanged.

Perhaps the most vulnerable argument for the claims of this or any other method lies in the performance of the people who have been trained with it. In 1979 I went to Irvine to learn more about the Natural Approach and to compare its success in terms of the proficiency of the students in Spanish there with the success of Spanish programs I have observed at other universities. I came away with the opinion that Tracy Terrell and his Natural Approach have set a mark of student achievement in beginning college Spanish that may not be equaled anywhere. For that if for no other reason I recommend to the reader a careful consideration of Terrell's approach and of its rationale.

Beverly Galyean's Confluent Approach: "Language from Within." Beverly Galyean, another of the innovators who favor a "gem-gathering" approach, has focused on different aspects of learning than the others. As with Lozanov, Asher, Curran, and Gattegno, the roots of her introspective "Language from Within" approach are founded neither in language teaching methodology nor in linguistic science, but rather in humanistic and transpersonal psychology. Like Curran, she acknowledges being profoundly influenced by Carl Rogers. But she discovered in the psychology of Perls, Maslow, Assagioli, and Jung also the basis for a radically different understanding of learning and found that it suggests a radically different approach to adult second language learning.

As she expressed it in a private communication, beyond the influence of Rogers evident in this approach are elements of

(a) Gestalt Learning Theory (Fritz Perls), whose basic premise is that all self-knowledge is possible through self-awareness. It is a matter of learning how to look within to discover organismic needs and subsequently how to fill these basic human needs. Our language forms emerge as a concrete expression of these needs. Thus "Language from Within" calls for introspection and self-disclosure types of activities.

(b) Humanistic/transpersonal psychology (Abraham Maslow), whose theory indicates that humans have five basic needs around which all learning energies coagulate. The three highest, close affiliation with others, self-esteem, and transcendence, are treated in a unique way in the "Language from Within" approach.

(c) Psychosynthesis (Roberto Assagioli), whose theory demonstrates how various inner levels of consciousness express themselves in symbolic imagery. In "Language from Within" programs Assagioli's influence is seen in the use of many guided imagery and fantasy activities.

(d) The psychology of Carl Jung, who first initiated the concept of "whole person learning," calling for a balanced interplay among sensory, cognitive, feeling, and intuitive experiences in the learning process. Thus the "Language from Within" approach calls for sensory, feeling, and intuiting experiences along with others of a more cognitive sort.

Recent brain research seems increasingly to indicate that knowledge may originate in the right or intuitive hemisphere of the brain but is then organized and expressed in the left brain. Since nontraditional learning activities such as fantasy, imagery, meditation, movement, music, deep breathing, poetry, art, and drama serve to "open up" the right hemisphere, a variety of these are used in confluent teaching.

Galyean encapsulates her perspective on language learning as follows:

The language program is set up to accomplish these coequal goals of self-knowledge or identity, self-esteem and interpersonal sharing through crystal-clear communication. It is based on the assumption that a positive self-concept and the ability to love both self and others is dependent on the ability to issue positive thoughts (based on positive words) about oneself and others. By changing the nature of language programs to include primarily those words and concepts that are powerful emotive evocators of self-affirming responses, we can change (or help individuals to change) their way of perceiving their strengths, potentials, and subsequent future choices. All good therapy is based upon "positive languaging" about oneself and others. Thus our simplest language programs can be powerful vehicles for human development.

Confluent education in languages (or any other subject) is concerned then with the personal growth of each learner in self-awareness through self-reflection and sharing with others in interpersonal dialogue. From skillfully guided activities in which these are emphasized, the mastery of the curriculum emerges naturally: the three flow together. The term "confluent education" refers to this merging or flowing together of cognitive, affective, and interactive goals and objectives into the learning experience.

Interestingly, in both Galyean's and Curran's approach the curriculum of a language course is largely generated by the learners themselves; however, a major difference between the two approaches is apparent in how and with what aims that learner-centered curriculum is generated. You will note the differences in her paper.

I find in confluent teaching an approach which ennobles learners and helps them to progress not only in linguistic skills, but even more importantly in self-realization. For me that is important. It has much to do with affect and is, I suspect, the key to successful language learning for many people who if they attempted to learn a language through a more conventional approach would be frustrated. I believe that a confluent approach and the techniques Galyean uses can significantly increase the power of language learning not only for the slow and frustrated, but also for the gifted. It is entirely consistent and compatible with Community Language Learning, and I think adds important new dimensions to it. Also I suspect that the attainment of the "spa effect" aimed for in suggestopedia can be aided by the aims and approach of confluent teaching.

HOW NOT TO INTERFERE
WITH LANGUAGE LEARNING

Leonard Newmark

In the applied linguistics of the past 20 years much has been made of the notion of first language interference with second language learning. Our dominant conception of languages as structures and our growing sophistication in the complex analysis of these structures have made it increasingly attractive to linguists to consider the task of learning a new language as if it were essentially a task of fighting off an old set of structures in order to clear the way for a new set. The focal emphasis of language teaching by applied linguists has more and more been placed on structural drills based on the linguist's contrastive analysis of the structures of the learner's language and his target language; the weight given to teaching various things is determined not by their importance to the user of the language but by their degree of difference from what the analyst takes to be corresponding features of the native language.

A different analysis of verbal behavior has been motivated in psychology by reinforcement theory; the application of this analysis has led, of course, to programmed instruction, step-by-step instruction based in practice on the identification of what are taken to be the components of the terminal verbal behavior. What could be more natural than the marriage of linguistics and psychology in the programmed instruction of foreign languages, with linguistics providing the "systematic specification of terminal behaviors" and psychology providing "the techniques of the laboratory analysis and control" of those behaviors?

If the task of learning to speak English were additive and linear, as present linguistic and psychological discussions suggest it is, it is difficult to see how anyone could learn English. If each phonological and syntactic rule, each complex of lexical features, each semantic value and stylistic nuance—in short, if each item which the linguist's analysis leads him to identify had to be acquired one at a time, proceeding from simplest to most complex, and then each had to be connected to specified stimuli or stimulus sets, the child learner would be old before he could say a single appropriate thing and the adult learner would be dead. If each frame of a self-instructional program could teach only one item (or even two or three) at a time, programmed language instruction would never enable the students to use the language significantly. The item-by-item contrastive drills proposed by most modern applied linguists and the requirement by programmers that the behaviors to be taught must be specified seem to rest on this essentially hopeless notion of the language-learning process.

When linguists and programmers talk about planning their textbooks, they approach the problem as if they had to decide what structural features each lesson should be trying to teach. The whole program will teach the sum of its parts: the student will know this structure and that one and another and another. . . . If the question is put to him directly, the linguist will undoubtedly admit that the sum of the structures he can describe is not equal to the capability a person needs in order to use the language, but the question is rarely put to him directly. If it is, he may evade the uncomfortable answer by appealing to the intelligence of the user to apply the structures he knows to an endless variety of situations. But the evasion fails, I think, against the inescapable fact that a person, even an intelligent one, who knows perfectly the structures that the linguist teaches, cannot know that the way to get his cigarette lit by a stranger when he has no matches is to walk up to him and say one of the utterances, "Do you have a light?" or "Got a match?" (not one of the equally well-formed questions, "Do you have fire?" or "Do you have illumination?" or "Are you a match's owner?").

In natural foreign language learning—the kind used, for example, by children to become native speakers in a foreign country within a length of time that amazes their parents—acquisition cannot be simply additive; complex bits of language are learned a whole chunk at a time. Perhaps by some process of stimulus sampling the parts of the chunks are compared and become available for use in new chunks. The possible number of "things known" in the language exponentiates as the number of chunks increases additively, since every complex chunk makes available a further analysis of old chunks into new elements, each still attached to the original context upon which its appropriateness depends.

It is not that linguists and psychologists are unaware of the possibility of learning language in complex chunks or of the importance of learning items in contexts. Indeed it would be difficult to find a serious discussion of new language-teaching methods that did not claim to reform old language teaching methods in part through the use of "natural" contexts. It is rather that consideration of the details supplied by linguistic and psychological analysis has taken attention away from the exponential power available in learning in natural chunks. In present psychologically oriented programs the requirement that one specify the individual behaviors to be reinforced leads (apparently inevitably) to an artificial isolation of parts from wholes; in structurally oriented textbooks and courses, contrastive analysis leads to structural drills designed to teach a set of specific "habits" for the proper formation of utterances, abstracted from normal social context.

Our very knowledge of the fine structure of language constitutes a threat to our ability to maintain perspective in teaching languages. Inspection of language textbooks designed by linguists reveals an increasing emphasis in recent years on structural drills in which pieces of language are isolated from the linguistic and social contexts which make them meaningful and useful to the learner. The more we know about a language, the more such drills we have been tempted to make. If one compares, say, the spoken language textbooks devised by linguists during the Second World War with some of the recent textbooks devised by linguists, he is struck by the shift in emphasis from connected situational dialogue to disconnected structural exercise.

The argument of this paper is that such isolation and abstraction of the learner from the contexts in which that language is used constitutes serious interference with the language-learning process. Because it requires the learner to attach new responses to old stimuli, this kind of interference may in fact increase the interference that applied linguists like to talk about—the kind in which a learner's previous language structures are said to exert deleterious force on the structures being acquired.

Consider the problem of teaching someone to say something. What is it we are most concerned that he learn? Certainly not the mere mouthing of the utterance, the mere ability to pronounce the words. Certainly not the mere demonstration of ability to understand the utterance by, say, translation into the learner's own language. Even the combination of the two goals is not what we are after: it is not saying *and* understanding that we want but saying *with* understanding. That is, we want the learner to be able to use the language we teach him, and we want him to be able to extend his ability to new cases, to create new utterances that are appropriate to his needs as a language user.

Recent linguistic theory has offered a detailed abstract characterization of language competence; learning a finite set of rules and a finite lexicon enables the learner to produce and interpret an infinite number of new well-formed sentences. Plausible detailed accounts also abound in the psychological and philosophical literature to explain how formal repertoires might be linked referentially to the real world. But the kinds of linguistic rules that have been characterized so far (syntactic, phonological, and semantic) bear on the question of well-formedness of sentences, not on the question of appropriateness of utterances. And the stimulus response or associational- or operant-conditioning accounts that help explain how *milk* comes to mean "milk" are of little help in explaining my ability to make up a particular something appropriate to say about milk—such as *I prefer milk*—in a discussion of what one likes in his coffee, and even less my ability to ignore the mention of milk when it is staring me in the face. An important test of our success as language teachers, it seems reasonable to assert, is the ability of our students to choose to say what they want. It has been difficult for linguists and psychologists to attach any significance to the expression "saying what you want to say"; our inability to be precise about the matter may well have been an important reason for our neglect of it in language teaching. But importance of a matter is not measured by our ability at a given moment to give a precise description of it: we can be precise about the allophones of voiceless stops in English after initial /s/, but it seems absurd to claim that it is basically as important—some textbooks imply *more* important—to teach students to make these allophones properly as it is to teach them, for example, how to get someone to repeat something he has just said.

The odd thing is that despite our ignorance as experts, as human beings we have always known how to teach other human beings to use a language: use it ourselves and let them imitate us as best they can at the time. Of course, this method has had more obvious success with children than with adult learners, but we have no compelling reason to believe with either children or adults that the method is not both necessary and sufficient to teach a language.

If we adopt the position I have been maintaining—that language is learned a whole act at a time rather than learned as an assemblage of constituent skills— what would a program for teaching students to speak a foreign language look like?

For the classroom, the simple formulation that the students learn by imitating someone else using the language needs careful development. Since the actual classroom is only one small piece of the world in which we expect the learner to use the language, artificial means must be used to transform it into a variety of other pieces: the obvious means for performing this transformation is drama—imaginative play has always been a powerful educational device for both children and adults. By creating a dramatic situation in a classroom—in part simply by acting out dialogues, but also in part by relabeling objects and people in the room (supplemented by realia if desired) to prepare for imaginative role playing—the teacher can expand the classroom indefinitely and provide imaginatively natural contexts for the language being used.

The idea of using models as teachers is hardly new in applied linguistics; and nothing could be more commonplace than the admonition that the model be encouraged to dramatize and the student to imitate the dramatization of the situation appropriate to the particular bit of language being taught. The sad fact is, however, that the drill material the model has been given to model has intrinsic features that draw the attention of the student away from the situation and focus in on the form of the utterance. Instead of devising techniques that induce the model to act out roles for the student to imitate, the applied linguist has devised techniques of structural drill that put barriers in the way of dramatic behavior and a premium on the personality-less manipulation of a formal repertoire of verbal behavior.

If what the learner observes is such that he cannot absorb it completely within his short-term memory, he will make up for his deficiency if he is called on to perform before he has learned the new behavior by padding with material from what he already knows, that is, his own language. This padding—supplying what is known to make up for what is not known—is the major source of "interference," the major reason for "foreign accents." Seen in this light, the cure for interference is simply the cure for ignorance: learning. There is no particular need to combat the intrusion of the learner's native language—the explicit or implicit justification for the contrastive analysis that applied linguists have been claiming to be necessary for planning language-teaching courses.

But there is need for controlling the size of the chunks displayed for imitation. In general if you want the learner's imitation to be more accurate, make the chunks smaller; increase the size of the chunks as the learner progresses in his skill in imitation. We do not need to impose arbitrary, artificial criteria for successful behavior on the part of the learner. If we limit our demand for immediate high quality of productions, we may well find that his behavior is adequately shaped by the same ad hoc forces that lead a child from being a clumsy performer capable of using his language only with a terribly inaccurate accent, and in a limited number of social situations, to becoming a skillful native speaker capable of playing a wide variety of social roles with the appropriate language for each.

To satisfy our requirement that the student learn to extend to new cases the ability he gains in acting out one role, a limited kind of structural drill can be used: keeping in mind that the learning must be embedded in a meaningful context, the drill may be constructed by introducing small variations into the situation being acted out (e.g., ordering orange juice instead of tomato juice, being a dissatisfied customer rather than a satisfied one, changing the time at which the action takes place) which call for partial innovation in the previously learned role. In each case the situation should be restaged, reenacted, played as meaning something to the student.

The student's craving for explicit formulization of generalizations can usually be met better by textbooks and grammars that he reads outside class than by discussion in class. If discussion of grammar is made into a kind of dramatic event, however, such discussion might be used as the situation being learned—with the students learning to play the role of students in a class on grammar. The important point is that the study of grammar as such is neither necessary nor sufficient for learning to use a language.

So far, I have been talking about the use of live models in language classrooms. How can such techniques be adapted for self-instruction? The cheapness and simplicity of operation of the new videotape recorders already make possible a large portion of the acquisition of a language without the presence of a model; it has been shown convincingly that under the proper conditions it is possible for human students to learn—in the sense of acquiring competence—certain very complex behaviors by mere observation of that behavior in use. Acquiring the willingness to perform—learning in a second sense—seems to depend to a greater extent on reinforcement of the student's own behavior and is thus not quite so amenable to instruction without human feedback at the present time. However, extension of techniques (originally developed to establish phonological competence in step-by-step programmed instruction) for self-monitoring to cover whole utterances with their appropriate kinetic accompaniment may suffice in the future to make the second kind of learning as independent of live teachers as the first and thus make complete self-instruction in the use of a language possible.

THE POWER GAUGE
IN LANGUAGE TEACHING

Earl W. Stevick

Even when basic courses are written in the most enlightened manner, the melancholy fact remains that "the language teacher is not likely to find a textbook adjusted to his needs," and even with the advent of texts that are more and more satisfactory, Gurrey observes that often "teachers . . . merely follow the book. . . . The reason for this is not only that [they] are so often trained to follow the book, but [that] so many of them are not confident enough to rely on their own skill and understanding." As a result, "teachers, in following the book, teach in a half-hearted way." Politzer, in reference to the widely approved learning of specific utterances, tells the student that "if the textbook you happen to be using follows an approach that connects sentences with specific situations, you have only to follow the book," but it is doubtful if a textbook can go even that far under its own power. Closset may have been nearer the mark when he said, "a pupil tends to remember only what he has actually experienced and what is in harmony with his personality."

It seems to me that in planning how to train teachers in the use of a specific basic course, we should keep this view of the textbook in mind. It is in this context that I would like to suggest a formula for good language teaching. To be sure, the numerical values that I shall use in illustrating it are wild guesses, and the whole thing is in any case a grand oversimplification. But at least it will help me to develop a perspective which is sometimes lost.

Let me begin with a series of five simple-sounding statements about teacher training.

1. The purpose of a training program is to produce people who will do something that we may call, for want of a better term, "good teaching."
2. The "best teaching" is that teaching from which the students get the most "benefit," whatever that is.
3. Other things being equal, the benefit B derived from a language course is proportional to some power x of the number of words learned. Write this with a capital V for vocabulary.

4. Other things being equal, the benefit derived from a language course is proportional to some power y of the number of structures mastered. Write this as capital S:

$$B = VxSy$$

This much of the formula stands for information that the student gets about the language. But "the teaching of a language should be considered more as the imparting of a skill than as the provision of information . . ." and, our recent tradition tells us, "language is a skill, and skill is the result of habit." "The key to language learning is (well-planned and lively) drill, drill, drill."

The recognition of drill as an essential component leads to the fifth of our statements:

5. Other things being equal, the benefit is also dependent on the power P of the teaching:

$$B = VxSyPz$$

It is this elusive concept of "power" that I want to examine more closely. A close approximation to what it means is found in any high school physics textbook:

$$P = f\,d/t$$

"Power is proportional to the amount of force and to the distance per unit of time." In terms of language teaching, d/t in this formula is still time, measured in conventional units. The symbol d is distance measured in syllables, or in responses, or in sentences. (The d/t part of "power" is what I had chiefly in mind when I wrote about "Technemes," and many other writers have also emphasized the need for a large volume of "drill, drill, drill" within the time available.)

What has not been so often remembered is that f (force relative to the student's personality) is also a variable. Yet "the use of language (unlike most skills) calls for the contribution of the whole personality." The class is "the scene of various activities"; it is "society in miniature"; each student's body is "a living, active organism" and not just a receptor for the forms, structures, and cultural content that make up the course. If the response that a student gives is based on something in the textbook, let us say that the value of f is somewhere between 10 and 19; if the response refers to something outside the book, the value of f is greater, say, somewhere in the range of 20 to 29; if the subject is of personal relevance to the student, f is perhaps 30 to 39; if the topic is suggested and sustained by the student himself, f is perhaps 40 to 49. This means what we all know, which is that you can afford to spend more time per response on interesting material. "Habit strength is a function of *how many* of the stimuli produced by a response possess *how much* . . . so called reinforcing potential." Why then labor so hard to put it into a pseudo-mathematical formula?

The point, briefly, is that the best possible teaching is not done by using the best possible materials according to the best possible procedure. What we sometimes forget is that neither material nor procedure is appropriate as the chief object of attention. What the teacher (and the teacher-trainer) should keep his eye on at all times is the power gauge. Familiarization with the materials, as in a training course, is justified insofar as it shows the trainees what resources are available for making their teaching more "forceful"; indoctrination with procedures is similarly justified because it shows the trainees how to get more responses per unit of time (d/t), and because it enables them to save their attention for nonprocedural matters. If we train teachers in phonetics or in some branch of linguistics, we are helping them to understand what goes on under the hood. If we train them in writing drills and exercises, we are preparing them to make their own modifications and repairs along the road. In Bennett's words, "It is as much a part of each teacher's professional responsibility as anything else . . . to feel competent to supplement or gradually replace material whenever it is found wanting."

Our formula says, among other things, that the most powerfully taught course would be one in which from the outset everything that was said or done would be on subject matter initiated by the students and of intense interest to them. I think this is perfectly true. If it were also possible, we would not need textbooks, but it is not possible and so we do.

The reason why it is not possible is the same as the reason why we can't start a car on a steep upgrade in high gear. The textbook is as necessary to language teaching as a low gear is to an automobile. But no one would drive cross-country entirely in low gear. One aim of a 1-day or 2-week driver education course should be to teach people how, with the particular mechanism that we are placing at their disposal, to shift gears gracefully.

COMMUNITY LANGUAGE LEARNING*

Charles A. Curran

The present report on a 3-year research project represents both a study in some facets of the counseling relationship and a somewhat different approach to the learning of foreign languages. This research involves basically an effort to determine if methods adopted from counseling skills and relationships could be used to facilitate the learning of foreign languages.

This paper will report briefly on:

1. Some concepts behind the research.
2. Some counseling methods and sensitivities adapted to foreign language learning.
3. A discussion of some of the results as indicated by evaluation data and personal protocols.
4. Some tentative implications and hypotheses that may be drawn from the results thus far obtained.

The relationship between counseling and learning has of course been widely discussed in the literature. These discussions suggest the likelihood of a very real learning component in the counseling process. These areas therefore hold promise for valuable research in the process of human learning. Consequently the present research project (sponsored by a grant from the Society for Human Relations Research) was devised to interrelate, if possible, the counseling process itself with an actual learning situation.

One aspect of recent research in the counseling relationship is placing increasing emphasis on the intensity of belonging and commitment that exists between counselor and client. Words like "warmth" and "acceptance" are growing to have increasing meaning and significance for the counseling process as more evidence begins to appear to show how their presence or absence influences significantly the effectiveness of the counseling dialogue. When there

*Presented to the Menninger Forum, February, 1960.

is a blocking in the counseling relationship, it can apparently sometimes be due to basic factors impeding the counselor from a deep and complete commitment to the relationship because of undefined needs and resistances in himself. The client, sensing this, withholds from the relationship too, and barriers are maintained that can sometimes seriously impede the counseling process.

One aim of this project was to study not only the learning process but also some of the subtleties of the relationship between the language expert and the learner, particularly those factors that decreased the learner's sense of trust, belonging, and identification with and security in the relationship with the language expert.

The learning of four languages, German, French, Spanish, and Italian, was chosen as the direct goal of the project. The methodology was not from the usual methods by which languages are taught but rather was patterned upon counseling techniques and adapted to the peculiar anxiety and threat as well as the personal and language problems a person encounters in the learning of foreign languages. To put it another way, the problems a person faces and overcomes in the process of learning a foreign language were conceived as similar to the problems one faces and overcomes in a personal counseling process.

Consequently the learner was not conceived as a student but as a client; and the native instructors were not considered as teachers but rather were trained in counseling skills adapted to their roles as language counselors.

The learning of foreign languages as such was chosen as the goal of this project, first because it is one of the major deficiencies that seem apparent in our present educational methods and process, and second because it represents a testable situation, where standardized written tests, controlled comparisons with ordinary college class progress and individual tests are possible. A third and far more compelling reason, however, was the observation made by many people, particularly in learning to speak a foreign language, that they found themselves in a high degree of personal threat and anxiety. They described their reactions in terms of personal confusions and emotional conflicts that often seemed similar to, if not identical with, the same expressions people used in beginning counseling interviews, as they described complex personal involvements.

These four particular languages were chosen not only because they are the common languages of Western civilization but especially in order to make the learning problem more complex, and at the same time because they bore a basic relationship to the Saxon and Norman origins of most English words. In this we were also attempting to see, therefore, if these four languages could in a sense be considered as somewhat unified in English and if they were capable of being learned as a somewhat unitary process. This, in a sense, might be considered similar to the ways separate and apparently unrelated problems and life situations often seem to become more interrelated as a person gains insight into himself and his situation in the counseling process.

If the reactions to threatening situations and their concomitant stress and anxiety and the control of these reactions seem, as some writers have suggested, to be basic to the process of solving personal problems in counseling, then something of the same threat stress and anxiety seems to exist, to some degree at least, if one is asked to communicate in a foreign language in which one has little or no competence.

This threat is not only psychological but in its somatic components seems to suggest many of the reactions that Selye has described in his stress syndrome. The whole psychosomatic system is directly engaged in the first stage of language learning, particularly if one must speak that language in the presence of others who know it well. Distortion of sounds, for example, and being unable to hear and distinguish words distinctly, as well as the inability to pronounce the new sounds accurately, could therefore not only be considered the result of the newness of these sounds but could also follow from the distortion which the person's threatened state could produce. Many people may hold onto a false sound because it is similar to a familiar sound in their native language. They perhaps get security from this sound, whereas the completely new sound is too strange and unfamiliar. Other similar questions are also raised by this consideration of personal threat in language learning.

Stated another way, one might say that this would imply a twofold problem intrinsic to the learning of foreign languages, and perhaps to the learning of many other things too. There are the immediate problems of the learning process itself. But if a person is also in a highly threatened state, there would be the much more complex problem of the psychological and somatic effects of this threat on the person himself and the degree to which his defensive and tense emotional state impedes adequate learning.

This concept of threat could also give additional clues why the small child learns one or more languages so readily. He is apparently not so easily threatened by new sounds, since he has as yet no familiar language. He is, at the same time, generally surrounded by an atmosphere of warmth and understanding from his parents and from some older children or adults from whom he learns, which atmosphere would be conducive to the diminishing of his threatened state.

The small child's natural willingness to be dependent on others and the warmth and affection which give him security as he begins to learn his native language is quite different from the way an adolescent or adult approaches the learning of a foreign language. The adolescent or adult has already acquired basic security in a set of sounds and expressions with which he is comfortable and which are more or less adequate to express all that he wishes to say. He is not, therefore, like the small child, linguistically handicapped. He does not ordinarily fear rejection or feel insecure. But the instant such an adult is expected to speak in an unknown foreign language, he is in a severely handicapped state in which all his normal linguistic securities and proficiencies are absent. His anxiety mounts, apparently because he is faced with a personal situation with which he has little or no adequate means of coping.

If this is so, one can see that such a person, linguistically considered, is in a state similar to that which people often present at the beginning of counseling interviews. They too, in one or more important areas of their lives, feel basically inadequate, fear the rejection of others, and generally feel they lack means of coping adequately with problems in these particular areas.

Further, as the psychological client is moved more or less strongly in the direction of a personal solution and at the same time frustrated by his confusion, the language client is anxious to speak the language and is at the same time equally frustrated by his lack of linguistic tools. Both seem also in conflicting emotional states of on the one side wishing to be dependent and to have someone else solve their problems, and on the other feeling hostile and resistant to such dependency in their own urges to find an independent self-directed solution.

If we ask what, among other things, the counselor's skill brings to a person threatened and anxious about personal problems, we might answer first of all that it consists in conveying to him, through the counselor's own empathy, a deep understanding and acceptance of his feeling of inadequacy and the anxieties and insecurities it produces.

Through the counselor's commitment and dialogue, there grows slowly in the client a deepening sense of security that his inadequacies will not be turned against him but will somehow be understood and reflected by the counselor in such a way that he can slowly grow in self-understanding and gradually acquire better means of coping with his threatened situation.

This then would give us one of the first basic factors in the language counselor–client relationship. The counselor's whole manner must convey the same deep empathy for the language client's beginning threatened state and must at the same time provide him with increased security and more adequate means for coping with his linguistic anxiety and threat.

The language counselors were consequently first trained in the general psychological background and theory of personality threat reactions and in a general understanding of the techniques of counseling with particular emphasis on warmth and acceptance. They were also made aware by a series of experiments how one feels in a threatened state for which one can find no solution. As subjects of these experiments, they all recognized in themselves these same reactions of conflict and confusion and their ambivalence to have to be dependent on the one side and yet at the same time to resist this dependence, in their own urge for an independent solution. Since the native counselors in German, French, Spanish, and Italian were themselves foreigners in America, they also recognized clearly in themselves the same reactions to threat in the various general experiences in English which they were having. Some spoke English quite proficiently, while others were in various stages of learning. Yet all were sharply aware of numerous experiences which brought forward their feelings of threat and anxiety and the various accompanying emotions and somatic components.

One further factor was revealed in some of the language counselors whenever their own native language became the focus of a discussion. Being forced into submission and an inferior state in an atmosphere where everyone spoke native English, they sometimes observed in themselves compensatory urges as soon as an opportunity to speak and instruct in their own language presented itself. They were often, for example, either overly protective and reassuring or alternately too abrupt and quick. One of the first things the psychological background and counseling training gave them was the awareness of this compensatory drive. Somewhat as the untrained psychological adviser can make a client resistant even when he is giving good advice, so these language counselors grew to see that in their unskilled efforts to help language learning, they were often really disturbing the language client and making him alternately hostile or too dependent.

The language-counseling relationship began therefore with the client's linguistic confusion and conflict. The aim of the language counselor's skill was first to communicate an empathy for the client's threatened inadequate state and to aid him linguistically; and then slowly to enable him to arrive at his own increasingly independent language adequacy. Consequently the more expert and sensitive the language counselor became in conveying warmth and empathy that was, however, not condescension or pity, the more effective he would seem to be in aiding the language client to begin to move in the direction of language independence.

The actual methodology was therefore devised so as to create relationships with the language counselor which enabled the client to grow linguistically from a state of dependency, insecurity, and inadequacy to an increasingly independent, self-directed, and responsible use of one or more foreign languages.

Having discussed some of the basic concepts behind the research we can now briefly describe the actual methods by which this language-counseling relationship was carried on.

In the language-counseling process the counseling relationship itself and the real-life experience in the use of the language were combined. In other words the same experience in which the language client needed acceptance of his threatened emotional state and aid in his linguistic confusion was actually combined with a situation where he needed immediate use of his foreign language to take part in a group conversation.

By this arrangement we had in fact what came out to be both language counseling and at the same time a relationship with a group of from 6 to 12 people in a group discussion. This group process, however, was heightened by the fact that the group interrelationships were carried on in four different foreign languages. What might, from this brief description, sound like the mixing of tongues after the Tower of Babel, turned out, in fact, to become a surprisingly smooth and consistent growth in communication and language security, as the language-counseling process developed.

One of the advantages of this arrangement that is immediately obvious, but nonetheless very significant, is that each person was taking part in a real group experience. This was a natural relationship with people he knew only slightly and grew to know better as they talked together as any group of adults might talk. But all the talking took place in four foreign languages.

To arrive at this, we devised five stages of adaptation:

Outline of Stages in Language Counselor–Client Relationship
from Counselor Dependency to Independence

STAGE 1

The client is completely dependent on the language counselor.

1. First, he expresses only to the counselor and *in English* what he wishes to say to the group. Each group member overhears this English exchange, but is not involved in it.
2. The counselor then reflects these ideas back to the client *in the foreign language* in a warm, accepting tone, in simple language in phrases of five or six words.
3. The client turns to the group and presents his ideas *in the foreign language.* He has the counselor's aid if he mispronounces or hesitates on a word or phrase. This is the client's maximum security stage.

STAGE 2

1. Same as above.
2. The client turns and begins to speak the *foreign language* directly to the group.
3. The counselor aids only as the client hesitates or turns for help. These small independent steps are signs of positive confidence and hope.

STAGE 3

1. The client speaks directly to the group in the foreign language. This presumes that the group has now acquired the ability to understand his simple phrases.
2. Same as 3 above. This presumes the client's greater confidence, independence, and proportionate insight into the relationship of phrases, grammar, and ideas. Translation is given only when a group member desires it.

STAGE 4

1. The client is now speaking freely and complexly in the foreign language. Presumes group's understanding.
2. The counselor directly intervenes in grammatical error, mispronunciation, or where aid in complex expression is needed. The client is sufficiently secure to take correction.

STAGE 5

1. Same as stage 4.
2. The counselor intervenes not only to offer correction but to add idioms and more elegant constructions.
3. At this stage the client can become counselor to the group in stages 1, 2, and 3.

In the first stage the client was totally dependent on the counselor. He had to receive from the language counselor, much as a small child receives from a mother, every word or phrase he intended to use in the group discussion. This was achieved by having the counselor sit a little behind him to his right or left (see Figure 1, arrangement 1) in such a way that he could express his ideas in English as a personal communication between the counselor and himself. The counselor then reflected these ideas in a warm, accepting, and sensitive tone in the foreign language which the counselor represented and the client was to speak. So, for example, if the client chose to speak French, he had a native

ARRANGEMENT 1

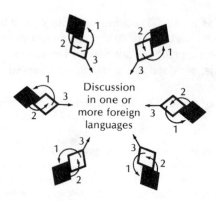

Possible foreign languages: German, French, Spanish, Italian

1 = idea in English
2 = idea in foreign language
3 = idea in foreign language to group

(White: Language clients, Black: Language counselors)

ARRANGEMENT 2

Figure 1 Counseling—foreign language research design of the different positions in language-counseling discussions.

French counselor. German, Spanish, and Italian counselors were also available. Each member of the group could, however, overhear the English exchange between the language counselor and client, and he therefore knew what each person would say to the group in the foreign language.

After the client received his idea in the foreign language form, for example, French, he turned to the group and presented this idea in French, still having the counselor's aid if he mispronounced or hesitated on a word or phrase. Expressed in other terms, stage 1 was the client's maximum security stage in the sense that

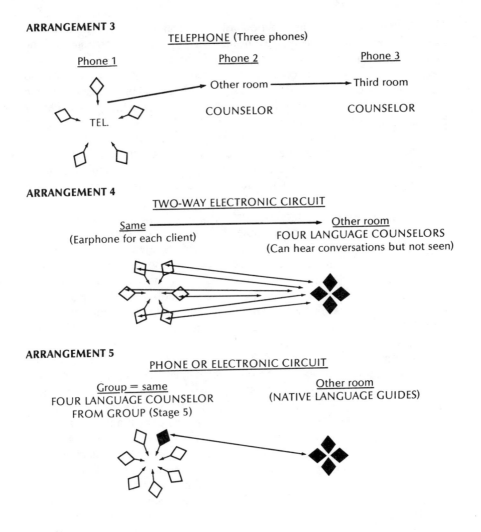

ARRANGEMENT 3

TELEPHONE (Three phones)

Phone 1   Phone 2   Phone 3

Other room —————→ Third room

TEL.   COUNSELOR   COUNSELOR

ARRANGEMENT 4

TWO-WAY ELECTRONIC CIRCUIT

Same ——————————————→ Other room
(Earphone for each client)   FOUR LANGUAGE COUNSELORS
                                    (Can hear conversations but not seen)

ARRANGEMENT 5

PHONE OR ELECTRONIC CIRCUIT

Group = same   Other room
FOUR LANGUAGE COUNSELOR   (NATIVE LANGUAGE GUIDES)
FROM GROUP (Stage 5)

Figure 1   *(continued)*

while he participated in the group by speaking either French, German, Spanish, or Italian he was in fact sure that he was speaking this language without error, and pronouncing it accurately. There was no way in which error could be reinforced; on the contrary, the whole relationship was intended to reinforce accuracy and correctness.

All the groups began with insecurity, hesitation, and caution. They were self-conscious and very aware of each other, since they were all comparative strangers at the first session. Because no one was forced to speak unless he wished, there were inevitable periods of silence and then difficult struggles together to begin to talk freely with one another. At first artificial topics like the weather were monotonously repeated, until the group, tiring of this, began openly to discuss why they could not speak more freely about themselves and their present language fears and insecurities. This kind of breakthrough, which occurred in each group, gradually brought the individuals in the group to deeper feelings of security and belonging.

This slowly developing sense of group belonging seemed to be one of the major helps which each member received from the group. This feeling of being understood and accepted by the group, while they were fearful and inadequate linguistically, gave them confidence that they could speak and understand these languages, and it increased their desire to be able to do this.

We notice that this method of combining both language counseling and a real-life situation in speaking a foreign language to a group introduced the language learner into two interrelated but different experiences. In one he began as a dependent and insecure handicapped person who received security and clarification and overcame his handicap through the language counselor's warm, secure manner in supplying him linguistic tools which he needed. This was done in such a way that he not only gained increasing psychological security and confidence but also was able gradually, step by step, to grow in his own independent language competence.

Simultaneously, in a group that began as strangers to him, he gradually learned to communicate in one or more foreign languages and at the same time grew to understand their foreign-language communications in return. He was, in this sense, always exposed to a double threat. He had the threat of his relationship with the counselor as he was struggling to communicate in one or more foreign languages. But he had an even sharper threat from the group itself, where he could not protect himself by presenting his ideas in his own native language. In fact, as the group members explained their reactions later, they felt they quickly became secure with the language counselors but remained for a much longer time insecure and threatened by one another.

The language counselor's sensitive understanding of the client's handicapped and dependent state was therefore especially important in stage 1. Sentences or phrases had to be gently halted at six or seven words, and the parallel translation kept very simple. Where possible, cognates were employed to give immediate recognition and security. Very simple constructions were used, and where possible, idioms were avoided.

So while the client himself, knowing little or nothing of the foreign language, was understandably insecure and fearful about speaking that language in a group, yet he had the counselor's warm acceptance and language ability to reflect immediately and accurately in simple phrases what the client wished to say in the foreign language. As a result clients were, in fact, soon able to speak to the group with rapidly growing confidence and security.

Here in the four foreign languages, the individual grew in his relationship with the group and in his independent use of his language skills, as he realized each member of the group felt just as he did, and each had his own personal struggles and anxieties around the same language threat. He could then begin to express his own ideas to the group, even at a personal and intimate level, through the medium of one or more foreign languages. This, as we can see, furthered not only his own confidence in communication but also his own growing reassurance. He could also understand with increasing accuracy everything being said in the four languages, since he already knew the words in English from overhearing the prior client-counselor communication.

Once this ease in stage 1 was reached, sometimes after two 1-hour sessions, the conversations flowed along in an easy, normal manner. These people were often unaware for long periods that they were in this cumbersome, handicapped arrangement, much as amputees and other handicapped people play basketball, go bowling, drive cars, etc., as soon as they sufficiently adapt to their handicap. For a number of students, in fact, the acceptance of this kind of "handicapped state" in itself seemed to be a fundamental point in their belonging and sharing in the foreign language.

A further interesting point here was that this type of normal conversation, once established, defeated fatigue. Conversations could continue for 2 or 3 hours much as if they were in English. Boredom also was avoided as more intimate, personal, and stimulating discussions and cross-cultural interchanges began to occur.

Sometimes too at a later stage the group would choose discussions that illustrated particular tenses such as a discussion of a future trip to the moon, to enable most of the verbs to be formed in the future tense.

All the sessions were tape-recorded, enabling the group to play back their discussions. As this was being done, the language counselors sometimes copied each client's sentences and gave them to him on a series of 4×6 cards with points of grammar briefly indicated. At other times an opaque projector was used so the whole group could see the sentences as they listened to the playback of their conversation. The main emphasis, however, was much more on the conversational exchange itself. This seemed to be far more really interesting and valuable to the group, according to their own evaluation.

Obviously some time was spent in stage 1. Each one was free, however, as he pleased, to move to stage 2. Those who had had some previous language classes in a particular language tended after a time to begin to speak a few phrases on their own. Stage 2 was devised to correspond to this natural and understandable transition toward independence and language maturity.

Stage 2 was therefore the counselor's adaptation to the client's beginning positive confidence, hope, and desire to take independent linguistic steps. The language client began slowly to gain confidence in his capacity to speak the foreign language and in the feeling of reassurance that he could begin to do this, in a small way, by himself. At this stage he spoke directly to the counselor in English. The counselor reflected his ideas in the foreign language only when he clearly hesitated or turned for help. One of the surprising counselor-client reactions here was the sensitivity and empathy that often existed between the two. The counselor seemed usually to know when the client needed help and when he did not. If help was given too soon, the client was made momentarily hostile. If, on the other hand, it was delayed too long and the client was left in a helpless state, he was equally momentarily hostile on the other side.

In the third stage, having gained greater confidence, independence, and proportionate insights into the relationship of phrases, grammar, and ideas, the client spoke immediately to the group in the foreign language without any English communication of his ideas to the counselor. Only when he clearly needed help did he turn to the counselor with the English expression of what he wanted to say in the foreign language. Here the counselor with a surprising intuition sometimes already knew the word or phrase the client was struggling to use and could often supply it to him without any English communication between them. The very intensity of the concentration of their communication together, and the deep relationship and security which both had seemed to produce this joint understanding. The following excerpt from one of the language counselors describes a subjective reaction to the client relationship at this stage:

I had to relax completely and to exclude my own will to produce something myself. I had to exclude any function of forming or formulating something within me, not try to do something, but instead letting enter into me without any restriction, what the person says and being completely open to everything he might say, foreseeing with calm, not hoping or wishing that or this word might come forward; not concentrated on what the person might say, i.e., on the contents of the speech, but on the person himself, completely accepting him and at the same time trying to understand what *he* wants to say, not *what* he wants to say.

Together with the client, I concentrate on his process of trying to find this word or that expression joining into this process with sympathy and understanding. I do not allow myself to feel embarrassed about his hesitation, momentary silence or stuttering, in order not to bring up any tension which would make him self-conscious, but I sort of try to find the word myself, and as I do not know what word is wanted I am just joining in the process of thinking with the other person. Thus, so to say, both of us are thinking in combined effort. It is important that there be in me no willing or wishing, but a relaxed state of almost passiveness, which is however creative as it provided additional creative force to the other person. I try to be relaxed, without any personal anxiety. . . . . I am almost indifferent to what is said, or better, to how the other person puts it, as there is a deeper level of communication which need not cling so much to words, which are the outward appearance of what is communicated. I feel like I am walking along a path with the other person towards a common goal.

And from another language counselor:

Being a counselor to two people who want to have a conversation in my native language: Their conversation is flowing through me. I am participating in one continuous flow of thoughts that goes through me in two directions. I have a humble role: people refer to me only when they need help. The rest of the time they are having a conversation among themselves. Nevertheless I am not excluded from the conversation. I am participating in a passive role, giving myself to what they want to say, not producing something myself. Giving myself to the others, helping them so smoothly that they forget to realize that there is somebody without whom they would not be able to perform all this, somebody who gives them their security.

In stage 4 the client had arrived at a rather independent ability to express what he wished to say to the group in the foreign language itself. By this time, too, the whole group had correspondingly gained sufficient comprehension of the other languages involved that they understood without translation what was said directly in the foreign language. Consequently the counselor's role here was the reassurance that a native person was observing with intense concentration everything the client said and yet offering aid only when help was needed in some complex expression, grammatical error, or mispronunciation.

In stage 5 the counselor intervened not only to correct the now more rare mistakes but also to add idioms and more elegant constructions where necessary.

There were no rigid lines between the five stages. One was quite free to move from one to the other as he pleased. General fatigue or some temporary insecurity might cause a person to start again in stage 1 after he had been for some time previously in stage 2, 3, or even 4. Changing languages would, of course, often change stages. A very fluid process actually existed in which the five stages served only as clues to the relationship between counselor and client, and client and group at the moment. This could change whenever the individual client desired.

Having more clearly in mind the five stages of the counselor-client relationship, we can now study briefly the other ways communications were made in addition to arrangement 1 (see Figure 1).

We see that arrangement 2 simply allows for more people in the group—one counselor to three persons. The counselor stands and walks over to each at a signal from the client. Arrangements 3, 4, and 5 correspond loosely to stages 3, 4, and 5, since they imply increasing language proficiency in the group.

In arrangement 3, by the use of the telephone, the counselor or counselors are in other rooms, or sometimes in other parts of the city, to be contacted by phone when needed. The phone is dialed in (live) so that when a mistake is heard the counselor whistles and the client picks up the phone to get the correction.

In arrangement 4 each client has one earphone connected to the other room. If he makes an error or needs help, only *he* hears the counselor—the others may not even know he was helped. The counselors, however, hear everything in the client room.

Arrangement 5 corresponds to stage 5 in the counselor-client relationship. At stage 5 the client sometimes became counselor for a group in stage 1, 2, or 3 with the native language counselor or counselors (in this case called guides) on a third circuit or in a room, but only to offer necessary correction or aid to the counselor. The group's entire relationship was with the counselor, not with the native expert. The native expert, removed from the group either psychologically or physically, was heard only by the counselor.

Evaluation and Outcomes. Since this research has now been carried on for 3 years with a number of graduate and undergraduate groups from three colleges, and with certain changes in methods and procedures as new data and awareness came forward, there is a certain understandable variation in both the results themselves and the methods used to achieve them. The first experimental group, carried on for one semester 3 years ago, was more primitive and exploratory in its methods than the most recent experimental group of last semester. Consequently in the beginning we were dependent almost exclusively on subjective methods of evaluation. We asked each one to put a level-of-expectancy number (from 1 to 10) for what they expected to achieve in each language. At the end of the semester each one was asked to put another figure for what he felt he had actually achieved in each language, and then to discuss this. All the discussions were tape-recorded. This procedure was followed with each group after the first group, and provided somewhat similar results.

From these evaluations it was quite evident that the general picture was one of much greater gain and actual achievement than the individual student had expected. Since no particular screening device was used to pick the members of these groups, except to list the project in the catalogue and make it available to interested students, there was naturally much insecurity, skepticism, and even anxiety among the students when they were informed that this was to be an attempt to learn four foreign languages at the same time by counseling methods. Consequently in the recorded protocols each student expressed his or her amazement not only that it was possible for this to be done, but that he or she had been able so freely to participate in such a discussion in four foreign languages. The students were equally surprised to discover that they could understand and could feel that they belonged to the foreign languages and to one another by the end of the sessions.

They expressed not only an intense sense of sharing with the others but also a profound identity with the four languages. They in fact gained an increasing sense of the unity of these languages and their own identification with this common civilization.

In the language-counseling groups each student had a deep sense of being accepted and of belonging. There was also an intense feeling that each person could be himself, even though he himself was speaking a foreign language. This symbolic sense of acceptance and belonging which, by the interchange of English and the foreign languages, the group symbolized for one another, was one of the things most commonly commented upon by all American and non-American students. Or, to put it another way, it was only in this group that each foreign student could feel himself the equal of the American and in the same respective position, since all were more or less equally handicapped in four languages and an authority in one.

In the first group no objective measures of progress were used. A member of the group, however, having had no previous courses in French, on applying to another university passed the examination and received the highest possible level of French credit. In her subjective evaluation of herself she felt she had made even more gain in Spanish and equal in Italian. Other group members had similar convictions of their gain in competence in these four languages. Two members of the second group won the Spanish and French prizes in the college.

The following excerpt of a recorded evaluation by one of the students can be considered typical of the general reaction to the experience in language counseling. This excerpt includes only the comments on German and French.

I was very much surprised at the fact that I would get anything out of the language research in German. I was more surprised by my ability to understand German as the different speakers spoke it in our conversations. I found it much simpler than I had expected, because I began to see its relationship to English and to understand it in terms of its relationship to English. I noticed that I did not so much discover a facility of detecting words as I discovered a facility in detecting general ideas. . . . I could discover that the words were flowing through me and were an extension of my English vocabulary.

Part of this I attributed to the facility of the counselor, who enabled me to feel very much at ease in the language, and consequently allowed the words to flow from herself through me into the group. I also was extremely surprised at the ease with which I could discuss in German, although I did not do this very often. I believe I only spoke German three or four times, but I had come to German after speaking French in the group, and I was amazed at the lack of noticeable difference in the flowing of either of the languages through me. Also I noticed that I had developed an interest—really more than an interest—in German. . . .

With regard to French, I noticed several things, one of which was definitely more of a facility in speaking French. I made more attempts to speak French. Before, I would be blocked in speaking with anyone from France. I found myself now wishing to converse in French and not being so much impeded by my lack of knowledge. . . . I noticed no difficulty with the pronunciation whatsoever, and this was, I believe, due to the encouragement of the counselors. . . .

I was also very much amazed that when I addressed the group in conversation there was in me no notice of the fact that I was speaking French, but rather, simply an extension of myself into the group. . . . I was not conscious of what word I was using or choosing, but in one span of time I found myself becoming more aware of the words which occurred more frequently and found myself more anxious to speak on my own without the counselor's aid.

Forty-five students actually participated in the experiment either for one semester or for as many as six semesters. Four followed the program straight through for all six semesters. These four therefore made the maximum gain in four languages; three of these arrived at stage 4 or 5 in all four languages. One of the four who was absent from a number of sessions arrived at stage 5 in comprehension in all four languages, at stage 4 in speaking one, and at stage 3 in speaking the other three. One of these four did not take the test evaluations. The other three ranked extremely high in the four languages.

At the other end of the scale of those tested, 18 took the program for one semester only. They made the most gain in those languages which they had had previously at least one semester in high school or college, even though at the beginning some felt they had almost completely forgotten whatever they had learned in the previous courses.

The greatest gain in actual competence was made of course by those who already had some knowledge of a particular language. Of the 45 people, 11 who had previous knowledge of French showed high gains. The same proved true for five who had previous knowledge of Spanish and five who had previous knowledge of German.

For those who had no previous language courses or experiences in a particular language, while definite gains were made in learning, the most remarkable gain seemed to be the passing over the threshold of positive identification with the new language.

This meant that they were no longer afraid of the language and now felt sure that if they took it in a regular class—as some did—they would like it and could learn it. Or, put another way, the first semester experience alone seemed to have as its greatest result a strong positive reinforcement to learn the language through a positive identification with the language counselor and the experience of being able to speak the language and communicate ideas to the group with the counselor's help.

Some years ago Brachfeld pointed out the turning point evident in language learning:

Many years of experience in learning languages has given me the conviction that there is a "turning point" in language study. This "turning point" has very little to do with intelligence, talent, and so forth. Psychologically it is rather akin to courage. In three foreign languages I can clearly remember my "turning point." In a fourth one, I believe that I have not yet arrived at, but am very close to the "turning point."

This "turning point," or what we called the language threshold, was very evident in our research. Some students even recalled the precise day when this sense of belonging, this passing over the threshold, occurred in one or the other of the foreign languages. It was closely related to a deep sense of psychological belonging and sharing with the language counselor.

In fact one of the main results of this counseling-learning relationship was that it seemed to enable students rather rapidly to pass over this threshold of confidence and away from fear, uncertainty, and strangeness. In one semester they seemed to acquire a very positive identification with the four foreign languages and a confidence and security that they could learn to speak and understand them. In other words, they felt strongly that they belonged to these languages. These languages were no longer strange and threatening for them.

A second result, interrelated with the first, was the overcoming of strong personal blocks against a particular language itself or the people it represented. These blocks existed in at least one language for over half the students. These resistances were caused either by unfortunate earlier experiences in trying to learn the blocked language or by national or cultural hostilities to a particular people.

In actual language learning, the written and oral tests, as we saw, indicated a definitely significant gain in written and spoken language competence. This compared favorably with the scores made in individual languages by control groups of college classes taking only one of these languages alone.

This suggests the possibility that learning all four major European languages by a language-counseling method would be possible and in fact perhaps more efficient than learning each one through a separate process. Each group of students at the end of the semester experiment in language counseling were quite convinced of this themselves. They were, in fact, surprised at the ease with which Saxon-English words and many German words and many Norman-English words and French, Spanish, and Italian words were related. Once they began to hear these similarities in the counselor's responses, they were helped by this to feel much more secure in the foreign languages. These foreign words did not seem nearly so removed from their own language, and they were therefore much less threatened by language strangeness.

Another result was an increasing awareness that language is really "persons." That is, the focus shifted from "grammar" and "sentence formation," as might be contained in a language textbook, to a deepening sense of personal communication. Language became a means of sharing and belonging between persons. The concept of "communion" was restored to communication, first through the acceptance and understanding received from the counselors and then from the gradual sense of belonging and freedom in one or more foreign languages with the group.

Another basic result of this research would seem to demonstrate that the process of foreign language learning does have much in common with the process of psychological counseling. It begins at the same stages of negative emotion where conflict and confusion predominate and the person is unable to cope by himself with his language problem, much as a beginning client finds himself frustrated and even defeated in a particular area of personal problems. From here there is steady growth toward confident, independent language activity and insight. This moves the client in the direction of increasingly less need of any dependence on the counselor.

There is also a change in self-reference and self-image. The language-client begins with a negative self-reference in his fear of or resistance to the foreign language. He slowly begins to see himself speaking this foreign language, and he emerges with a positive self-reference to the foreign language.

This process was definitely furthered by the language counselor's ability to establish a warm, understanding, and accepting relationship. When this happened, the counselor ceased to be another foreign person and became an "other-language self" for the client. This, in the clients' own evaluations of their experiences, seemed to be the most important agent in the client's gains in language proficiency and security. As in psychological counseling the client's growth was most effectively furthered when there was an intense empathy between himself and the language counselor. Through this he could slowly grow in a more independent understanding of and coping with his language problems. He could thus grow in language maturity and responsible independence.

A LINGUISTIC MODEL
FOR LEARNING AND LIVING
IN THE NEW AGE OF THE PERSON

Charles A. Curran

We can begin with a conceptual model drawn from the familiar experience we have all had of dropping a stone into a pool and watching the ripples or circles slowly move out from the center. For our purpose the stone will be seen as the teacher-learner relationship in the process of which people learn to speak a second langauge. The circles radiating out from the center will represent our present new age with its overlay of influences from the previous age just recently ended.

We will talk about these two circles. The larger of the two represents the previous age—from the seventeenth century until now. The inner or small circle we can consider the new age—the age of the person—into which we have now entered. We have entered into this new age, however, with many carry-overs, many unanalyzed models from the earlier age. Later, after the analysis of these two circles, we will come back to the stone itself in the center, namely, the personal relationship between the knower of English, or any other language, and the learner who is a speaker of another language.

ASTRONOMY: THE IDEAL MODEL OF SCIENCE

Many of the unconscious as well as conscious models of our present age have their origin in and are related to the concept "scientific." This has been the dominant model throughout the last four centuries. Obviously the word "scientific" can mean many things. For example, it can mean genuine openness to new ideas, an enquiring mind questing for whatever is valid and helpful, freedom from bias. Such concepts we want, of course, to retain. But if I were to ask you to free-associate about the origin of the word "scientific"—and if your free associations are similar to mine—you might see the familiar picture of Galileo looking at the stars and moon; you might see various instruments for calculations, say, figures on a blackboard with an analysis of the planetary system.

Our outer circle, then, represents the scientific age in which astronomy has been seen as the ideal model of science since the seventeenth century. This model is objective, impersonal, and mathematical, and it stresses the great value of the observer position—removed and uninvolved. Without question, this model has brought enormous benefits. It enabled us to go to the moon—a goal that mankind has had since the beginning of time. It began by observing the moon from afar, and ended by going there.

If we look at this outer circle then, we can see that much of what we are now doing, even though we have moved into the age of the person, is interwoven with attitudes and values which flow from that model. What the scientific age and the model of astronomy stressed most was the way in which the knower, through his instruments, stood off and examined what was happening "out there" and then calculated from what was observed. These observations were put into a mathematical formula; they were turned into a series of problems worked out and answers arrived at. To have "answers" ended the process.

The astronomy model also puts the knower totally in charge of the process. What is "out there" can be figured out and predicted. We know from our own experience that this is exactly what happens when the scientist, using careful calculations, accurately predicts an eclipse and it takes place exactly as predicted. According to this ideal model, the knower then, if he makes the right formulation of the problem and figures it out properly, will come up with the right answers, and "things out there" will happen just as the knower has concluded they should. The astronomy model, then, puts all emphasis on the knower. It also highlights the point that the uninvolved, the distant position, the observer, the unengaged, is the one who is apt to yield the most accurate answers to the problems and even produce the most accurate formulations of the problems.

PROBLEM-SOLVING MODEL

It is not hard to jump into our own time and realize that without the word "problem" we would be rather lost. You cannot pick up a newspaper without reading about international problems, personal problems, business and economic problems. If we move to language teaching, we almost immediately think in terms of grammar problems, pronunciation problems, vocabulary problems. In most textbooks, the process and exercises by which the students are helped to focus on these "problem" areas are thoroughly spelled out to both student and teacher.

But if we are not consciously aware of when the problem-solving model is or is not appropriate, we can unconsciously be affected by it to the point of conceptualizing almost all personal relationships basically as problem-solving ones.

This analysis of the hidden model implications behind common words such as the word "problems" we have called "linguistic value analysis." This process enables us to see that common words we use tie us unconsciously to ways of thinking and acting in relation to ourselves and one another.

You can test this influence of "problem solving" in yourself. If someone makes an appointment to see you and in some way they have implied they want to talk about some personal thing or some learning situation and if after a few polite exchanges there is a silence, you will probably have a strong urge to say, "Well, what's your problem?" This suggests that the only way to get to the nitty-gritty of something is to formulate it into some kind of problem. Then we can proceed to some kind of answer. We see here a mathematical model unconsciously determining our thinking process and our relationships.

Another dynamic that seems to follow from a problem-solving model is a "selecting-out" process. The way it works is that we tend to select out or not hear other models of relationship that our language still suggests to us. We have tested people in their reaction to the following type of sentences. Again if your reaction is similar to theirs, you will see that in some measure you have largely "selected out" what the sentences in their totality imply. The sentences might go:

Our intention in this paper is obviously not to come up with any final answers to anything. The problems are far too vast for that, but hopefully we can come up with some new ways of looking at these problems. It is not that these new ideas will be fruitful immediately, but hopefully over a period of time, they will have sunk in and taken root, eventually to bear fruit in your own experience when you have had time to put them into practice.

Now, if sometime later someone were to ask you what I had said in those sentences, you might say, if your reaction is similar to that of others who have done this:

Well, he said we are going to take a fresh look at some particular areas of problems and come up, not with any final answers, but with answers that, at least in some practical way will be helpful, and then we would have a chance to try these answers and various solutions and see how they work out for us.

If in hearing this you say to yourself, "Yes, that's about what I thought he said," then you will have illustrated how deeply the outer-circle age has embedded itself into our model of thinking. While it is true that the first part of the sentences talked about problems and answers, the second part talked about ideas sinking in, taking root, and bearing fruit. Two totally different models were presented, one from the mathematical notion of problems and their answers in the back of the book and the other from an agrarian model of seed entering soil.

AGRARIAN MODEL

The agrarian model suggests a very different dynamic from the problem-solving one. In the model of seed entering soil there is an equal stress on germination as well as insemination, with all the nutrients of the soil coming forward. First the soil must open up to let the seed enter. Then the soil must bring all its cooperation for the seed to have any hope of being fruitful. So while the first model puts the focus on the knower-person and, almost like the stars in astronomy, considers the learners merely objects of the predictions and answers of the knower, the second model has the learner deeply engaged and responsible for bringing fruit out of this seed that the knower has planted.

So we can see that in a certain sense we have moved from the outer circle—the scientific age—to the inner one—the age of the person—by looking at an older model, seed and soil, which we still use. What is interesting, though, is how seldom we reflect on this earlier model in itself and how we can select it out in a series of sentences and interpret it according to a problem-solving one.

We can now come at this somewhat differently and also move into the inner circle by looking at what has happened in the last 50 years in the basic sciences. The present knowledge of science has found great difficulty with such a depersonalized model, even though it proved so valid and rich up into the first part of the twentieth century. At that time a change came about in science. This change was due to the realization that in physics predictability and therefore the problem-solving model no longer held when one got to individual particles and individual instances. The purely observational relationship was no longer possible.

One of the leaders in this awareness was Heisenberg. His famous summary of the issue was called the "uncertainty principle" and was presented as an alternative to the scientific notion of rigid predictability and depersonalization. A quote from Heisenberg, and then we will go on:

Natural science does not simply describe and explain nature—it is part of the interplay between nature and ourselves. It describes nature as exposed to our method of questioning. This was a possibility of which Descartes could not have thought, but it makes the sharp separation between the world and the "I" impossible.

Said in another way, in many instances the "I" has to get involved, much as the seed must enter the ground, and the two must become engaged if the conceptualization of fruitfulness is to emerge. And this "I" is not an abstract intellect, but an emotional, instinctive, and somatic being as well—filled often with anxiety and anger as well as positive feelings and urges to learn. I simply want to suggest that this awareness was the beginning of the break that leads us from the outer circle to the inner one and introduces us now to the age of the person.

KEY-AND-LOCK MODEL

So let us look directly now at our present age. We can see clues to the inadequacy of the problem-solving model if we notice how the substitution of one word for another can give rise to a new model. This is what has happened with the common and often unnoticed substitution of the word "key" for the word "answer." There is revealed in the way people use the words the mysterious process by which a people begins to sense the inadequacy of models which have been set up by certain words. We have been talking about the "key to the problem" as well as the "answer to the problem."

The phrase "key to the problem" creates a quite different operational relationship than "answer." If one pauses to reflect, one can see that this phrase relates more to the "seed-entering-soil" model than to the "answer-in-the-back-of-the-book" model. We can be profoundly grateful for the great achievements and gains of the previous age that allow us to solve problems, predict going to the moon, and finally walk on the moon. But if we are to remain true and responsive to this new age of the person, we need to see that putting a "key" in the door and opening the lock does not end a process as does an "answer" to a problem. It rather begins one.

In other words, we need to recognize that when we have the "key to language learning" or the "key to proper pronunciation," for example, we are not at the end of a process. One cannot rely on the predicted outcome as in the problem-answer model. Each key has a particular lock. It is in this sense then that certain words and phrases can imply a totally different operational system.

Let us look further at this relationship between the key and the lock and the process that is inherent in that model. No matter how valuable, well constructed, or accurately cut a key is, it will be effective only if it has the total cooperation of the lock. A rusty lock, one with a damaged tumbler system, or simply a key that looks as if it ought to fit but does not for some reason can all cause nonentry into the room or whatever the lock is locking.

So with this shift in modality we are no longer talking of teachers who would solve problems, offer the right solution, and then expect learners to respond in a predictable way to those solutions. We are saying rather that if we use the problem-solving model we need to consciously recognize that having arrived at certain keys to various problems we are still in need of the committed and involved cooperation of the learners. A key does not give answers but enters in.

We can see then that moving from the "answer" to the "key" to the problem, we have come to the same conception that Heisenberg has given us, namely, that the "I" is in every relationship, and no matter what problem-solving process we may go through, we come finally to two persons relating together: the person of the knower, who has some keys to some problems and therefore is absolutely essential, and the person of the learner, whose cooperation in letting these keys enter, submitting to the aggression of the key-turning process of the knower, and then in turn actively being aggressive to pull the bar in the lock, is equally important to the entire process.

Therefore, in so understanding this mutually cooperative and responsive process, we have not only a model for the knower-learner relationship but in a basic sense a model of what science is now maintaining. That is, we can have the objectivity of an observer up to a point, but beyond that point we enter into an interpersonal relationship where the "I" of the knower and the "I" of the learner are as equally and intensively intertwined as are the key and the lock. If both are to be effective in what they are trying to do, they must work closely, sensitively, and graciously together.

THE ADULT TEACHING/LEARNING RELATIONSHIP

This leads us then to the stone itself—the knower-learner relationship. To have two persons deeply engaged with one another at the level of complexity and subtlety of their whole personalities is a totally different relationship from having one simply to provide answers to the other's linguistic problems. It is far more complex and far more challenging than the simpler astronomical model drawn of the knower as observer problem solver.

Here we might take a look at some implications in the acronym TESOL. What we see is a name which intriguingly catches the person not only of the knower but also of the learner. Let's look carefully. "Teachers of English"—it could end there, couldn't it? Most of us would have no difficulty in understanding teachers of English meeting together to discuss their problems and coming up with better answers and hopefully better ways of teaching.

Now look at the rest of the acronym: "To Speakers of Other Languages." If we put an equal emphasis on the word "speakers," we suddenly realize that we have two experts in this relationship—not just one. In using the word "expert" here, what we mean is that we have two persons quite experienced in their own languages. Therefore, we are talking about adults—an adult-knower/adult-learner relationship.

An adult or adolescent learner, as we know, is not simply a person who is passive and who is going to be automatically receptive to the suggestions, answers, and solutions we, as expert teachers, have worked out. He or she is an emotionally charged, intensely conscious adult aware of how much they already know in their own language. To take on a whole new communicative system—to learn to speak English—at least in the first stages of this process, means to have this competence and confidence threatened. While we all know that this is in most instances not traumatic for the child, since the child seems not that invested yet in self-identity with his own language, for the adolescent or adult it can be.

Going back, then to the acronym TESOL, we can see that it implies another acronym to express the other person in this relationship, namely, LESOL—Learners of English as Speakers of Other Languages. So what we are looking for in the key-and-lock or agrarian model is the fruitful interrelationship and constructive cooperation between TESOL and LESOL. LESOL must willingly accept the seeds of knowledge that TESOL can offer if there is to be an entering into the target language.

We know that this ideal is not always achieved; it is nonetheless, like 300 in bowling, the ideal goal of this creative learning relationship. We might say, however, that the realization of this ideal is furthered to the degree that there is delicate and sensitive understanding of both the teacher-knower and student-learner.

THE FIVE STATES OF HUMAN CREATIVE LEARNING

Let us now look at a way we can combine the agrarian sowing seed model or what we have called the "inseminational-germinational" model of learning with the more mechanical but similar model of the key entering the lock. In the beginning of the agrarian model, the seed enters the soil and is totally encapsulated by it. We have called this stage 1. In the human model one can talk about the embryonic position. Here, because the learner is so inadequate in the new language, he or she is seen as totally dependent on the knower of the target language. So in stage 1 the understanding skills in the knower enable the learner, often in a state of anxiety and threat, to make a commitment to the knower in security, confidence, and trust.

The adult and adolescent learners are self-conscious of identity with their own language, in contrast to the preadolescent child, who seems able to interchange grammatical constructions and language sounds without resistance. The self-conscious adult must therefore be encouraged by the sensitive and skillful understanding of the knower if the knower's seed is to be given a chance to take root or if the key is to function successfully in the lock.

In stage 2 one sees beginning attempts toward separation from the knower, but still there is a great deal of dependence. As we move to stage 3, especially toward the end of stage 3, we see ambivalence and ambiguities. To help imagine this, think of a circle with a line through the center, and make one half of the circle black and the other half white. The black indicates how much, at the end of stage 3, the learner has already absorbed. The subtlety here is that now the language learner is in a crucial position. He can now "get along," have a job, and enjoy a certain level of wage earning and personal success in the new language. The danger now is that because the immediate pressure is off, the strong motivation to move into the white part of the circle—the refinements of the language—is not there. So if we meet such students 10 years later, they may be speaking much the way they did 10 years before, even though previously they had made noticeable progress up to that point.

Therefore, at this point in the process a whole new relationship has to emerge. Going back to our analogy of the key and lock, we would propose that here is where we begin to get a reverse process. The lock now must respond aggressively and begin to put pressure on the bolt to withdraw the bolt so that the lock may be opened. Looking at the sensitive and complex personal relationship involved, this point in the human learning process is crucial for both knower and learner. The learner, now quite conscious of what he knows, can become increasingly resistant to what he still does not know. The knower, on the other hand, increasingly conscious of the learner's resistance, the learner's pride in what he already knows, is apt to begin having difficulty in offering corrections, or in our terms, filling out the white side of the circle.

Stage 4 comes about when this ambiguity has been resolved constructively; when the learner's anger, aggression, intense struggle to work out for himself his achievement in the target language has been quietly encouraged. This is done not so much by overt approval but by an obvious willingness on the part of the teacher to leave *learning space*.

So at the end of stage 4 the learner is secure that he can be self-assertive, committed, even angry in the new language, much as he is in his own, and in no way will this assertion of self be misunderstood or interpreted negatively by the knower or other members of the learning community. At the same time, the learner is sure he will receive the knower's necessary corrections and precisions.

This leads, then, in our experience, to the creative relationship where at the second half of stage 4, the beginning of stage 5 and beyond, minute discriminations and corrections can be made and absorbed. At this point there can be a total investment of the learning self in all the fine discriminations, idioms, subtleties of construction, and better style that the knower can still give. But, for this to be best fulfilled, the learner's defensiveness must give way to open understanding of the knower's hesitance and insecurity in making such corrections. The understander now becomes the learner in this subtle aspect of the relationship.

As you can see, here we have moved from the model of the knower who has the "key" to linguistic "problems" and the learner who is seen as the cooperative lock, to a more human creative learning model. In this creative relationship a new learning self is born through the delicate union between a sensitive knower and equally sensitive learners.

Before we move on to those conditions that most favor this kind of creative growth of a new learning self, let's look at one further point about the speaker of another language. One can still remain somewhat of an observer in studying grammar and vocabulary and in learning to read another language. While it is less true in writing, because one's knowledge of grammar and vocabulary is in some measure on the line, yet even in that case there is usually a chance for correction before we make a total commitment of ourselves in writing.

It is when one speaks another language that one is linguistically naked. One is vulnerable to the skilled knower, who can immediately catch the mistakes. It is this special risk in being a speaker that heightens the necessity for an atmosphere of personal security permeating all five stages.

MUTUAL SECURITY FOR BOTH KNOWER AND LEARNER

To catch the conditions that in our experience over years of research seem to be necessary to best produce this creative relationship, we have devised the acronym SARD. The "S" is the mutual *Security* that both learner and knower have with one another. We have found this best achieved by imitating counseling and psychotherapy in the relationship of deep understanding between learner and knower. We wish to arrive at the same kind of commitment and methodic trust that the client has toward the counselor and in turn the same unconditional positive regard on the part of the counselor toward the client. This seems to result in a creative security equally shared and mutually supported by both knower and learner. This does not mean the knower needs to be a psychotherapist or even a skilled counselor. But certain understanding skills that bring this knower-learner security can be learned by practice and effort.

There are a number of subtleties in how this security is produced. But in our experience two basic attitudes held by the knower-teacher seem important. The first is an attitude of total trust and confidence in the learners. Along with this must go a nonjudgmental attitude about the person of the learner. In this kind of atmosphere, learners can let the sounds of the target language as they come from the knower-teacher flow through them in total and relaxed imitation. We might add here that this total trust may be especially difficult in our time because of advertising and similar daily barrages that tend to force us to continual skepticism and doubt. But unless the learner trusts the teacher, he will tend to filter, distort, and even misunderstand. So, confusedly, the learner proves his doubts right, when in fact in an attitude of doubting resistance he never clearly heard and so never learned what the teacher had really said.

While there are many ways in which this initial trust and nonjudgmental atmosphere can be brought about, we have found one of the best ways is to have learners begin speaking the target language in small groups (4 to 7) at a time through a skilled language counselor. The same trusting atmosphere can be generated in larger groups. Out of this sense of support grows the independent knowledge of the learner, as we have described earlier, by reason of a slowly assertive independence. These conversations, recorded, played back, and put in writing, can serve as a text, if desired, for grammatical and vocabulary reflection. We will say more about this when we talk about reflection.

The second attitude which is basic to security has to do with the teacher seeing himself as giving "seeds of knowledge" which must have their unique germination in each learner. This view is in contrast to the model "knowledge is power." The giving up of teacher power is crucial here and not easy, since power brings status and self-security. But the knower's willingness to give this up is a major factor in student growth.

In the agrarian seed model, then, power is not an issue at all but rather an entering-in process. If there is to be a harvest, the farmer must put seeds into the ground, cover them up with dirt, and then depend on the soil and the natural process to do its work. Once plants begin to emerge, the farmer must then do other things than he did at the beginning if they are to grow sturdy and strong.

Learner security seems to emerge in much the same way. When learners have tested the teacher by openly imitating the strange sounds or, later, making up phrases and sentences by themselves, and they discover total acceptance through the nonjudgmental attitude of the teacher, the learners seem to gain confidence. Confidence grows and takes on a different value, especially in stage 3, where the learners feel that they can be aggressive and angry. They can even project this on the knower, as a surrogate for what they are hostile to in themselves—namely, the mistakes they continue to make—and yet still not be rejected by the teacher or the other group members.

Once this kind of security has been established and affirmed, the learner seems increasingly motivated to work on his own vocabulary lists and grammar structures and able to sort out what he knows and what he still needs to know. It is in this sense that he is freeing himself more and more from a dependence on the knower. In this way too the teacher grows more confident and secure making discriminating corrections. It is this mutual confidence and security then which is characteristic of stage 4. However, it is at this point in the process, as we have indicated earlier, that the learner begins to recognize that his very confidence may, in turn, begin to threaten the teacher.

This is a pivotal point in the relationship. It has been our experience that in proportion as the learner takes the responsibility of making it easy for the teacher to make these final corrections, to give idioms and different subtleties of expression which could not be given earlier, a final mutually fulfilling creative learning experience occurs. All these changes in the learning process we have placed under the heading of Security.

The second letter in the acronym SARD can be understood as *Attention-Aggression*. While it is true that the word "aggression" in popular parlance has a pejorative tone, we mean it to signify an active posture on the part of the learner in contrast to a more passive one. The very fact that learners in this process begin by speaking puts them in an assertive or aggressive position. It also puts them in an attentive position. As the learner speaks and hears back his own sentences, as well as those of the other learners in the group, he is constantly made aware that he is guiding the conversation, not the teacher. It is this sense that attention and learner aggression coincide. The more actively involved the learner, the greater the attention.

Moving to the "R" of SARD, the core element here is the concept of *Reflection*. While retention flows from reflection and is also represented by the "R," for our purpose in this paper we will talk about two types of reflection. One we will call "text reflection" and the other "experience reflection." The text reflection can be carried out in a number of ways. One way we have found quite helpful is to listen back to a tape recording of the conversation—in the target language. The learner, partly by guesswork, partly by memory, and partly by recognition, realizes that he has understood almost all of its contents—in the target language. This is a great satisfaction.

This experience alone, which can occur in one of the first sessions, becomes one of the most important of all security sources by way of reflection. The learner can say to himself, "I understood that and it was all in the target language." Even though he had said it originally in his native language, having now heard himself speaking the new language, his new-language self is already beginning to be born. This initiates the process through which this new-language self steadily grows to finally become as confident a speaker in the new language as in the native language.

The second type of reflection, reflection on the learning experience itself, is also important. This is where the teacher needs some special skills in psychological understanding. The learner often needs time to take counsel with himself around his conflicts, anger, anxiety, and general emotional states brought about by the learning experience. We have found it extremely valuable if the teacher or another skilled person who can speak the native language of the learner is able to allow the learner to clarify his anger, discouragement, or alternatively, feelings of encouragement and hope and similar reactions, even if that exchange is only two or three minutes.

This exchange, however, is best carried out if the teacher has acquired some skill in understanding both affective and cognitive communication. This kind of communication can bring forward remarkable gains in self-awareness and can free the learner to go on unimpeded by a certain emotion, conflict, or self-accusation. This kind of understanding seems especially to help the learner overcome an urge to withdraw in shame and embarrassment at making mistakes.

We are not proposing that reflective understanding demands a complex and esoteric psychotherapeutic skill. Rather we are saying that such understanding can be learned, with effort, by any dedicated and sensitive teacher.

The last letter in the acronym SARD is related to *Discrimination*. We feel that one of the most common reasons why learners do not discriminate in a language and therefore continue all their lives to make the same mistakes is that they were never totally secure and so never completely attentive. Consequently they never had a chance to reflect on what the exact sound, spelling, and grammatical construction were. In the rare instance when they had a chance to do this, say, after 10 years of speaking the language, they are amazed that they never knew that the word sounded like that even though they may have used it thousands of times.

The adult language learner is, at first, often impatient with the minute details of perfecting the target language. We propose, therefore, like the small child, the adult learner is allowed to be secure in the first three stages as long as he or she can be understood. But we are not suggesting any neglect of precision, grammatical accuracy, and careful pronunciation. Rather we are suggesting waiting for an adult learning readiness for this kind of discrimination. We are suggesting that we wait until a stage of adequate learning security has been achieved—in our process, stages 3 and 4. It would be at this time that precise discrimination in various areas would emerge as part of the creative new-self growth. By this time too, the learner is secure enough to concentrate on and so really hear this discrimination.

Now that we have discussed those conditions contained in the acronym SARD, you may be saying to yourself, well this kind of model for learning demands far more advanced psychological skill than the ordinary teacher would have. Our experience has been the contrary. This is part of the reason for the title of this paper, "A Linguistic Model for Learning and Living in the New Age of the Person." We are in a new age, an exciting new age. We can begin to consider now not only methodologies aimed at helping teachers to be more skilled teachers, but also methodologies aimed at helping learners to be more skilled learners. These methodologies also further those deep personal relationships that we have called "community learning." The acquiring of this kind of creative skill is not beyond the ability, understanding, and degree of commitment that any dedicated teacher would normally have.

From our experiences with teachers we are proposing that it is most valuable training and skill not only for learning but for living in this new age of the person.

YOIN

We return now to the model with which we began—the stone dropped in the pool. The Japanese use this to illustrate what they mean by *yoin*. In the concept of *yoin*—one of the most sensitive relationships among cultured and educated Japanese—a knower delicately suggests only the minimum of what he thinks an enquirer would need. The enquirer, then, is left on his own to pursue, in his own uniqueness, fineness, and sensitivity, all that this quest would lead him to. The height of *yoin* is for the knower to hold back and in no way enter the sanctuary of the learner's quest.

This, perhaps, is what we in the West are beginning to learn now in this new age of the person—something of the Japanese conception of *yoin*. Or stated another way, we are beginning to understand the conditions of fineness between persons who are in a deep creative relationship. Whether it is the creative relationship of having children in love or producing a manuscript together, or knowers and learners deeply engaged together in the language-learning process, the conditions that convalidate each one's worth seem to be the same.

This is the heart of counseling-learning/Community Language Learning. We are proposing that a truly creative learning relationship, like any creative relationship, must give evidence not only of imsemination, as most basic and essential, but also of germination and a continuing delicately demanding cooperation. What we are talking about then—if I may use the word, not sentimentally but in a constructive sense—is a love relationship between TESOL and LESOL, giving birth to a whole new English self in the Speaker of the Other Language.

To truly learn something then is to grow a new self—from infancy to adulthood. this we know is best accomplished in an atmosphere suffused with mutually reflected fineness, worth, consideration, and deeply shared regard.

SUGGESTOLOGY
AND SUGGESTOPEDY*

Georgi Lozanov

Suggestology is the comprehensive science of suggestion in all its aspects, but for the time being it deals mainly with the possibilities of suggestion to tap man's reserve capacities in the spheres of both mind and body. Consequently it is the science of the accelerated harmonious development and self-control of man and his manifold talents.

SUGGESTION

The word *suggestion* derives from the Latin word *suggero, suggessi, suggestum,* to place, to prompt, to hint. This word has acquired a more or less negative meaning in many languages, but in English a shade of meaning has been given to the word which is close to our understanding of it: to offer, to propose. Thus, according to our understanding of the word, suggestion is a communicative factor which is expressed in "proposing" that the personality should make its choice, should choose both rationally and intuitively and according to its structure and disposition from among a wide range of possibilities among complex stimuli which are being intricately associated, condensed, coded, symbolized, and amplified. The choice is founded upon the external orchestration of the stimuli which come from outside of or arise within the personality itself, not only within the limited sphere of consciousness but also, simultaneously and to a fuller extent, in the various and numerous levels of *paraconsciousness.* In fact the utilization of the conscious-paraconscious stimuli, well organized, psychologically orchestrated, and harmonized with the personality, is suggestion in its

---

*Abridged from "The Lozanov Report to UNESCO." Full text can be ordered from Lozanov Learning Institute, 1110 Fidler Lane, Suite 12125, Silver Spring, Md. 20910.

most manifest and positive form. Such utilization can reveal the personality's universal reserve capacity and stimulate its creativity. A visual representation of suggestion is art. For is art not the greatest form of suggestion?

Reserve Capacities

Suggestion in its most positive manifestation and when well organized can uncover the personality's reserve capacities. By reserve capacities we understand the unmanifested but genetically predetermined capacities operating mainly in the paraconscious and surpassing the normal ones several times over. The laws governing these capacities are to a certain extent different from the ordinary psychophysiological laws.

Among the many examples of suggestively tapped reserve capacities we can mention the following: (1) *Hypermnesia* or supermemory (in long-term memory). This supermemory surpasses the possibilities of ordinary memory several times over. Sometimes it occurs in psychotherapy, in hypnosis, and when applying methods of catharsis. Mass hypermnesia can be brought about under the conditions of suggestopedic instruction with both healthy and sick people, when the educational-curative process is carried out properly. Hypermnesia as an important reserve capacity is characterized by the following specific psychophysiological laws: (*a*) manifestation either after a latent period and without any conscious effort, or suddenly and spontaneously; (*b*) increasing recollection without reinforcement (reminiscent curve); (*c*) amnestic covering and sinking of the basic sense-bearing nucleus of the complex stimulus into paraconsciousness until it is "raised" out of paraconsciousness into consciousness; (*c*) making the first recollection easy under the conditions of emotional impetus, of the associative connections of the peripheral perceptions and of concentrative psychorelaxation; (*e*) great durability of the reproduced memory traces; (*f*) decreased susceptibility to fatigue; and (*g*) a considerable psychotherapeutic, psychohygienic, and psychoprophylactic effect. (2) *Provoked hypercreativity* or suggested or autosuggested creative superproductivity. Intuition is activated and states similar to inspiration arise. These are outwardly expressed in a decidedly greater creative manifestation of personality. A number of experiments have shown that the manifestation of artistic, musical, and even mathematical abilities (in accordance with any given person's manifested and potential abilities) increases considerably both quantitatively and qualitatively. Suggestological experiments have shown the possibility of accelerated creative self-development. Here again we find the same psychophysiological laws as are characteristic of hypermnesia. (3) *Suggestive control and self-control of pain, bleeding, the functions of the sympathetic nervous system, metabolism,* etc.

The tapping of man's reserve capacities can be achieved only under the conditions of excellent suggestive organization, orchestration, and harmonization of the conscious-paraconscious functions. Though inseparably connected with consciousness, yet the basic "store" of the reserve capacities is paraconsciousness.

Paraconsciousness

By paraconsciousness we understand more or less unconscious mental activity. Here we include everything that, for the given moment, is outside the scope of consciousness. When we operate with various concepts, when we read or solve problems and are, on the whole, consciously concentrating our attention on some activity, we are not aware of the many unconscious components which constitute these activities, for example, the ideas which build up notions; the letters and even the words of sentences which we happen to be reading; the unconscious judgments and premises hidden in the shortened formulas of thinking; the codes and symbols. The concept of paraconsciousness comprises also the numerous unconscious forms of associating, coding, and symbolizing which have an informational, algorithmical, and reprogramming effect on personality. Paraconsciousness embraces the unconscious sides of creativity as well as intuition and inspiration.

All these sides of paraconsciousness penetrate each other and take part in the desuggestive-suggestive process.

Antisuggestive Barriers

There is no suggestion without desuggestion, without freeing paraconsciousness from inertia of something old. The means of suggestion are usually referred mechanically only to subliminal stimuli or only to emotional involvement. One often loses sight of the fact that the whole personality takes part in every reaction. Then this means that no effect can be expected if the subliminal perceptions, the peripheral perceptions, and the emotional stimuli are not in accord with the manifold and often conflicting dispositions of the personality, both inborn and acquired. It is difficult to realize a suggestive situation if it is not in accord at the moment with the particular needs of the instincts and with the motivation, attitude, mind set, expectancy (with the placebo effect), interests, and in general, all the factors of the personality which take an unconscious part in building up the *antisuggestive barriers.*

As a manifestation of conscious-paraconscious unity, the antisuggestive barriers are a peculiar characteristic of personality. They are, in fact, overcome through harmonization with them. The three antisuggestive barriers, *critical-logical, intuitive-affective,* and *ethical,* are inseparably connected and are subject to continual dynamic changes.

Social Suggestive Norm

Overcoming the antisuggestive barriers means also overcoming the social suggestive form of one or another of the limitations set to what we can do.

Caught in the net of the numerous social suggestive norms in most cases, we do not even attempt to do anything that is at variance with them. We do not believe that it is possible to increase our memorization in volume and soundness, to accelerate our creative development, to have more self-control over both our mental and our physiological functions. The social suggestive norm teaches us that it is impossible, and contains a note of warning not to attempt it. And if it really happens somewhere it is considered a miracle, an exception, or a falsification. That is why suggestology in its development as a science for liberating the personality's reserve capacities (and hence for displacing the social suggestive norm and for freeing the larger fields of personality) encounters great opposition.

THE MEANS OF SUGGESTION

The means by which suggestion overcomes the antisuggestive barriers and tops the personality's reserve capacities are complex. It is very difficult to separate them and show them mechanically, all the more so because their realization is a question of both the personality's abilities and its qualities. If we do, however, try to separate them in order to study them, infantilization and pseudopassivity belong to one group of controlled states of personality which can be provoked from the outside suggestively or which arise by themselves autosuggestively.

Infantilization is a controlled state of intuitive activity, emotional plasticity, increased perceptiveness, and confidence in the possibility of freeing one or another of the reserve capacities in a given situation. Infantilization arises when a highly harmonized contact is established with a person possessing authority (prestige), but it can come about unaided.

Pseudopassivity (concert pseudopassiveness) is a controlled state, resembling the state in which we find ourselves when listening to classical music. It is a state of concentrative psychorelaxation. We are speaking neither of hypnoidal relaxation nor of muscle relaxation that is an end in itself, but of a calm mental state, lacking any stress, free of needless thoughts and action, with lowered ideomotor activity. On the background of this calm mental state a pleasant, untiring concentration is realized similar to our concentration at a concert.

The part played by authority in creating confidence and emotional stimulus and the part played by harmonious intonation and rhythm do not call for any explanation here.

Peripheral Perceptions and Emotional Stimulus
(Double-planeness and Psychological Orchestration)

If we try to simplify our understanding of the means of suggestion, we can reduce them, somewhat schematically, to two basic physiological mechanisms: peripheral perceptions and emotional stimulus. The peripheral perceptions are caused by stimuli that are in strength—supraliminal stimuli which at the moment of perceiving have got into the periphery of attention and consciousness. They do not fall in the focus of consciousness because of its limited volume. The receptive fields of the sense organs and the brain are, however, much wider than the scope of conscious perceptions. Consequently the peripheral perceptions fall into the sphere of paraconsciousness. They are characterized by considerable dynamism. At any moment they can enter again into the realm of conscious perception. The peripheral perceptions are realized not only outside the receptive field focused by the consciousness, but also in the field itself. Having reached the brain, this information emerges in the consciousness with some delay, or it influences the motives and decisions and is operative in tapping the reserve capacities. This peripheral information included in the paraconsciousness underlies long-term memory.

The peripheral perceptions suggest and control unconsciously but reliably, while the emotional stimulus impregnates all the activities of the personality as a whole. Complex desuggestive-suggestive situations can be controlled and self-controlled through the unity of the two basic psychophysiological mechanisms: the peripheral perceptions and the emotional stimulus.

The Basic Principles (Foundations) of Suggestology

Suggestology has developed as an attempt to translate the ancient and perennial searching to tap reserve capacities genetically predetermined in man into a modern reality. It combines desuggestive-suggestive communicative psychotherapy with the liberating and stimulating aspects of art and some modifications of the old schools of concentrative psychorelaxation. The experimental research and the new theoretical meaning given to the phenomena researched have led to definite psychophysiological conceptions. In close connection with this research, the following three *inseparable* psychophysiological fundamental principles of suggestology have been formulated: (1) *Interpersonal communication and mental activity are always conscious and paraconscious at the same time.* (2) *Every stimulus is associated, coded, symbolized, and generalized.* (3) *Every perception is complex.*

We dealt with the first principle in discussing the problem of paraconsciousness, its unity with consciousness, and the role it plays in harmonizing the entire personality for the purpose of stimulating its harmonious and creative development.

The second fundamental principle shows that with the continually increasing abstraction a number of the original levels of perceptions, the original ideas and notional generalizations of a lower level, are being constantly pushed into paraconsciousness in order to make room for the following higher codes and symbols.

The three basic principles of suggestology, no matter how schematically given, are indicative of the possibilities of the two basic psychophysiological mechanisms: the peripheral perceptions and the emotional stimulus.

SUGGESTOPEDY

On the basis of this general theory of suggestion which we have outlined we have worked out an educational and curative desuggestive-suggestive pedagogical system—suggestopedagogy or suggestopedy (suggestopedia).

The socially and historically built-up norm concerning above all the level of man's memory and the speed of skill mastery as well as the idea of the "throes" of creative work have brought into being a suggestive mind set which in fact slows down the development of man's genetically conditioned mental powers. That is why one of the most important aims of suggestology is to liberate to a considerable extent, to desuggest all students from the social suggestive norm, desuggesting the accumulated inadequate ideas about man's limited capacities.

Instead of creating conditions for the joyous satisfaction of the personality's basic need—the thirst for information, and instead of bearing in mind the way the brain functions, teachers often seem to want to "teach the brain how to function."

The following are some of the things in ordinary education which are inconsistent with the physiological, psychological functions of personality:

1. It is well known that in no case does the brain function only with its cortex structures, or only with the subcortex, or with only the right or the left hemisphere. The functional unity of the brain is unbreakable no matter that in some cases one activity or another comes to the fore. Therefore, the emotional and motivational complex, the image thinking and logical abstraction, must be activated simultaneously. But most often there are the following two kinds of deviation from this natural fact:

a. The teaching is addressed only to the cortical structures and the left hemisphere of the learner, as if he were an emotionless and motivationless cybernetic machine.

b. Although the learner may be taken as a psychophysiological entity, the educational process is not directed globally to all parts of the brain simultaneously.

2. It is well known that analytical-synthetical activity under normal conditions is accomplished simultaneously—there is no such thing as a stage of pure analysis or of pure synthesis. This simultaneous and indivisible connectedness of the physiological processes has its own psychological expression. It also underlies cognitive—from the general to the particular and back to the general. But these natural laws often undergo "correction" in pedagogical practice in one of the following ways:

a. Elements are studied separately, in isolation from the sense-bearing whole; they are automated through tiring exercises, and only then are they connected one after the other and systematically to form the whole.

b. The whole is studied without paying attention to its component parts and to the mistakes arising in this way. In both cases attempts are made to break up the natural simultaneity of the processes of analysis and synthesis.

3. Man's personality takes part in every communicative process simultaneously at numerous conscious and paraconscious levels. This nature-granted fact is "utilized" in pedagogical practice most often in the following two ways:

a. The principle of conscious participation in the educational processes is formalized and turned into a fetish. According to it the learners must learn and automate each element of the material in a strictly conscious and rational manner in spite of the fact that it can be learned to a certain degree spontaneously and intuitively at the first perception of the globally given lesson.

b. Weight is laid only on the paraconscious and intuitive powers of the learner, and the necessity for a conscious finalizing and creative reassessment of the material is overlooked.

In contrast to the above inconsistencies which violate the physiological and psychological functions of personality, the three basic principles of suggestopedia take into account psychophysiological laws: (1) the global participation of the brain, (2) the simultaneous processes of analysis and synthesis, and (3) the simultaneous and indivisible participation of the conscious and paraconscious processes. If we do not abide by these unchangeable psychological laws and by the basic principles of suggestology, the education process becomes an inhibiting factor and one causing illness. Any educational process of that kind precludes any tapping of the reserve capacities. What is more, some sociopsychological factors are added to the psychophysiological ones, and this increases the difficulties. For example:

1. The mind set of fear of learning. Many nations have some kind of proverb that means "learning is torture." Making the process of teaching and learning more intensive often intensifies this fear and also the inner counteraction, in both learners and teachers.

2. The social suggestive norm of the personality's capacities being limited. According to this norm, man can supposedly assimilate new material only to a definite, fairly low level.

The combination of a fearful mind set and the social suggestive norm of man's limited capacities under the conditions of a nonmedical pedagogical approach results in mass "covert didactogeny": Pupils suffer to a greater or lesser degree from "school neurosis." They have no confidence in their powers; they do not trust their own inner reserves. For them education has been turned from the natural process of satisfying the personality's essential need—the thirst for knowledge—into a psychotrauma.

It is only too natural that with this mind set the nonmedical attempts to intensify the educational process may lead to reinforcing inner mental conflicts, to the fixation of neurotic states, and instead of the results of the educational process getting better they get worse.

The mind set of fear of learning and the social suggestive norm of man's limited capacities make the erroneous approaches and methods worse. The following are some examples of how far some of these erroneous approaches and methods can go:

1. The material to be studied is broken up into smaller and smaller elements. These elements must be grasped, memorized, and automated and then are gradually united into larger entities. In this way are formed some useless primitive habits on the lowest level, which have to be given up in order to build up habits on a higher level, and then the latter have also to be got rid of. And thus it goes on until at last we acquire habits and skills on the necessary highest operating and creative level. This building up and fixing of elementary habits which have to be given up afterward in order to acquire fresh higher-level habits is due to the mind set of fear of our limited learning capacities. But creating a "hierarchy of habits" worsens this mind set and lowers motivation. The hierarchy of habits in any nonmedically organized pedagogy is dangerous for the health. Consequently dry recapitulation results in demotivation and delaying the effect of the instruction instead of accelerating it.

2. Often teachers, aware of the harmful effect which the negative mind set of students toward instruction and learning brings with it, deliberately introduce intervals for relaxation and joking. But by introducing these intervals they in fact suggest that the learners need some relaxation and distraction. They suggest to him that his inner mind set of fear of learning and his fatigue and displeasure with it are justified. Gaiety that is an end in itself when introduced in lessons, no matter how refreshing it may be, brings a risk of still more deeply inculcating the conviction that their basic negative mind set toward instruction is justified.

3. Attempts to accelerate the process of instruction are being made through mechanizing and programming it. The learner communicates with the machines and obtains feedback through the programmed materials. But in this the learner is isolated from the social environment and the wealth of emotion provided by the group. Regardless of the favorable aspects of mechanizing and programming instruction, the feedback information which the learner obtains about how well he has assimilated the assigned material, because of its lack of warmth, not only does not stimulate him but even reinforces his negative mind set toward learning.

This cursory analysis of some of the methods aimed at bettering the efficiency of the process of teaching and learning shows that in pedagogical practice in fact pressure is often exerted on the learner's personality. He reacts against this pressure. The motivation for learning is lowered. Pupils begin to learn only when they are pressed by the necessity to obtain some kind of qualification for the sake of the practical requirements of their plans in life. Thus the satisfaction of their basic need, the thirst for information, is accompanied with displeasure instead of pleasure.

Becoming aware of these negative sides of the process of instruction, teachers in some countries have switched to the other extremes: advocating full freedom for the learner. The learner should be free to choose what and how he is going to learn. However, this search, in its essence justifiable, leads in practice to the absence of any sound form of education. Why should the learner be given freedom in the process of instruction and not be freed from his inner fear of his own limited powers of assimilating new information? Freedom accompanied with fear of learning is equal to giving up learning.

The Psychotherapeutic, Psychohygienic, Physiological, and Sociopsychological Aspects of Suggestopedy

The most important thing in our opinion is to do away with mass didactogeny and bring the process of instruction into line with the laws governing the functioning of the brain. If an educational system succeeds in liberating the learner from fear and from the social suggestive norm of his limited powers, and is brought into line with psychophysiology, it will easily achieve its other pedagogical aims. But the difficulty arises not so much from considering how to bring about the initial liberation, as from how to create a system of sustained, continuous inner liberation. The learner's confidence in his own capacities for learning should grow constantly, and in this way instruction gradually develops into self-instruction. It will gradually go beyond the limitations of the social suggestive norm and penetrate into the sphere of human reserve capacities.

It is this trend toward inner liberation and self-discipline that suggestopedic education develops. It creates conditions for developing skills and habits of inner concentration on the background of optimal psychorelaxation. Man's global capacities are utilized. The emotional stimulus is enhanced; motivation, interests, and mind sets are taken into consideration and activated; the purposeful participation is organized of as many conscious and paraconscious functions of the personality as possible. For example, in regard to attention as an integral element of the learner's activity the process of instruction is organized in such a way that not only the close active attention of the learners is made use of, but also their incidental passive attention, and particularly the peripheral perceptions, which take an unconscious part in both active and passive attention.

Suggestopedy looks for ways to overcome the social suggestive norm. It taps reserves also through organizing the paraconscious elements in the conscious-paraconscious complex. In this respect it leans on the suggestological theory of the paraconscious basis of long-term memory and also on the part played by paraconsciousness in motivating intellectual activation, creativity, and global stimulation of personality. In this way it tries to respond better to the globality characteristic of the natural psychophysiological laws and above all the three basic principles of suggestology.

Suggestopedic Reserve Complex

All the factors mentioned above make it possible for the suggestopedic educational system to release a *reserve complex* with the following obligatory characteristics:

1. Memory reserves, intellectual activity reserves, creativity reserves, and the reserves of the whole personality are tapped. If we do not release many-sided reserve capacities, we cannot speak of suggestopedy.

2. Instruction is always accompanied with an effect of relaxation or at least one without a feeling of fatigue. If learners get tired in lessons, we cannot speak of suggestopedy.
3. Suggestopedic teaching and learning is always a pleasant experience.
4. It always has a favorable educational effect, softening aggressive tendencies in pupils and helping them to adapt themselves to society.

Principles and Means of Suggestopedy

The principles and means of suggestopedy take into account the age characteristics and the pedagogical aims of students. The principles are: (1) joy, absence of tension, and concentrative psychorelaxation; (2) unity of the conscious-paraconscious and integral brain activation; and (3) suggestive relationship on the level of the reserve complex.

The principle of joy, absence of tension, and concentrative psychorelaxation presupposes joy with learning, mental relaxation, and "nonstrain concentration." The emotional release creates conditions for undisturbed intellectual and creative activity without causing the fatigue and the consumption of energy that accompanies strained attention.

The observance of these principles means that the teacher should teach his pupils how to learn.

We must emphasize that this principle means neither passiveness in the sense of lack of will, lack of discrimination and subordination, nor gaiety per se. It calls for calmness, steadiness, inner confidence, and trust.

The principle of unity of the conscious-paraconscious and integral brain activation is in fact a principle of globality. Not only are the learners' conscious reactions and functions utilized but also his paraconscious activity. This principle recognizes the simultaneous global participation of the two brain hemispheres and the cortical and subcortical structures, and also the simultaneously occurring analysis and synthesis. When this principle is observed, the process of instruction comes nearer to the natural psychological and physiological regularities in personality. The consciousness, in the sense of attitude and motivation, is lifted to a still higher level. Under the conditions of the suggestopedic educational system the process of instruction is not set against the natural inseparability of the conscious and paraconscious functions.

The principle of suggestive relationship on the reserve complex calls for a reorganization of the educational process which will make it similar to group psychotherapy with the particular relationship established in it. The level of suggestive relationship is measured by the degree of the tapped reserves in a learner. The qualitatively different characters of these reserves (a new type of assimilation of material, considerably great volume and retention of what is assimilated, positive psychohygienic effect, useful educative influence, etc.) make them reliable criteria for the realization of this principle.

This principle makes it imperative that the process of instruction should always run at the level of the personality's unused reserves. This cannot, however, be achieved if the principles are applied separately (if each principle is observed in isolation from the others). Many good teachers create a pleasant atmosphere in the classroom. It would seem that they are following the first principle of suggestopedy. But assimilation of the material in this atmosphere does not reach the level of the suggestopedic assimilation with its new objective laws governing the processes and with its psychohygienic effect from the process of instruction. In these circumstances one gives one's smiling confirmation to the validity of the brain's limited capacities and backs up the accepted ideas that studying can only be made more pleasant. Such confirmation of the old norms, in spite of the gentle approach, can be of little advantage. Under suggestopedic conditions joy springs not so much from the pleasant outward organization of the educational process, but rather from the easy assimilation of the material and the easy way it can be used in practice. The observance of the three principles simultaneously in every moment of the educational process makes learning joyful and easy, and leads to the tapping of complex reserves.

There is another important and characteristic feature of suggestology involved here: while attention is drawn to the consciously understandable, generalized unity and the sense of it, the processes of paraconscious perception and thinking process the implied elements included in the general code: for instance, in teaching foreign language the learners' attention is directed to the whole sentence, to its meaningful communicative aspect, to its place and role in the given life situation. At the same time pronunciation, vocabulary, and grammar remain to a great extent on a second plane. They are also assimilated, but the well-trained teacher draws the students' attention to them only for a short time and then goes back quickly to the sense of the whole sentence and situation. A considerable part of these elements is learned along with the whole structure without any specific attention being paid to them.

When children are taught to read, they do not learn the separate letters first in order to be able later to join them to form syllables, words, and sentences. But neither are they taught by the so-called "whole-word" method where no interest is shown in the letters that form the words. The children learn meaningful units—words and short sentences—and they discover the letters on the second plane, in the form of finding the answer to the picture puzzle which illustrates the material. Thus they stimulate the whole in its elements simultaneously, their attention being directed in most cases to the meaningful whole.

When the educational process is of a linear nature, which suggestopedy rejects, it consists of dry logicalized teaching that is separated from the essentially inseparable "emotional presence." An educational process of a linear nature has an especially harmful effect in regard to the misunderstood "principle of consciousness," having led to an unsuccessful attempt to break the inherent unity of the conscious and the paraconscious processes. At the same time it has resulted in demotivating and unpleasant conscious learning of isolated, senseless elements before the learners have grasped the idea of the meaningful whole, of the pleasant and motivating global unit which is eventually formed out of these meaningless elements.

Suggestopedic Foreign Language System for Adults

In every suggestologically well-organized communicative process there is a leading procedure with a ritual of "placebo" meaning. The other stages are more or less subordinate to this focus.

The conviction that the new material which is to be learned will be assimilated and become automatic and creatively processed without strain and fatigue is suggested by the weight and solemnity given to the carrying out of this session. This session must, above all, facilitate the memorizing and psycho-hygienic sides of teaching and learning, although these are of necessity bound up with the whole personality. The suggestopedic session is adapted to the subject taught and to the age of the learners. Such a session for little children is quite different from the one for grown-ups. (For children this session is most often a didactic opera performance.) One of the most important of the peculiar characteristics of the suggestopedic session is that it is a source of aesthetic pleasure for the learners.

The recital-like character of the session has advantages over all other types of "special" procedured seances.

1. The session is acceptable from the point of view of the ordinary level of culture and of practical experience, in this respect resembling certain forms of art.
2. There are no hypnotizing procedures, nor does the student feel any undesirable suggestive pressures on his personality.
3. The liberating-stimulating, desuggestive-suggestive influence of specific selected music and specific histrionic mastery, adapted to the requirements of suggestopedic teaching and learning, are used.
4. Ritualization of the musical-theatrical performance, with its rich possibilities of additional positive associating and revised according to the requirements of the educational process, is made use of.
5. At the same time students are learning, their aesthetic interests are aroused and their ethical development is improved.
6. Instruction is made pleasant, is never tiring, and has favorable motivation strength.

The suggestopedic session in the regular foreign language courses for adults comprises two parts. In the first part the students listen to classical and early Romantic music of an emotional nature, while in the second part they listen to preclassical music, of a more profound and more philosophical nature.

The new material that is to be learned is read or recited by a well-trained teacher, once during the first part of the concert and once during the second part of it. At the same time the teacher must, while taking into account the features of the music when reading the material with intonation and with behavior, convey a feeling of conviction to the students that the material will be mastered very easily.

There are three principal phases of the suggestopedic lesson in a foreign language: the presession phase, the session phase, and the postsession phase.

The presession phase takes about 15 to 20 minutes. In this phase the students are made familiar with the key topics of the new material for the first time. The organization of this "first encounter" is of particular importance in creating a positive mind set for reserve capacities. A great part of the material is memorized during this phase. (The anticipation of the next phase, the one consisting of the real "first encounter," arouses pleasant emotions.) The teacher explains the new material very briefly, i.e., deciphers the thematic dialogue in a few supporting points. In doing this, he must suggest through his behavior that the assimilation has already begun and all is pleasant and easy. Already during the deciphering, which is a stage of giving the primary information, the following stages should be noted: fixation, reproduction, and new creative production.

The session phase comprises the session itself, which has already been described above. It lasts for 45 minutes, and with it the day's lessons always come to an end.

The postsession phase is devoted to various elaborations of the material to activate its assimilation.

The elaborations comprise reading and translation of the text, songs, games, an extra text (a monologue), retelling, and conversation on given themes. All this merges into role-playing, but the role-playing should take place only when the students themselves express the wish to do it. The activation must be spontaneous. Thus the teaching and learning acquires sense and meaning.

The suggestopedic system for teaching foreign languages to adults is subject to a number of psychological principles which should be observed, for example, good, authoritative organization; purposeful, double-plane behavior of the teacher; motivating initial instructions which are read to the students; directing of the students' attention to sense-bearing wholes; no obligatory homework, though permission can be given to the students to go through the new lesson for about 15 or 20 minutes in the morning and in the evening, but only informatively, the way one skims through a newspaper.

The textbook is also of importance. Its contents and layout should contribute to the success of the suggestopedic process of teaching and learning. A lighthearted story with a pleasant, emotional plot should run through the textbook. The greater part of the new material is given in the very first lesson— 600 to 850 unfamiliar words and the greater part of the essential grammar. In this way, at the very beginning the students have a wide choice of language possibilities at their disposal, to cope with the communicative elaboration. Thus they do not feel themselves "conditioned" to speak within the limits of a few words and patterns. Each line of the textbook contains parts that can be substituted by others. Thus hundreds of patterns are assimilated at once and under natural conditions. The pictures used as visual aids are connected with the subjects of the lesson and not with elements of it.

The translation of the lesson in the mother tongue is given to the students at the beginning of the lesson to look through cursorily, and is then taken away. In this way the instruction is modeled on what is natural for adults—to have a translation of the text in the foreign language. But we do not stay long at this stage; we quickly pass on to the stage in which there is no translation at all.

There can be different variants of the suggestopedic foreign language system, from courses with several lessons a week to courses of whole days' "immersion" in the suggestopedic foreign language atmosphere. The leading factor is not the number of lessons but the psychological organization of the process of instruction.

If we take as a basic pattern the 24 days' foreign language course with four academic hours a day, either no homework or only some informative reading allowed for 15 minutes in the evening and in the morning, the following results can be expected: (1) The students assimilate on th average more than 90 percent of the vocabulary, which comprises 2,000 lexical units per course. (2) More than 60 percent of the new vocabulary is used actively and fluently in everyday conversation and the rest of the vocabulary is known at translation level. (3) The students speak within the framework of the whole essential grammar. (4) Previously unseen texts can be read. (5) The students make some mistakes in speaking, but these mistakes do not hinder the communication. (6) Pronunciation is satisfactory. (7) The students are not afraid of talking to foreigners who speak the same language. (8) The students are eager to continue studying the same foreign language.

A NATURAL APPROACH

Tracy D. Terrell

The purpose of this paper is to suggest a "natural" approach to the teaching of a second language (L2) in an academic situation. I have used the adjective "natural," since most of the support for the suggestions I will make stems from observations and studies of second language acquisition in natural, i.e., nonacademic, contexts. Not all these suggestions of this approach to the acquisition of L2 in academic contexts are new, of course; however, I believe that a combination of all of them results in a course which is strikingly different from those with which I have been acquainted.[1]

The organization of this paper is as follows. First, I will briefly sketch the view of communicative competence and language acquisition in the context of academic L2 learning which underlies this approach. I will then turn to a discussion of three basic guidelines. Finally, I will discuss some practical implications of these guidelines with regard to classroom teaching.

COMMUNICATIVE COMPETENCE

My premise is that it is possible for students in a classroom situation to learn to communicate in a second language. This assertion may surprise those who would argue that this is indeed already the premise of L2 teaching in most institutions. However, there are many who question "whether any significant level of communicative competence may be attained in the very constraining environment of the classroom" (Valdman 1975:424). This same writer further suggests that the goal of communication "may best be deferred to more advanced levels of instruction and to special purpose courses." In addition, the final products of most of our language classes unfortunately support this suggestion. The reality is that the majority of our students in 1- and 2-year language courses do not attain even a minimal level of communicative competence. In most first-year courses a very small part of the time is spent on actual communication; most of the efforts are directed toward exercises and drills to teach morphology and syntax. It is highly doubtful, however, that the amount of structure (morphology and syntax) which is taught in most first-year language courses (first and second year for high schools) is in any real sense absolutely essential for normal communication with native speakers.[2] Further-more, it is probably true that normal first-year language students are not capable of learning to control in their speech the immense amount of grammatical complexity taught in most classes in a single year.

The key to any discussion of this topic is an agreement on the definition of "communicative competence." I use this term to mean that a student can understand the essential points of what a native speaker says to him in a real communicative situation and can respond in such a way that the native speaker interprets the response with little or no effort and without errors that are so distracting that they interfere drastically with communication. I suggest that the level of competence needed for minimal communication acceptable to native speakers is much lower than that supposed by most teachers. Specifically, I suggest that if we are to raise our expectations for oral competency in communication, we must lower our expectations for structural accuracy.[3]

Let us assume that the primary goal is communicative competence. For the purposes of listening comprehension, morphology is by necessity ignored by the language learners at beginning levels. Syntactic differences are noticed only insofar as they differ drastically from L1, and even these differences cause little problem for comprehension if the major lexical items of the sentence are known and if the sentence is uttered in a meaningful context.[4] With regard to production, only on rare occasions will errors in surface morpho-syntax, such as verb subject or noun-adjective agreement, cause the native speaker difficulties. Errors with the elaborate case system of German or the gender and number agreement systems of the Romance languages normally cause no interpretation difficulties by a native speaker if the sentence is uttered in a meaningful context. Most of the problems in interpretation stem from the fact that the sentences uttered in the classroom by the teacher or student have no communicative context, since they are created for the practice of some morphological or syntactical item being studied.

The preoccupation with grammatical correctness in early stages of L2 teaching is essentially a felt need of language teachers and is not an expectation of either language learners or most native speakers of L2, who with few notable exceptions are usually quite happy to deal with foreigners making any sort of effort to speak their language.[5]

SECOND LANGUAGE ACQUISITION

The student at any point in a natural L2 acquisition process possesses a developing system of grammar rules, which parallel to adult grammars permits him to process input in L2 and to make appropriate responses.[6] At first this grammar is extremely rudimentary. Most probably the first governing principle is to "string the known and appropriate lexical items together in more or less the same order as L1 or in the order in which the words are thought of." The sets of grammatical principles termed by Nemser (1971) "approximative system," by Corder (1971) "idiosyncratic dialect," and by Selinker (1972) "interlanguage" evolves in the direction of the adult speaker. At any point in time, however, the output cannot be expected to be perfect. On the other hand, in the traditional classroom the student expands his grammar one rule at a time, learning each as perfectly as possible and progressing from a simple to a more complex output. The output at any one point is restricted but as grammatical as possible. In natural L2 acquisition the output is as varied as possible and expresses quite complex ideas at all times. It is the grammaticality of the utterance which increases with time and experience.

If communicative competence is an immediate goal, we must establish as quickly as possible a large lexicon with very general syntax rules. Vocabulary acquisition is relatively simple. It also gives the student the ability to comprehend utterances and at least some ability to respond in real communicative situations. Once the student is communicating, however imperfectly, the teacher can then direct the materials and experiences toward the development of the student grammar ("interlanguage") in the direction of the adult grammar.

LEARNING AND ACQUISITION

Language knowledge stems from two sources: what is learned and what is acquired.[7] Learning is the conscious process of studying and intellectually understanding the grammar of L2. Acquisition, on the other hand, refers to the unconscious absorption of general principles of grammar through real experiences of communication using L2. It is the basis for most first language ability and in terms of L2 is commonly known as "picking up a language."

In most L2 classrooms the emphasis is on learning, not acquisition. However, since no one has ever completely described the grammar of a language much less taught it to anyone, all L2 ability must also involve acquisition. The most obvious incontestable example of acquisition is the ability to "pick up" a nativelike pronunciation with minimal exposure. Not all students are equally adept at acquisition, but the important point is that while acquisition is present to some degree in all L2 ability, learning may or may not have played a major role.[8]

If we consider the diverse situations in which adults communicate in second languages, it is probably true that most second languages are not learned in academic situations but are acquired naturally. A speaker of one language must use another in the marketplace. Often one language is used at home and in everyday communication but another must be learned for educational or business purposes. In many cases the adult speaker has moved to another language area and must learn that language for much of his or her daily communication, as is the case for most immigrants. The main point is that people of all ages and backgrounds do acquire second languages, often without the help of formal education or special courses. One factor common to all these situations is that language learning takes place when there is a real need and motivation for it.[9] There is no doubt that the ability to acquire a second language perfectly decreases as one grows older, but the overwhelming empirical evidence from L2 learners in cultures all over the globe in the most diverse situations shows that adults can acquire languages and that indeed the acquisition of other languages in some societies may be the norm (Hill, 1970).

L2 acquisition in adults may be quite similar although not identical to L2 acquisition by children. Bailey, Madden, and Krashen (1974) found that adults acquire grammatical morphemes in the same way as do children (using Dulay and Burt's 1973 study); they concluded that "children and adults use common strategies and process linguistic data in fundamentally similar ways."[10]

Taylor (1973), after a review of the relevant research, concludes that "what may be necessary for the adult to acquire real native proficiency in a second language is a persevering motivation, the desire to identify with another cultural group integratively and the ability to overcome the emphatic barriers set up by ego boundaries." He added that "it seems likely that affective psychological variables may constitute the major reason why adults are not always as successful as children in language acquisition." Evidence from Gardner and Lambert (1972), Guiora (1971), and Nida (1971) indicates that a positive attitude with regard to affective variables not only may be necessary to acquire language, but that it may actually function independently of factors such as aptitude and intelligence.

The evidence at this point indicates then that the primary factors which influence L2 acquisition are affective, not cognitive. Therefore, the overriding consideration in all the components of any natural approach must be to make the student feel at ease during activities in the classroom.[11]

In summary, I have suggested that (1) immediate communicative competence (not grammatical perfection) be the goal of beginning language instruction, (2) instruction should be directed to modifying and improving the students' grammar (rather than building it one rule at a time), (3) students should be given the opportunity to acquire language (rather than be forced to learn it), and (4) affective (not cognitive) factors are primary forces operating in language acquisition.

In the following section I will discuss some practical guidelines designed to implement these suggestions.

GUIDELINES FOR A NATURAL APPROACH
TO L2 TEACHING

1. *Distribution of learning and acquisition activities.* All teachers have tried to deal intelligently with the problem of how much time to dedicate in the classroom to the various sorts of activities which are involved in gaining communicative competence. For purposes of discussion I have classified these activities into three groups: explanation, practice, and application. Activities of

explanation and practice (drills, exercises, etc.) are of course mostly directed to learning, not acquisition. Application may involve both learning and acquisition.

Methods differ, sometimes drastically, with regard to the amount of time spent on each activity and the manner in which each kind of activity is approached.[12] Even the order of presentation may be different. For example, in the early days of audiolingualism it was recommended that practice precede explanation (habits established before the generalization, to use the jargon of the period). There are differences of opinion on which language, L1 or L2, to use for the explanation, and what sorts of practice are useful (pattern drills, written exercises, translation, etc.). In most cases, the teacher directs the learning process and all three components (explanation, practice, and application) are covered first in the classroom. Out-of-class activities are generally restricted to practice of various sorts. In the audiolingual approach it was important that this out-of-class practice not involve new elements.

Since the teacher takes the responsibility for explanation, practice, and application (in addition to the emphasis on correctness in speech), most of the classroom time is necessarily spent on explanation and practice, and very little on communicative situations in which the student may use what he has learned. Nor do I see any way of changing this pattern, if the teacher must assume responsibility for all explanation and practice in the classroom.

In fact, I claim that the situation in most beginning L2 classrooms is even worse than I have implied. In most if not all approaches the learning of the "form" of the sentences, i.e., correct morphology and syntax, becomes the focal point for almost all class activities. Even on those rare occasions in which the student manages to escape from a drill activity to an interesting topic, the teacher's response is usually "muy bien" or "sehr gut," once again underlining to the student the fact that he was interested more in the form of the utterance than in its content.[13]

There can be no real change in this pattern unless a change in attitude is made toward the relative importance of communication versus correct form at this level. If communication is more important, then it follows that most if not all classroom activities should be designed to evoke real communication. In fact, unless the students live in an area in which L2 is spoken, it is only in the classroom that the student will have a chance to exercise any natural ability to acquire the language.

For these reasons, I suggest that the entire class period be devoted to communicative activities. Explanation and practice with form are essential if we expect any improvement in the output of the students' developing grammars, but they can be done for the most part outside of class. This outside work must be carefully planned and highly structured. The explanations must be clear enough to be understood by most of the students without using classroom time. Exercises must be self-correcting or, at least, a liberal use should be made of keys for correction. Specific assignments should be completed, collected, and evaluated in some systematic way.

The student should realize that the primary responsibility is his for improvement in the quality of his output. The teacher can provide the materials, guidance where needed, and even some extra motivation in the form of quizzes or tests, but it is the student who must decide when and where to improve his speech by implementing what he has learned. It should be remembered that conscious knowledge of structure does not automatically lead to the ability to use that knowledge in speech. This often takes a considerable amount of time.

2. *Error correction.* Much has been written on error correction (Cohen 1975). However, there is no evidence which shows that the correction of speech errors is necessary or even helpful in language acquisition. Most agree that the correction of speech errors is negative in terms of motivation, attitude, embarrassment, and so forth, even when done in the best of situations.

Even Valdman, who voiced the opinion that errors should not be tolerated in formal language learning (Valdman 1975:423–424), admits that "in a natural setting, communicative competence may be achieved despite deviation from surface structure well formedness." In normal second language acquisition the speech of a learner is almost never corrected.[14]

On a practical level it must be recognized that the possibility of carrying on an intelligent conversation with students in L2 without errors is close to zero. For the beginning student it is doubtful that even one sentence will be well formed unless the topic of conversation is severely limited. This is to be expected; the student is working from a partial grammar in the process of development; output is limited in all components. If the student's speech at this stage is corrected, he will soon learn that he will be able to respond adequately only in very severely restricted contexts; certainly no added remarks will ever pass the teacher's inspection. Consequently, most students avoid trying to communicate anything which goes beyond simple direct answers. Communication in the real world with native speakers bears little resemblance to this sort of classroom exchange.

I suggest that error correction be done only in written assignments which focus specifically on form and never during oral communication. As far as I am aware, only Holley and King (1971) have ever proposed to eliminate entirely the correction of speech errors from the classroom. This sort of proposal would be impossible, of course, in a class which is based on the drilling of form.

A student should be encouraged to say new and interesting things with the knowledge that he will never be embarrassed in front of his peers. This kind of communication in a second language depends entirely on the imagination and creativity of the teacher and an ability to interact in real communication with the students.

3. *Response in both L1 and L2.* In most L2 classrooms the student is completely immersed the first day in the use of all the components of a grammar. For the audiolingualists, this usually means a dialogue and pronunciation drills. For practitioners of the direct method, it means simple questions and answers using correct pronunciation and structure. The possibilities of any real communication for the first few weeks are virtually nil in these approaches. The

natural insecurity of a new classroom, new peers, a new teacher, and a new subject is compounded by possible failure in any or all components of the grammar itself: the student may not comprehend what the teacher said, he may make pronunciation errors and structure errors, and he will probably be corrected for both.

A situation in which the learner is overwhelmed in this manner with new information rarely happens in natural second language acquisition, since he can usually begin his acquisition of L2 by spending a large number of hours simply listening to the language, avoiding direct participation in a conversation. Slowly, he can become accustomed to rhythm, intonation, pronunciation, and so forth. He has time to acquire a basic vocabulary. His strategy is to try to grasp the meaning of a sentence with the lexical items he recognizes without understanding all the lexical items in the sentence or its grammatical structure. Indeed at first, he may not pay attention to any structure at all, except perhaps for word order. His initial responses are normally very short, and in general the learner tries to gain experience with comprehension until he feels more confident in understanding the questions or comments addressed to him. He may spend many hours listening to speech which does not require complete comprehension or a direct response.

It would be nearly impossible to duplicate completely this sort of situation in a classroom. But we can concentrate first on listening comprehension. I suggest that the student be allowed to respond in his native language. If the student is permitted to concentrate entirely on comprehension by permitting response in L1, he can rapidly expand his listening comprehension abilities to a wide variety of topics and still be comfortable in the communication process. There is no evidence that the use of L1 by the student retards in any way the acquisition of L2. Indeed my experience has been that it speeds up this process, since it allows for concentration on one component at a time.[15]

In summary I have suggested three general guidelines which could facilitate L2 acquisition for communicative competence: (1) all classroom activities should be devoted to communication with focus on content, (2) no speech errors should be corrected, and (3) students should feel free to respond in L1, L2, or any mixture of the two.

I will turn to a more detailed discussion of the techniques used in a natural approach to teach the various aspects of language skill.

COMPREHENSION

Virtually all teachers of a second language realize that listening comprehension (and reading, for that matter) of a second language is a matter of learning to comprehend what is being heard (or read) without knowing all the structure or all the lexical items of the sentence. This is true for all second language contact up to the very last stages of perfection of the second language ability.

Although this fact is known usually through personal experience to almost all language teachers, the complex process of learning how to comprehend an idea without understanding all the components of the sentence is rarely explained in any detail, much less explicitly taught to the students. In fact, the opposite is usually true. The language is simplified by the teacher so that the student can with normal effort understand all the elements of the sentence. Students are rarely confronted with situations which approach real-life language use, or if such situations arise, the teacher and students simply dismiss the noncomprehension by explaining that the sample of language was too advanced, i.e., "they haven't studied that yet." The idea is that if one studies the grammar long enough, he will someday magically understand the language. This is not true, but we continue to teach as if it were. Few textbooks deal in any systematic way with the teaching of comprehension in terms of grasping the idea of a sentence without complete comprehension of all the elements in it. The question is how we can aid the natural process of the acquisition of listening comprehension abilities.

An adequate explanation of what the student is expected to do and assurances that he can be successful are indispensable. The student should be told at the very beginning that he will hear a lot of L2 which he will not understand and that this is both natural and necessary. It can be demonstrated to him that, with a moderate amount of attention to certain cues, essentially lexical at first, he will be able to follow the gist of the utterances he hears. The main objective in the first class sessions is to convince the student that he can understand utterances in the second language and that he can be comfortable with only a partial understanding of the components which make up the utterances.

The teacher may do several things on a practical level to achieve these goals. For example, he may set the context for the communication by beginning in English (or whatever the native language happens to be), and then switch naturally to L2, accompanied by gestures, diagrams, visual aids, and so forth. His speech does not necessarily have to be slow, but it should be as expressive as possible, lingering on key words or phrases. From time to time he may have to add a few words by mixing naturally the native language (in somewhat the way bilinguals normally mix two languages) to clarify key points in the narrative. The main objective is that he understands what he hears. Even if this is not strictly true, with enough experience it will be. It cannot be stressed enough that building a toleration for listening to a second language which one is only partially understanding is not especially easy; however, the satisfaction the student derives from comprehension usually ameliorates the tension caused by the hearing of unfamiliar lexical items and structure.[16]

The learning of vocabulary is the key to comprehension and speech production. With a large enough vocabulary the student can comprehend and speak a great deal of L2 even if his knowledge of structure is for all practical purposes nonexistent. It would be difficult to overestimate the extremes that the foreign language teaching profession has gone to in emphasizing grammar. For example, Dalbor (1972) has this piece of advice for the beginner: "If you are a typical foreign language student . . . you probably tend to worry a great deal about vocabulary. Please don't, because it is the least important aspect of your study. . . ." Bolinger (1970:78) comments that "this bit of doctrine has been preached to students for half a century, but I doubt that anyone but a first-year dropout has ever been convinced by it." I might add that if most teachers don't believe it, they certainly operate as if they do. Bolinger says that anyone who has mastered a foreign language knows well that the majority of time is spent mastering the lexicon of that language. He further suggests that "the quantity of information in the lexicon far outweighs that in any other part of the language, and if there is anything to the notion of redundancy it should be easier to reconstruct a message containing just the words than one containing just the syntactic relations. The significant fact is the subordinate role of grammar. The most important thing is to get the words in." The student's first task is to learn a large number of common words so that he can understand what the teacher is saying to him. Words in common semantic groups are easiest to learn. For example, one might say, "Let's think of things we see in our homes every day." If the word "table" is suggested, the teacher repeats the word several times in L2 and uses the word in sentences, talking naturally about tables, what they're used for, kinds and varieties, what can be put on top of them, and maybe an incident in which a table figures. The main point is that the students follow the gist of the conversation, and that as the conversation proceeds, other important words are also explained and added to the list the students will memorize. I have found that college students can learn to recognize 25 words a day with little difficulty. (For younger or older students this figure would have to be reduced.) This amounts to a minimum of 100 to 125 words per week, so that in 4 weeks it may be possible for the student to recognize 500 words or more, which is certainly sufficient to understand many conversations.

PRODUCTION

I have suggested that the student should be allowed to respond in L1 or in any combination of L1 and L2. When, then, will the student begin to speak the second language? The answer must be: whenever he makes a decision to do so, i.e., whenever his self-image and ease in the classroom is such that a response in the second language will not produce anxiety. The most common reaction to this suggestion is that students will never reach this stage unless forced to do so. I claim that this possibility is a product of the student's fear of the teacher's expectation of complete manipulation of the various components of the grammar plus fear of correction. Peer pressure from those who begin to use L2 successfully can be a strong factor in encouraging progress.

There are positive results of allowing the student to respond in the first language. Most importantly the standard problem of embarrassment is reduced considerably if not almost entirely eliminated. This point cannot be emphasized too much. The fear of ridicule by peers is very great in an L2 classroom, especially on the high school level (although adults are not immune to this phenomenon). Much of this fear comes from being required to produce new sounds without having had a sufficient amount of time to absorb the system naturally. This should never happen if the student is allowed to choose the occasion in which he will attempt to respond in L2. My experience is that for college students the switch to L2 is made after about 1 week.

The key to the student's progress is his success in communication. In the classroom success should mean exactly what it does outside the classroom: the communication was understood and responded to in an understandable fashion. As I have stressed, at no point in the natural communication process does error correction play a significant role. If the response is totally incomprehensible, the teacher may request a clarification of the idea exactly in the same manner as if the exchange had taken place outside the classroom in a real-life situation.

There is another important difference between second language presentation in the classroom and natural second language acquisition. In the classroom short answers to questions are discouraged and answers in complete sentences (so that the student can practice) are encouraged. For example, the student is asked, "Where is the book?" and he replies, "The book is on the table." A more normal response is "It's on the table" or simply "On the table."

Students should be encouraged to respond in any way they wish to the stimuli of the teacher: short answer, long answer, or no answer at all. They should be permitted to use their native language, the second language, or any mixture of the two. The goal is that the teacher produce a meaningful utterance (but not just meaningful in an abstract sense) and that the student respond in any way his partial grammar (or no grammar at all for the first few days) permits. The teacher focuses always and only on the exchange of ideas and away from the form of the communication. By using both languages, communication can take place even the first day without resorting to interchanges of the most inane variety which by necessity must occur if the student is forced to respond "correctly" in L2.

I do not mean to suggest that the classroom activities not be organized. Structure which is studied by the students outside the classroom cannot be applied unless there are opportunities to communicate using these structures.[17] For example, the teacher may wish to focus the conversation on past tense(s) by asking the students to describe their actions of the previous day. In order to elicit different "person-number" combinations the students may be divided into groups and instructed to find out what others did at some past time and then report this to the class using L2. Good teachers in all approaches have always been able to focus certain types of structure covertly in classroom conversation. The important point is that the opportunities are presented to the students to acquire and use these structures in a natural way in the classroom, restricting exercises and drills to outside class activities.

An important part of language acquisition and learning is the use of "strategies" by the student in order to generate sentences which go beyond the student's grammatical capabilities. Given that in the production of any utterance a student must focus attention on (1) message, (2) lexical items, (3) structure, and (4) pronunciation, the learning of details of complex grammatical rules is mostly a hindrance to communication. For this reason general strategies or rule approximations are extremely helpful on a practical level to further communication of the message, and on an affective level to enhance the students' own self-confidence in their ability to speak using L2.

In our pilot Spanish classes, we have organized the teaching of verb forms from general use of a single form, the third person singular, through various stages of more and more discrimination. In the case of gender assignment, we encourage them to follow the following strategy: if the word ends in -a, assign it feminine gender; assign all other words masculine gender. At a more advanced stage when they begin to use many words in -cion and -d, these can be added as a part of the rule. Finer distinctions can be added as the fluency allows.

In languages like German or Russian with case systems, the student would do well to speak with one case form (probably the nominative) at first and then begin to distinguish other forms as his fluency, and therefore time to process grammar rules, increases.

It should be kept in mind that grammars of different students will evolve at different rates. For example, one student may finally be able to master present versus past distinctions (at least in first person singular forms) in his speech, while another still relies on adverbs to signal past tense. Both may have "learned" the past tense paradigm and be able to produce the forms for tests, but in the case of the second student, his level of overall fluency does not allow for time to generate past tense forms.

It is a mistake to believe that students can become proficient enough to use the large number of detailed grammar rules in their speech which are taught in a first-year class. They can, however, learn general strategies which will reduce the number of errors made.

READING AND WRITING

There is, of course, no "natural" approach to the teaching of reading and writing a second language. However, although our goal is oral communication, most students also wish to read and write the language they study. In addition, reading and writing provide opportunities to expand the topics of conversation, facilitating thereby vocabulary acquisition, and to reinforce both the learning and acquisition processes. It should be noted that if vocabulary acquisition is emphasized instead of grammar, the student is able to read simple prose after only a few weeks of study. Likewise, real compositions are possible much earlier if the student is not judged on the basis of grammaticality.

TESTING

If communication is the goal, then it is the overall ability to communicate, not grammatical accuracy, which must be tested. This is not easy to do, of course; but to resort to grading based on grammatical accuracy is to avoid our responsibilities. Judgments of fluency will in many cases be subjective; however, if we cannot make those judgments with a reasonable degree of accuracy, our title as teacher of a second language means very little.

In a course in which oral communication is the goal, the test must be oral. This is difficult when one has many students, but the problem must be faced. Some are fortunate enough to have laboratories with cassette machines on which the individual responses of each student to an oral examination may be recorded. In other cases, the final may have to be conducted on an individual basis. However the logistics are solved, it is clear that written grammar tests are no measure of oral fluency—either comprehension or production.

CONCLUSIONS

I have argued that the goal of most students studying a second language in an academic situation is to acquire the ability to communicate effectively in that language. There is ample evidence that many teachers, but not native speakers or language learners, define effective communication as near perfection in structure and phonology, and thus doom the student to ultimate failure. I have suggested that students be given the chance to acquire language as well as to learn it. To this end I have proposed three guidelines: (1) students should be permitted to use L1 (with L2) in the initial stages of learning to comprehend L2; (2) students' speech errors should not be corrected; and (2) class time should be devoted entirely to communication experiences, relegating learning activities to outside the classroom. A reappraisal of the goals of foreign language teachers to bring them in line with students' and native speakers' expectations is long overdue. Most adults can learn to communicate effectively in a second language if they are given the opportunity to do so.

NOTES

1. This paper is essentially the outgrowth of an experimental introductory Dutch course at the University of California, Irvine. Although I speak Dutch, I did not feel competent enough to become an audiolingual drill master nor did I have any desire to return to the grammar-translation method even under the guise of a new name, "cognitive code." Therefore, I turned initially to a modified form of the "direct" method. The experiences of that year were subsequently modified and applied to seven sections of beginning Spanish at the University of California, Irvine.

2. Unfortunately not only is the knowledge of grammar not necessary for basic communication, it is definitely not sufficient for successful interaction with a native speaker in the language. The profession is unfortunately full of teachers who know the grammar of L2 quite well but cannot communicate effectively with native speakers (see also Newmark 1966). In addition, the emphasis on covering all the grammar in one year (two for secondary schools) may well be an idiosyncrasy of the American educational system. Wilkins (1972:1), in a description of one system used in various

parts of Europe, describes a trend away from this sort of lockstep instruction. He claims that we must "abandon the conventional grammatical syllabus which attempts to teach the entire grammatical system without regard to its application to specific language needs and to the fact that not all parts of the system are equally important to all learners."

3. We have little specific research on exactly what is necessary for basic communication. In one study of the Spanish subjunctive, it was shown that subjunctive forms were totally irrelevant for native speaker comprehension but that correct placement of pronominal forms as well as the position and use of the clause relator *que*, "that," was important (Terrell, Perrone, and Baycroft 1977). More such studies will be necessary if we are to choose intelligently the crucial structural items.

4. There is some empirical evidence to support this claim. Bellamy and Bellamy (1970) found that children do very poorly in interpreting certain morphemes such as past tense in sentences not in context. These same morphemes are comprehended quite readily in a full semantic context. It may be that even in adult speech the morphemes which mark essential grammatical categories may not always be the primary cue for interpretation. It may be the case that much grammatical information is determined primarily from context and that only in cases of ambiguity do we actually make full functional use of the grammatical markers for purposes of comprehension.

5. Others have also advocated the development of communicative competence. Brown (1974) stated that "we are also at a crucial moment in the history of language teaching: a new methodology—based on 'communicative competence' and on cognitive and affective factors—is being developed in reaction to the rote, oral-aural methods which began in the 1950's." He goes on to say that "the current L2 research will indeed have a great impact on shaping a new method." Many teachers do try to adapt whatever materials they use for producing communication as real as possible. This is far short of the major revisions I propose in this paper. Usually the proposals of the communicative competence school of thought suggest only that the drills and exercises should be as close to real communication as possible.

6. This approach to the analysis of second language acquisition was first introduced by Corder (1967) and has inspired a large amount of research since that date. The basic literature has been collected in two anthologies: Schumann and Stenson (1974) and Richards (1974). See also Hanzeli (1975) and Corder (1975).

7. I have followed the general usage of these terms. In addition, my proposals parallel Steve Krashen's model of second language acquisition in that what he terms acquisition I claim should take place in the classroom, and the device he terms the monitor should result from learning through specific kinds of exercises done by the students individually outside the classroom (Krashen and Seliger 1975).

8. This is not to deny that for some, learning may have been the principal component of language ability. This is probably the case for many language teachers for whom grammar was intrinsically interesting.

9. The hypothesis that adults may acquire a second language is somewhat contrary to the theory that there is a critical period for language acquisition after which little or no acquisition occurs or that it occurs with great difficulty. Penfield and Roberts (1959), for example, hypothesized that the difficulties which adults have in learning a second language are the result of the completion of cortical lateralization at puberty. At this point the language functions are localized in the left cerebral cortex, and it was suggested that the former plasticity of the brain, with regard to language acquisition, disappears. Lenneberg (1967), the best-known proponent of this hypothesis, used data from studies of mental retardation and aphasia to support this position. However, Krashen (1973) indicated that cortical lateralization may be completed by the age of five, and therefore, no matter what its relationship to L1 acquisition, it could not account for difficulties in L2 acquisition after puberty.

10. Also, Taylor (1974), with many others, has argued that L2 acquisition may be more similar to L1 acquisition than we have hitherto believed. If, for example, it turns out to be the case that there are no cognitive deficiencies with regard to L2 acquisition which separate adults from children, then we must look for a different explanation for the relative success for almost all children

and the relative failure for many adults, especially in academic contexts. Many have argued that an explanation of the differences lies primarily in the affective domain. A child's first language is really a means to an end: socialization and integration into both adult society and the society of the child's peers. Conversely the lack of such motivation and the absence of a strong positive attitude toward the culture of the language may be primarily responsible for the lower success rate for adult language acquisition.

11. See also Brown (1973) for a detailed discussion of affective variables in second language acquisition.

12. Interestingly enough, the research to date has not been able to show that any one method or approach produces better results in terms of language performance. The widely acclaimed Pennsylvania Foreign Language Research Project was able to conclude very little about the value of different approaches. In fact, according to their data not even the preparation of the instructor was correlated positively with success on the part of the students. Currie (1975) discusses two other projects designed to test the value of different teaching strategies: Casey (1968) and Levin (1969). In neither of the projects did method affect the results on a statistically significant level. In both the traditional grammar approach and the audiolingual oral approaches, which were the primary methodologies under consideration, the emphasis is on the teaching and learning of the structure of L2 and the student in neither approach is given the chance to acquire language and use it in meaningful situations.

13. Dulay and Burt (1973:257) expressed the same idea in relation to the teaching of morphology and syntax to children learning a second language, "Perhaps the most important characteristic of a natural communication situation that is most overlooked in language classrooms is that the attention of the speaker and hearer is on the 'message' or content of the verbal exchange rather than on its form. Yet most language teaching materials focus on the structures to be taught, often with the result that the message of the sentences taught, if there is one, is meaningless for both teachers and children.

14. Even in L1 acquisition situations correction apparently plays a very small role. Ervin-Tripp (1971:196) observed, for example, that "adults listening to children are usually listening to the message, just as they are when they listen to adults. Our evidence is that they comment on the form only in the case of socially marked deviations such as obscenities, lower class non-standard forms and in the case of Black families, forms believed to be 'country speech.' " Claudia Mitchell, the field worker at the University of California, Berkeley, is quoted by Slobin (1969:15) as follows: "Most of the corrections I observed by mothers to the group under five focused on speech etiquette rather than grammar. For example, a child enters the room and fails to greet the other adults present: 'Can't you say hello?'; a child interrupts a conversation: 'Wait until I am finished' or 'Say excuse me first'; child uses taboo word; child fails to maintain a civil tone when speaking to mother; child in excitement uses speech which is garbled although intelligible."

15. Postovsky (1970, published 1974, *Modern Language Journal,* 58: 229–239) reports that Robert Gauthier in Canada introduced the Tan-Gau method for teaching French to English-speaking students in which the teacher speaks French and the students respond in English until such time as each student individually approaches the state of "speaking readiness."

16. In the only study of L2 teacher speech of which I am aware, Henzl (1973) found that a "foreign Language Classroom Register is a linguistic subsystem that can be defined by rules of linguistic simplification similar to those of the Foreigner Talk and Baby Talk Registers." Thus it may be the case that we simplify intuitively for learners at different levels. Landes (1975), in a review of the studies of adult speech with children, concluded that "not only are adults sensitive to and affected by the need to communicate with their children, but that interaction patterns between parent and child change according to the increasing language skill of the child. Such features include sentence complexity, number of transformations involved, types of sentences addressed to the child, the use of repetition, modeling correction, baby talk register, and the speed of delivery."

17. It should not be assumed that the first time an opportunity is presented students will seize that opportunity to use the structures that they have been studying. Several opportunities will be needed before the student matches what he has studied with what he produces in free speech.

TECHNIQUES
FOR A MORE NATURAL APPROACH
TO SECOND LANGUAGE
ACQUISITION AND LEARNING

Tracy D. Terrell, Jeanne Egasse, Wilfried Voge

1. Instructional objectives. Objectives are defined topically. Structure is subordinated to semantic criteria.
2. Skill emphasis. All four skills are taught simultaneously. Emphasis is on the development of general strategies for comprehending and speaking the L2 in natural situations operating with limited vocabulary and structure.
3. Acquisition and learning. Instructions provide students with the many grammatical structures in the classroom; most approaches rely solely on learning.
4. Learning strategies. Both inductive and deductive learning strategies may be used depending on students' individual preference.
5. The language of the classroom. The target language is used unless there are extenuating circumstances.
6. Classroom activities. The main function of the instructor is to create a situation in which the students will want to communicate. The classroom is devoted primarily to communicative activities.
7. Vocabulary. A large recognition vocabulary is essential to the development of language skills. For a beginner, vocabulary range is more important than structural accuracy.
8. Response to instructor. The response should be appropriate to the situation; there is no point in repeating a sentence simply for the sake of repetition.
9. Language of response. Students in the beginning stages are allowed to pick the language of response. The shift to L2 is made when the student is ready.
10. Error correction. There is no evidence that error correction of student speech improves his "interlanguage." We believe that improvement will be faster without overt correction. Correction is limited to "expansion."
11. Pattern drills. These are fine activities for the language lab.
12. Written grammar exercises. These should be given as homework assignments.
13. Evaluation. The ability of the student to communicate is tested. Grades are based on range of expression and fluency, not grammatical accuracy, except when errors interfere with communication.

	Natural approach	Direct	Audiolingual	Gramtrans
1. Instructional objectives	Defined in semantic and communicative terms	Semantic-communicative	Defined in grammatical terms	Grammatical
2. Skill emphasis	4 skills simultaneously	Listening/speaking	4 skills ordered	Reading, translation
3. Acquisition and learning	Classroom: acquisition; homework: learning	Acquisition only	Learning only	Learning only
4. Learning strategies	Inductive and deductive	Inductive	Inductive	Deductive
5. Language of the classroom	L2	L2	L2 and L1	L1
6. Classroom activities	Meaningful communicative	Meaningful communicative	Drills, dialogues, recombination response	Grammar, exercises, translation
7. Vocabulary	(1) Semantically grouped (2) Emphasized (3) Free—according to class desires and needs	(1) Semantically grouped (2) Emphasized (3) Controlled	(1) Grouped by dialogue topic (2) Deemphasized in favor of structure (3) Controlled	(1) Grouped by frequency in reading (2) Emphasized (3) Controlled
8. Response to instructor	Short, appropriate, using reduced structure (interlanguage); simplification permitted at beginning levels	Appropriate, but in complete sentences; simplification permitted	Complete sentences restricted to known material, simplification not permitted	Not applicable
9. Language of response	L2, L1, or mixed	Only L2	Only L2	L1 in translation
10. Error correction	None (by natural expansion only)	Yes	Yes	Yes
11. Pattern drills	Restricted to language lab	Yes	Yes	Not used
12. Written grammar exercises	Assigned as homework; not used in class	Not used	Restricted use	Class and homework
13. Evaluation	Communicative competence; range of expansion	Communicative competence and accuracy	Structural accuracy	Grammar and translation

A CONFLUENT DESIGN
FOR LANGUAGE TEACHING

Beverly Galyean

Teaching for the threefold goals of self-reflection, interpersonal dialogue, and skills mastery is confluent language education. The term "confluent" is used to describe the process whereby the traditional educational goal of subject skills mastery is merged with the newly emerging humanistic goals of intrapersonal awareness and growth and interpersonal dialogue. In confluent language classes students practice structures that enable them to reflect upon their own needs, wants, concerns, interests, values, activities, and behaviors, and to share these with others. The content of all language practice is derived from student-offered material.

Four key processes are observable in confluent classes: (1) language practice immersed in the "here and now" reality of class interaction; (2) content of language practice based upon student-offered material, both cognitive (ideas, thoughts, facts) and affective (feelings, personal images, values, interests); (3) close relationships established among class members; (4) self-reflection and self-disclosure encouraged as a means to self-knowledge.

Empirical research studies and nonempirical observational reports indicate that students taught by teachers who use self-reflective and disclosing methods of teaching language tend to score higher on tests of communicative competence than those students working with methods calling for high levels of textual reference practice.

Imagine for a moment that you are a student in a language class. The teacher has just asked you to repeat "I am looking at the board." In reality you are looking at your book, but in response to the command you repeat "I am looking at the board." In this sense your language is lying to you. You are practicing sentences that are not true for you.

Now go to another language class. This time the teacher asks you, "What are you looking at?" You respond, "I am looking at you." T. "What do you see when you look at me?" S. "I see a woman. I see a blue blouse and white pants. I see long brown hair. I see sandals." The teacher now addresses you. T. "Now I am looking at you. What do you imagine that I see?" S. "You see me. You see my brown shirt and blue jeans." T. "What kind of person am I seeing?" S. "You are looking at a friendly, active, but sometimes nervous person."

You notice that this teacher talks to everyone in the class in such a personal manner. Conversation is real and centers on the persons and events emerging within the classroom. The language practice enables each person to communicate with the others concerning those items of personal and immediate relevance. At times, the teacher has you imagine situations. But even in this mode, imagined events are real to you and you become a unique means of discussion.

T.   Close your eyes and imagine you are hungry. You are looking around for your favorite foods. Eventually all of them appear before you. You select from these the ones you most want to satisfy your appetite. Watch, now, what you choose. (Pause) OK! Open your eyes and tell us what you are eating.

T.   What are you eating?

S1   I am eating pizza and salad.

S2   I am eating a chocolate sundae with cookies.

T.   Now think what you will probably eat for dinner tonight. List the foods and indicate after each if the food is: good basic (B); "junk" (J); fattening (F); diet (D); expensive (E); inexpensive (I).

T.   Let's compare our lists with each other. What are you going to eat tonight?

S1   I am going to eat spaghetti. It is fattening but inexpensive. I am also going to eat jello salad. It is not fattening.

S2   I am going to eat chicken, potatoes, and fresh corn. The chicken is good basic food but a little fattening. It isn't expensive. For dessert I am going to eat fruit salad. It is diet food.

The teacher then divides your class into small groups consisting of four students each. In this manner each of you has the chance to be the leader and to ask questions of the others.

S1 (leader)   What are you going to eat tonight?

S2   I am going to eat a tuna sandwich and some fruit. (B, I)

S3   I am going to eat roast beef, vegetables, and vanilla pudding. (B, E)

S4   I am going to eat barbecued ribs, rice, and French bread. (B, F)

When everyone has had a chance to respond, your teacher interrupts and begins asking a new set of questions based on your responses. As before, the class conversation is based on the interests and responses of the students.

T.   Think about the types of foods you prefer to eat. Remember what the other persons in your group said. I'll call out the foods and you respond with the names of those persons who like each type. You can mention yourself too! Who likes fattening foods? (Students call out names.) Who likes expensive foods? Etc. Now list your family members and tell what type of food each prefers to eat.

Sample responses:

T.   Who likes fattening foods?

S1   Veronica likes fattening foods.

T.   (To the class) What does Veronica like?

CL.   She likes fattening foods.

T.   Do any of you have family members who like fattening foods?

S2   My dad loves cakes and pies. I like doughnuts.

Let's take a moment, now, and examine what has occurred in this class. To begin with, this teacher structured all language practice in the "here and now" flow of interests of the students. Individuals addressed themselves to concrete aware- ness in the classroom, and cited their observations, feelings, and ideas, and also tapped and shared their imaginations. What is not a real occurrence in the class became such through imaginative powers.

The students made choices as to their preferences. Individual responses were encouraged and used as the basis of language practice. The original cognitive objective to reinforce the "I am looking at" and "I am eating" structures, and to practice question-answer dialogues for vocabulary expansion, was accomplished. The students spoke with each other, asking questions and prompting answers, thus fulfilling the interactive objective of student-to-student discussions. Finally, each person indicated a food preference (interest), meeting the requirement of the affective objective.

The teacher consistently followed the "output" of the students. All objectives were met by eliciting student responses to predetermined strategies; i.e., "What are you eating? What are you going to eat tonight? Cite family members and indicate their food preferences." These strategies not only invited personal dialogue but controlled the language practice to confine itself within the correct matrix of a given structure. In this manner, the language practice merged with natural interests, and at the same time, the form of the strategies assured correct practice.

With one student we saw an extension of the self-reflective process to include statements about oneself and one's personality. "You are looking at a friendly and nervous person." This student's personal perception is highly enough developed to articulate succinct statements about his/her self-aware- ness and acceptance. The teacher did not pursue this level of self-reflective activity in the class. In a moment we shall view a class where an in-depth look at self becomes the focus of the language practice.

The four key processes of humanistic teaching mentioned above were modeled by this teacher. Self-reflection and self-disclosure refer to those "growth" strategies which, when practiced by both teachers and students, allow understanding to flourish. Participating in these specially designed "growth" strategies enables one to focus on his/her inner world of needs, feelings, concerns, interests, and subsequent values, and to express these to others. These strategies originate in the theories and practices of humanistic psycholo- gy, and their curricular translations are insightful contributions of humanistic psychiatrists, psychologists, and educators who saw their potential for class- room use "to assure the maintenance of healthy mental growth among youth" (Alschuler 1973).

A few weeks later we enter this same class. The teacher has now added a "growth" component to the lesson. Although we shall see all four components of humanistic teaching, particular emphasis will be placed upon self-awareness and self-understanding.

Cognitive learning objectives for this class are: (1) to use correctly the imperfect tense "I used to"; (2) to form correct sentences using the structure "When I was _____ I used to _____ "; (3) to use correctly the verbs *to play, to go, to read, to wonder about, to look forward to*. Interactive objectives are: (1) to engage in paired (one-to-one) dialogue with others; (2) to ask questions and facilitate responses. Affective objectives are: (1) to reflect upon childhood activities and see how patterns of preferences have either been broken or continue into the present; (2) to determine for oneself if these preferences are freely chosen aspects of one's present life, and to see how they affect attitudes and behaviors.

The teacher begins by explaining the lesson plan to the students:

T.   On the board I have written a model sentence. Use it for your work, but supply your own answers. The purpose of this exercise is to help you practice the past form of "used to," and to think about similarities and differences between things you did as a child and those you do now. See what patterns, if any, you discover. In what ways have you changed? Remained the same? Do you think you are making free choices or are you trapped by past patterns of behavior? Here are the sentences. Offer your own responses and see what new information you might receive about yourself.

When I was a child I used to play _____ but now I play _____ .
When I was a child I used to go _____ but now I go _____ .
When I was a child I used to read _____ but now I read _____ .
When I was a child I used to wonder about_____ but now I wonder about_____ .
When I was a child I used to look forward to _____ but now I look forward to _____ .

Responses to these statements spark insightful discussions as to positive and/or negative attitudes and actions present in one's immediate life patterns; for example, one person mentioned that he realized for the first time how little value he placed on play in his adult life. Life was heavy, serious, and worrisome for him. Perhaps if he changed his life style to include more play, more relaxing activities, he would find ways of soothing his perpetually tense manner. A teenager mentions how, as a young child, she didn't have any worries because she sensed herself inadequate at performing most job skills.

Furthermore, through responses such as these, persons from various cultures learn much about the mores, customs, and values of persons from cultures other than their own. A Mexican youth tells of his experience with nicknames: "When I was about five years old and we lived in Oaxaca, my grandmother used to hug me tightly and she'd call me 'Mijo.' I remember when I first came to America and the teacher called me 'Juan' and I didn't know what to do. I thought she was angry with me." An Israeli girl adds that she'd always been called by her full name. In her religious practices, one's birth name is sacred and must not be changed.

Returning to our original lesson on "used to," the teacher now has the students work in pairs. One person elects to begin the dialogue. He or she asks the partner: "When you were a child what did you play?" The other person responds. When all questions have been completed in this manner, the askers become the responders.

When a high level of trust and comfort has been established among the students, and if the teacher has received sufficient instruction and practice in the use of "growth" strategies, those demanding even deeper personal reflection and understanding may be incorporated into the lesson. We see these operative in this next class. It must be added here that participation in the personal growth or awareness components of humanistic teaching is always voluntary. Individuals are free to choose their own degree of participating in the strategies. Students' readiness and willingness to self-disclose must always be weighed before incorporating the strategies into regular lessons.

T.   I will give you a list of statements. Complete each one with whatever words seem most appropriate for you.

I am a person who is _____ , who likes _____ , who wants _____ , who needs_____ , who feels_____ , who demands_____ , who fears_____ , who gives_____ , who hopes for_____ , who believes in_____ , who loves _____ , who says _____ .

When each student has completed this task, groups of six persons are formed. The students read their responses to each other. It is important to remind the students that their answers are only "of the moment," and in no way are intended to imply behavioral patterns. In fact, listening without judgment is encouraged. What one says today may differ from what one chooses to say tomorrow.

This strategy is then followed by a validation exercise. Given that the students know each other and have already engaged in personal sharing (the teacher has prepared them by previous self-disclosing exercises), they are invited to indicate what answers they expected to hear from the other persons.

T.   Read your lists again. Those of you who are the listeners, indicate which answers you expected the speaker to give about him/herself.

S1   I am a person who is lazy, likes pizza, wants affection, needs money, feels strong, demands a response from you, fears snakes, gives support, hopes for peace, believes in friends, loves his family, and says "I like you!"

S2   I knew that you would say you like your family.

S3   I thought you would mention your family and friends, but not laziness.

S4   I knew you would say something about your family, but I never thought you would call yourself "lazy."

This first student understands that the class members perceive him as a person who is close to his family. At least two persons have indicated that his self-perceived image of "lazy" is not in accord with their views of him. This does not imply that the student is lazy; the student now has input from the others that his self-perceptions are not totally congruent with theirs. The person may, in truth, be lazy, but not always show his laziness to others. Whatever the truth may be, the individual will determine for himself as he gains deeper insight into his own ways of being.

The teacher now elects to expand this exercise even further to generate various other self-perceptions.

T. Look at your own responses to "I am a person who_____." Imagine for a moment that you are allowed to use only three of these sentences to describe yourself to another person. Which three do you choose? (Students select responses.) Now form groups of four and read your answers to each other.

S1 I am a person who is kind, who likes parties, and who needs love.

S2 I am a person who is cautious, who wants money, and who hopes for wealth.

T. For this next part, select a partner with whom you'll share information about yourself. (Having the students work in pairs enables them to practice the communications skill of active-empathetic listening, and to feel the power of direct person-to-person dialogue.)

S1 (Facing the partner) I want you to know that I am basically kind, I like good friends, and I need love.

S2 (Repeats what S1 has said and then adds own response) You are kind, you like good friends, and you need love. I am athletic, I need friends, and I love my family.

S1 (Repeats what S2 has said.)

As a culminating validation activity, the teacher invites the students to mention to their partners what they've learned about themselves. The partners then respond by revealing what they have learned about the speakers.

S1 I've learned that I am kind, and that friends and love are important to me.

S2 I've learned that you see yourself as kind. I have always felt this way about you. You are kind to me.

In doing work that involves the giving and receiving of feedback, it is helpful to establish the rule of "positive" responses to each other.

So far we have seen the four cornerstones of humanistic teaching operative in this one class: (1) here and now teaching, (2) student output as class content for language practice, (3) interpersonal sharing, (4) self-awareness. The degree to which any one of these components is present in any given lesson depends on teacher preparation, teacher-student goals, readiness, and language development. Intricately bound to these variables is the teacher's knowledge of the students' goals for learning. Humanistic educators such as Borton (1970), Combs (1975), Weinstein and Fantini (1972), as a result of their extensive research on facilitative teaching behaviors, emphasize repeatedly the importance of teaching to student responses. The teacher's role becomes that of "orchestrator" of the various interests indicated by each student. Language is designated to carry the live exchanges among the students and to enable them to develop their own feelings and ideas in a communicative setting. In such a class, all class dynamics serve to fulfill the goal of student interest as the primary focus of teaching. One-to-one dialogues, use of student offered material, frequent mentioning of names, students addressing each other and working together, and selection of ongoing class phenomena as the subject matter of learning form the basis for language activities. The feelings, moods, ideas, interests, fears, joys, activities, and awarenesses of the persons in the class give shape to the live interaction within the class, and it is these interactions that teem with energy for learning. Language and communication in classes is enlivened and authenticated when used to express the vibrancy of these natural situations.

You will note this "aliveness" in the following class situation. The teacher will constantly draw upon the fresh resources and newly acquired ideas, and will use many teaching responses solicited from the students themselves.

T.   Today we are going to review the future tense. Let's use this occasion to think about our futures, how we'll be in the years to come. Complete the following statements with your feelings and ideas.

    Now I like to read _____ . Twenty-five years from now I will like to read _____ .
    Now I like to travel _____ . Twenty-five years from now I will like to travel _____ .

T.   Respond to these questions:
    What kind of food do you eat now? What kind of food will you eat in twenty-five years? What clothes do you wear now? . . . in twenty-five years? What kind of friends do you have now? . . . in twenty-five years? What kind of films do you prefer now? . . . in twenty-five years? What kind of music do you prefer now? . . . in twenty-five years? Where do you live now? . . . in twenty-five years? What is easy for you to do now? . . . in twenty-five years? What do you like best about yourself now? . . . in twenty-five years?

When the students have completed their responses, the teacher has them work with a partner to practice question-answer responses and to experience the personal sharing of information with another person. When the question-answer sharing seems finished, the teacher asks the students self-reflective questions to help them focus on the meaning inherent in their experiences. The teacher first models his or her own content. In doing this, the teacher coparticipates in the class dialogue and models for the students how he or she is asking them to be with each other. The questions "What did you learn?" and "What does this mean to you?" are central to self-reflective teaching. Teachers introduce the form in language learning so that the students will be able to evaluate their own insights while engaging in growth and awareness exercises.

T.   Take a moment, now, to consider what you've learned about yourself in doing this exercise. I know I've learned that I live very much in the present and I don't think very much about the future.
S1   I learned that I'll probably always like pizza. I hope my stomach survives.
T.   What did _____ learn about herself?
S2   _____ learned that she'll probably always like pizza, and she hopes her stomach will last.
T.   What did you learn about yourself?
S2   I learned that I like active people and that I'll always like active people.
T.   What did _____ learn about himself?
S3   _____ learned that he likes active people and that he'll always like active people.

The teacher has accomplished several "maximal" learning goals in this short exercise. The students have practiced the same basic structures several times. They have repeated and heard repeated various renditions of the "I learned" matrix, but each time, the sentences were changed with personal output of the students. Each student offered relevant information. The entire exercise flowed from personal responses to interesting and engaging life possibilities. By having the students repeat the contributions of the others, the teacher is fostering respectful attitudes to empathetic listening and understanding. Communication in this class is an exchange of lively situations emerging from the interest perspective of each person.

Another theory rich with possibilities for language teaching is the "meaning-needs" theory proposed by humanistic psychologists. Since meaning arises from an individual's urge to seek fulfillment for basic needs and attitudes, and perceptions and behaviors are shaped by these needs, then all learning is viewed as essentially self-enhancing. In a language class, for example, the student would tend to select those vocabulary items and those structures which would most assist him or her to express whatever interest seemed pressing at a given moment. Just as the human organism energizes itself to satisfy its own needs, so also does the speaker actively seek out those expressions most congruent with his or her desire for adequate self-communication (Curran 1972). Whenever a lesson focuses on a particular category of need, and if learners are actually experiencing that need during the lesson, maximum learning energy is available for grasping the cognitive content being presented. For example, if students are hungry, a drill involving food items would be particularly effective. If there is an important athletic contest after school, keying in on the students' feelings and enthusiasm would release natural focusing energies. The following lesson illustrates how an aware teacher combined the need for food with an opportunity for self-reflection. This class took place during the period preceding the lunch break.

T.   Think of your favorite foods. You might want to close your eyes and imagine what these foods look like. Feel them, smell them, taste them! See yourself eating this food. (Pause) Now imagine you can eat anything you want and you don't need to worry about calories. What do you eat? (Pause) Now think about this delicious food you are eating and see how you are like the food. How are you and food alike?

S1   My favorite foods are tacos, pizza, fries, cokes, and fresh fruit. Since I don't need to worry about calories, I will eat a large cheese and pepperoni pizza. Pizza is rich and satisfying and I am rich and satisfying.

S2   My favorite foods are hamburgers and fries, burritos, steak, and chocolate ice cream. Since I can eat anything I want, I will eat a large cheeseburger filled with tomatoes, cheddar cheese, and onions. I will drink chocolate shakes. Hamburgers are full, quick, and are great for beach parties. I am full, quick, and love beach parties with good friends.

Identifying with an object is a key process in Gestalt awareness training (Brown 1971, Galyean 1976, Perls 1973). The idea is to provide individuals with the means to project various aspects of themselves outward so as to recognize what images of themselves they carry within. One sees oneself projected onto the external object. Projection exercises such as these are central in the repertoire of growth and awareness exercises used in education settings. We might say, then, that the key to humanistic teaching is a personal awareness of what is interesting and energizing to oneself and to others, and the ability to encourage reflection upon and discussion of these momentary interests in the course of language practice. Teaching for self-reflection and meaningful communication demands a keen awareness on the part of the teacher as to what feelings, thoughts, and interests are current during each class. This teacher sets the tone of empathy (feeling with others), openness and trust, and support for living through various learning difficulties arising within the students. The skills of self-reflective-interaction teaching, closely paralleling the counseling skills taught in counselor education programs, are best learned in group experiences, and also in personal growth and awareness workshops and courses. Because of the newness of this style of teaching, however, there is a paucity of available teacher education programs sponsoring courses in related areas.

In the meantime, while waiting for language education to incorporate humanistic teaching modes into presently existing programs, interested teachers can enroll in courses such as "group dynamics," "valuing," "interpersonal relations," "guided imagery," "awareness labs," "individual and group counseling," and courses related to the development of "human potential." These are usually offered in college psychology and counseling departments, and are frequently sponsored in the extension offerings.

Even without formal education in humanistic practices, teachers can begin designing classes in the vein of humanistic theory and practice. It is vital to keep in mind the unfolding of three teaching-learning objectives: cognitive, affective, and interactive. These domains embrace the concept of "whole person" learning, and guarantee to the learner the opportunity to use his or her language as a mode for grasping and expressing what is uppermost on his or her mind; i.e., using language for self-enhancing purposes, which in its turn enriches the dialogue shared by the whole group.

The following set of questions is helpful for deciding upon the threefold objectives. They underpin humanistic practices and serve as guidelines for person-centered teaching.

1. What situations most interest my students?
2. What seems to be the predominant feeling or mood of today's class?
3. What activities and events are central in the students' world?
4. How am I feeling today? Where is my energy?
5. What's happening in my class at this moment? Where are the energies?
6. Have I planned a way in which each student will have the opportunity to speak with each other? With me?
7. Have I prepared some strategies that will bridge the grammar with the need for relevant conversation?
8. What outside resources am I bringing to class, and how do they merge with the students' interests?
9. How do the students relate with each other? With me? Is the classroom atmosphere primarily one of trust? Or of suspicion and guardedness?
10. As I observe the students during class, what am I seeing? Are they excited? Involved? Bored?

11. How much talking am I doing as compared with how much talking the students are doing?
12. Am I prepared to use the spontaneous happenings and expressions in the class as a part of the lesson?
13. Am I willing to share my own feelings and interests with the students?
14. In preparing my classes, have I stated, taught to, and evaluated objectives for the cognitive, interactive, and affective domains of learning?

Another way to provide for a "lively" class interchange that allows for learning in all three domains is to keep a "Life Style Preference Chart" for each student. These can be used for one-to-one sharing or small-group work, or the teacher can file the information for use in whole-class exercises. In this way, both the teacher and the students have a profile of the basic interests of each person in the class. This information is then used for conversation practice or for structured pattern practices. The students are helped to discuss their own content within the perimeters of linguistically correct structures.

	Me
favorite clothes	
favorite music	
favorite way to spend money	
favorite food	
favorite hobby	
something I hope for	
someone or something I love very much	
what I like best about myself	

Each person fills in his or her response in the far left column. Other columns may be used to note the responses of three other persons (if you are working in groups of four). Following the sharing of information, a question-answer drill led by one student in each group enables each person to practice structured patterns in a lively manner. The students also learn which other persons in the class share the same interests as they.

S1   What is your favorite music?
S2   My favorite music is _____ .
S1   What is your favorite hobby?
S3   My favorite hobby is _____ .
S1   What is your favorite food?
S4   My favorite food is _____ .
T.   Based on the information you have indicated on your charts, now decide who in your group is most like you and who is least like you. With whom would you like: (a) to study? (b) to spend Saturday? (c) to talk? (d) to hike? (e) to eat lunch? (f) to have as a teacher? (g) to have as your boss?

Since 1973, one of the major themes of professional language journals and yearly conferences has been "humanizing and personalizing" classes. The overstress on linguistic skills mastery to the deficit of genuine communication among persons in the class has been cited as one of the main reasons for students dropping their language study, or for giving low priority to language learning.

During the course of this article, several strategies and processes, as well as self-reflective questions, have been offered as examples of and guidelines to humanistic teaching. We advocate housing the communication of personally relevant messages within linguistically correct structures. We view communication of personal material and the ability to converse meaningfully and comprehensibly with others as symbiotic processes, intricately bound one with the other. By examining our own words, we understand more fully the musings of our own being, since words are tangible projections of the emerging Self. Full self-comprehension, however, takes place in dialogue with others who listen to what we are saying, and who validate our self-perceptions. For this dialogue to take place, clear communication is necessary. Thus, mastery of linguistically correct structures serves to enhance communication for personal growth.

Research projects conducted to determine the effects of humanistic programs and/or programs for communication indicate that students taught a second language in a communicative setting where the language is used to express their own needs, interests, ideas, and interactions in real events tend to score significantly higher on tests of communicative competence (Jarvis 1970, Savignon 1972, Joiner 1974, Schulz 1974). Nonempirical studies reported by the Confluent Education Research Center, and by Wilson and Wattenmaker (1973; see also Galyean 1975), citing teacher observations of the participation and achievement of their students after engaging in specifically designed growth and awareness exercises, concur with the results of the empirical studies. Students tend to talk more in the target language and show greater proficiency in using the language to express personal messages.

Because the field of humanistic teaching is relatively new, and research into the long-term effects of incorporating personal growth strategies and interactive dynamics into traditionally cognitive modes of teaching is in neophyte stages of development, certain cautionary considerations are issued: (1) readiness (2) privacy (3) holism (4) motivation.

Readiness for self-reflection and self-disclosure differs among individuals. Teachers should first be aware of their own comfort with affective sharing, and approach the students with the same manner of caution. The degree to which growth strategies and interactive dynamics are incorporated into regular lessons depends on the readiness level of both the teacher and the students.

Each person retains a sense of personal "life space." This space includes all meaningful events that one wishes to communicate with another, as well as those events that one selects to guard only for oneself. An individual may be quite ready and willing to engage in affective sharing and at the same time decide to keep certain information only for him or herself. Unbridled self-disclosure is not the aim of humanistic teaching. Rather, individuals are encouraged to share only what they feel they wish to share with others for their own benefit. Participation in self-disclosing activities should always be voluntary, and alternate activities should be provided for those who do not wish to engage in self-disclosure.

"Holism" in learning demands growth in intrapersonal awareness (affective), interpersonal sharing (interactive), and intellectual development (cognitive). The merging of all three realms into one learning process is called *confluent education*. In order to avoid weighting the class in one area over the other, teachers are reminded to consider all three domains in writing lesson objectives. The "what" of the lesson is combined with the "so what does this mean to me" of the personal response, and is validated in the "so what does this mean to us" of group interaction.

Finally, and perhaps most important, is teacher motivation in using the strategies. In themselves and as intended by the writers of humanistic curriculum, the growth strategies and interactive dynamics are intended to foster "whole person" growth, nourishing human relations, and to develop skills mastery in whatever subject is being studied. Each area is equal in importance. Teachers using humanistic methods of teaching are involved in profound personal growth, deepening awareness of feelings and energies within themselves, as well as within their students and the class itself. Commitment to humanistic teaching is also a commitment to personal growth. There is a danger that humanistic methods will be used to manipulate students into self-disclosure before they are ready, or to entice them into language practice by involving them in personal conversations that are beyond their level of comprehension. In order to guard against trespassing on private "life space," teachers are encouraged to examine their own motivations and to match their willingness with that of their students.

It has been my experience in some years of work to develop humanistic language programs that when teachers are sensitive to their own needs as well as to those of their students, and design their classes according to the readiness and interests of all present, learning is maximized. Combs and associates, in extensive research on "outstanding teachers," conclude that the "outstanding teacher" is one who is at one and the same time an expert in the subject, thoroughly knowledgeable in a variety of appropriate methods, consistently teaches to student energies (interests), establishes close interpersonal relationships between him or herself and the students, and fosters the same among the students themselves. This teacher is also keenly aware of his or her own needs as they affect student performance (Combs, Blume, Newman and Wass 1974). In short, the "outstanding teacher" is one who has within him or herself the goals of affective (knowing oneself) and interactive (nourishing relations with others) and cognitive (subject expertise) teaching. The realization of these goals is nurtured within humanistic programs.

I close with the words of one of my students. She expresses delight at discovering the power of her language, which is, in reality, the power of her own person. "I discovered I had something to say. At first I was surprised that others really cared about listening to me. But after a while I realized that listening is a part of caring, and that the harder I listened to others, the harder they seemed to listen to me. Sometimes I was amazed at my own honesty and that of the others. Somehow, because of our 'up front' sharing, we all became closer and learned to trust and care for each other. I'm amazed how my words could mean so much to me and to other people. They sort of tell me who I am, and who I am becoming. I just never thought words could be so powerful. In fact, I guess what I've learned the most is that I am the one who is powerful."

4

APPROACHES TO A RICH LEARNING ENVIRONMENT

INTRODUCTION

Krashen proposed the distinction between *conscious learning*, which is typical of the academic approach to knowledge generally fostered in language classrooms and language textbooks, and *acquisition*, which is the way children and adults naturally come by language without the benefit of formal instruction.

Part 3 dealt with acquisition-oriented instruction which attempts to introduce critical elements of natural language acquisition into the formal instruction environment. Clearly implied was the notion that teaching production directly is an inefficient approach and neither necessary nor sufficient to achieve the ends desired. If the Monitor Model and its assumptions about language acquisition are valid, then the main thrust of most academic language teaching today, together with the means used, is misguided, for its main thrust is toward the earliest possible development of proper oral communication skills, and the means used to promote these include modeling and imitation, teaching of grammar, drilling of simulated pieces of conversation, correction of errors, and the other practices that characterize audiolingual classrooms.

Krashen's model has been taken as predicting that if instead of filling classroom time with "formal learning" activities (such as drill routines, grammar explanations, and error correction) we concentrate instead on providing an informal learning environment saturated with large amounts of comprehensible input at the $i + 1$ level, for most learners oral production will emerge naturally, uninhibited by an overactive Monitor. (This suggests the aphorism: "a language can be caught but not taught.")

No doubt all language teachers have experienced impatience with slow and faulty student response and have known the temptation to explain the principles of word and sentence formation that seem so clear, simple, and helpful, to model well-formed utterances and invite imitation of the model, to correct faulty imitations and try to shape up nativelike production through much repetition and attention to proper form—in short to teach as they were taught and as seems so eminently logical, the way prescribed by most textbooks and still commonly

advocated in methodology courses. Would it not violate academic respecta-
bility to teach otherwise? How could these activities possibly be unproductive?
How could they possibly be less productive than alternative approaches which
do not focus on form and correctness? On the other hand, if these activities that
seem so inviting and so intuitively defensible to most language teachers are
really as effective as supposed, how can we account for the dismal record of
language learning in a system which has fostered these activities for decades?
And if their logic is so compelling, how can we account for approaches such as
those described in this book which use none of these, yet, if claims are to be
believed, succeed very well?

An obvious question is whether in a classroom an informal approach
modeled on supposed natural language acquisition strategies is sufficient by
itself to lead efficiently to communicative competence. Or whether the results
might not be enhanced by the injection of elements of formal learning into the
artificially created informal learning environment, tapping the powers of both
and accommodating the preferences, strengths, and learning styles of different
learners? It is not a question of whether either an informal or a formal approach
is necessary or sufficient to lead to mastery, but whether both combined may not
be superior to either alone.

In practice if not in theory, many teachers favor an approach which
integrates formal and informal learning in the classroom. John B. Carroll (1974)
proposed teaching toward a cognitive understanding of the structural elements
and functions of a language through a sophisticated and carefully structured
syllabus while at the same time immersing the learners in a rich acquisition
environment. He suggests a two-stream approach:

one devoted to exposing the learner to materials containing a relatively uncontrolled variety of
linguistic elements (for example, vocabulary and grammatical constructions) and the other devoted
to a rather carefully developed sequence of instructional content. The two streams would
presumably have interactive effects, in the sense that the second stream would give the learner the
specific guidance that would help him in his efforts to master the materials of the first stream (pp.
141).

Herbert Seliger (1979), suggests that language rules may in fact serve as
acquisition facilitators. And Alison d'Anglejan (1978) speaks positively of the
possible "consciousness raising" power of rules.

My own presuppositions as an experimentalist have led me so far to favor an
integrated approach whose dominant focus in the initial phase is fluent
comprehension of a wide range of discourse. Gradually this comprehension
emphasis is tempered with activities typical of the Silent Way, Community
Language Learning, the Lozanov Approach, the Participatory Approach, and
others which deal very directly with oral production and to some extent with
feedback on errors in oral production.

In my own experience as language learner, I have felt that I was not in full
possession of language items I had become conscious of until I tested them out in
meaningful use for my own purposes. And often I have found that attempting to

communicate with what I thought I knew from comprehension exposure makes me conscious of the gap between active control and passive recognition. (Much of the necessary "testing" of one's language knowledge should of course take place in interaction with native speakers out of class, but the activities I use, based on the approaches of Gattegno, Lozanov, Curran, Terrell, Galyean, Gomez, Lipson, and others, allow students to proceed in testing their own hypotheses, working from their own internal syllabus in class without disrupting the same processes of the others.)

From my experience I have found that it is only when I use the spoken language, when I "get it out in front" of myself and other speakers present, that I become fully conscious of where I am in the language and see what work I need to do. What I produce out of my own mind and heart, even though at first it is only to ask the time of day, that is what stays with me and can be recalled minutes and hours later, and that is what I most surely acquire as my own. Until I take that step to inner-motivated, psychologically real, oral communication, the hours of comprehension training put in are not visibly productive. To be sure, they provide the broad linguistic foundation and the intuitive sense of the language which I can then use to venture onto the much more demanding tasks of oral communication.

If, on the other hand, in oral production I am expected to work from and stay within the limits of the current and past lessons (someone else's syllabus), if I am called on to reproduce what is not within me, what I may not be ready for or what I may not be working on, then I often feel I am being put through meaningless calisthenics. I am not playing the real game. And I sense that I am not progressing at an optimal rate. The class is getting in my way!

These considerations, intuitively felt, reveal the reasons I am confortable in integrating elements of both formal and informal approaches.

Ultimately it may be, as Evelyn Hatch has proposed in one of her many illuminating articles (1978), that "language learning, even at one- and two-word stages, evolves out of learning how to carry on conversations." This suggests that acquisition of communicative competence in a second language evolves not so much from learning the rules of sentence formation, or even producing sentences, as from learning by experience the rules of discourse formation, learning the "structure of conversation and of speech acts" by participating actively in them. As someone put it: "Language is not acquired (by a child) through modeling and repetition as much as through a drive for acceptance, and that requires taking part." There is, of course, a very significant movement in language teaching today, known as the "functional" approach or the "communicative syllabus," which is rooted in such assumptions.

In Part 4 four ways of dealing with production are presented, each developed with the aim of creating a learning environment that accelerates the learning of specific production skills. They are: the Silent Way by Gattegno; a simulation-gaming approach developed by Harvey and Francis; and an inductive grammar study approach together with an "easification" or "priming" approach developed by Blair.

THE SILENT WAY

Caleb Gattegno burst upon my consciousness in 1967 when I read John Holt's book, *Why Children Fail,* containing an account of a demonstration lesson on arithmetic concepts taught by Dr. Gattegno to a class of severely retarded children. I recommend reading Holt's description of that class as background to an appreciation of the power and subtlety of Gattegno's unique teaching.

It was more than a year later that I obtained Gattegno's 1963 book, *Teaching Foreign Languages in Schools the Silent Way,* and began to appreciate how extraordinary Gattegno's ideas were. I wrote down a few of the ideas that really struck home in that first reading. These included:

• I advocate an approach that throws the learner upon himself, eliminates as far as possible the mechanical elements of teaching and learning, and minimizes the conditioning of learners.

• From birth the child's mind equips itself more and more adequately by its own workings, trial and error, and deliberate experimentation, by suspending judgment and revising conclusions.

• [My students] are allowed to try their hand and to make mistakes in order to develop their own criteria of rightness, correctness, and adequacy. . . . Correction is only seldom part of the teacher's work. The development of "inner criteria" can suffice to lead to correctness. The criteria of rightness, correctness, and adequacy are developed as we go along, not at the end of learning or at a given moment.

• I do not correct learners, I only throw them back on themselves to elaborate further their criteria and to use them more strongly.

• Against the demand for immediate correctness through so-called imitation, I take upon myself the burden of controlling myself so as not to interfere, but to give time to make sense of mistakes and to develop exercises that foster advance. Only self-education will lead a learner to the mastery of a skill. . . . To require perfection at once is the great imperfection of most teaching and most thinking about teaching.

I presented these notes to colleagues in the language department for their comments and found that few were ready to even consider such radical thought. If it had not been for the witness of John Holt and others to the power and effect of Gattegno's teaching, I might easily have rejected it myself. Intuitively, however, as I stated in Part 1, I was intrigued by Gattegno's notion of "subordinating teaching to learning," and I pursued his approach further, to my great satisfaction.

I have selected two pieces of Gattegno's writing, both describing a small part of his approach—enough, perhaps, that readers can in a preliminary way experience some of the excitement of trying out very basic ideas. There is, of course, much more to Gattegno's approach than is described here: the very useful concept of "ogdens," his use of word charts and pictures, the "words in color"—one could go on and on. The books and workshops on the Silent Way of course give a more complete view.

A COMMUNICATION APPROACH THROUGH GAMES II

There is hardly a language teacher alive who is not interested in tapping the power of games to elicit animated and motivated communication in language classes. Many books and papers have been written which describe games for language classes, and there seems to be a ready market for more books describing more games and other "fun activities" to "liven up" the language classroom.

I define two categories of games: Games I and Games II. The games that are typically described in books and articles I call Games I. Like learning native songs and dances, playing these games is usually viewed as a peripheral, adjunct activity, "dessert" to go along with the more nourishing main course, the textbook and the learning activities prescribed therein. These may be simple games like twenty questions, What's My Line?, bingo, Scrabble, crossword puzzles, spelling bees, or more complex games like Monopoly and Stratego. Functioning in the classroom as "pace changers" and "reward activities," their effect can no doubt be positive.

The other category of games, Games II, is not widely known or understood. Games II are central activities toward the skillful playing of which a whole lesson or series of lessons, even a whole course, may be dedicated. And the increasing skill at playing these progressively more challenging games requires, of course, ever-increasing proficiency in using the language. The game and the motivation to play it well constitute a major driving mechanism of the course.

I will let John Harvey's section below give you a fuller picture of the rationale of Games II as the concept was elaborated in the preparation of the monumental *Standard Chinese: A Modular Course*, in which Harvey played a key role.

There is not to my knowledge a long history behind Games II in language classrooms. John Harvey and John Francis worked together in developing the notion in the early 1970s. Besides those mentioned in Harvey's article, Delbert Groberg, Wade Fillmore, and Michael Sudlow have contributed significantly to the development of the concept and elaboration of Games II. At present simulation games in language instruction are being widely discussed and increasingly experimented with.

For readers who are particularly interested in the concept of "Games II" I would recommend taking a course in Chinese that uses *Standard Chinese: A Modular Course*. Interestingly, several of the most innovative language courses I have experienced are in languages that few people study: besides the above-mentioned Chinese course and Lipson's *A Russian Course*, Burling's programmed comprehension course in Indonesian; an experimental Swahili listening comprehension course designed by James Nord at Michigan State University; an experimental Chinese listening comprehension course designed by Harris Winitz at the University of Missouri at Kansas City; and an as yet unpublished course in Bolivian Quechua designed by Richard Crapo, a professor of anthropology at Utah State University. For any of these—and others too, no doubt—it would be worth studying the language just to experience the power of a new and different approach.

MUCH LANGUAGE
AND LITTLE VOCABULARY*

Caleb Gattegno

The title of this chapter has already indicated that it is possible to make a distinction between language and vocabulary. I claim that we can teach much language although we limit considerably the amount of vocabulary.

Let us imagine that we are looking at a class of interested students of any age (6 or 11 or 14 or adults), and that the teacher enters the room for the first time. The class knows that it will study a foreign language, and the teacher is determined not to use one single word of the vernacular, which he may know or which may even be his mother tongue.

The approach is, as I have insisted, most artificial. The box of colored rods that the teacher places on his desk is all he carries. He opens it and draws out of it one rod and shows it to the class while saying in the foreign language the word for rod, with the indefinite article if it exists in that language. He puts it down in silence and picks up another of a different color and says the same (one or two) words again, and so on, going through seven or eight rods and never asking for anything. The intrigued students have attentively noted the events and heard some noises which to them will seem the same while their eyes see only different objects and a repetition of the same action. Without any fuss the teacher then lifts a rod and asks in mime for the sounds he uttered. Bewildered, the class would not respond, in general, but the teacher says "a rod" and asks again in mime for another effort from the class. Invariably someone guesses (perhaps from the habits ingrained in traditional teaching) that the teacher wants back what he gave. When in his own way the pupil says something approximating what the teacher said, the teacher may smile or nod, showing how content he is at being understood. At the next trial almost the whole class repeats the sounds for a rod (very approximately in most cases). The teacher does not inquire whether some students are thinking of a piece of wood, others of lifting something, or something different. Contact has been established without the vernacular, and that is all that was wanted so far.

---

*An excerpt from *Teaching Foreign Languages in Schools the Silent Way.*

The teacher then introduces the names for four or five of the colors, giving the sounds for "a blue rod," "a black rod," "a red rod," "a yellow rod," "a green rod," or any other combination of the ten colors available. Because the names of the colors are now added, the pupils can no longer imagine that different expressions mean the same action and are forced to conclude that the teacher is giving the phrases that summarily describe these objects. The exercise is now shifted to practice in uttering the foreign sounds for the six or seven objects, so that as soon as one rod replaces another, one utterance replaces another, which would be the case in the vernacular.

This may be the end of the first lesson. Usually it is not, and the teacher motions two pupils to come and stand near him. He turns to one and says in the foreign language: "take a blue rod." (He has previously made sure that the set of rods on which this action is to be performed has more than one rod of each color.) Naturally, no response is to be expected, except perhaps the utterance of the words for "a blue rod." So the teacher says the words again while putting the pupil's hand over the set and making his fingers take a blue rod from the pile. Then he says: "take a brown rod" or "take a yellow rod," etc., and can expect a correct action as a response. He does this a number of times, for it is natural that while the pupil is concentrating on choosing the correct rod he does not produce the substitute in his own mind for the word "take." The teacher then turns to the other student and does what he did before but fewer times. Then dramatically he changes places with one of the students and indicates that the student should now utter the words first. Someone in the class usually gets the idea. If not, the teacher goes back to the previous situation and does what he did before once or twice again. The exchange of places this time yields the required results: the equivalent of "take a blue (or red) rod" is uttered by one or the other of the students. When the teacher complies with this, he is conveying an agreement that the rules of the game are being observed.

The next lesson usually shows that the time separating the two sessions has served the students well. The quick revision of the sounds for the names of the colored rods proves that the class pronounces them on the whole much better than the previous time.

Calling two other students, the teacher says: "take . . . ," and the action is performed at once, usually correctly. But this time the teacher adds: "give it to me," and indicates with his hand that he wants it. As he does it with different rods and alternately with each of the two students, the set of noises for "give it to me" is put into circulation. Then, after saying "take a . . . ," the teacher says: "give it to him" (or "her," according to the sex of the student). (The teacher may have to use his hands to convey the meaning.)

The class has heard phrases and sentences being used from the start by a number of students, or even all of them, more or less adequately, but at least approximately recognizably. The language covered is: a rod, a yellow, red, blue . . . rod, take a . . . rod, give it to him, her, me.

What is significant is that the set of rods has helped:

- To avoid the vernacular.
- To create simple linguistic situations that are under the complete control of the teacher.
- To pass on to the learners the responsibility for the utterance of the descriptions of the objects shown or the actions performed.
- To let the teacher concentrate on what the students say and how they are saying it, drawing their attention to the differences in pronunciation and the flow of words.
- To generate a serious gamelike situation in which the rules are implicitly agreed upon by giving meaning to the gestures of the teacher and his mime.
- To permit almost from the start a switch from the lone voice of the teacher using the foreign language to a number of voices using it. This introduces components of pitch, timbre, and intensity that will constantly reduce the impact of one voice and hence reduce imitation and encourage personal production of one's own brand of the sounds.
- To provide the support of perception and action to the intellectual guess of what the noises may mean, thus bringing in the arsenal of the usual criteria of experience already developed and automatic in one's use of the mother tongue.
- To provide durations of spontaneous speech upon which the teacher and the students can work to obtain a similarity of melody to the one heard, thus providing melodic integrative schemata from the start.

In the first few lessons this will be deliberate, but it will soon become a framework of conventional handling of this teaching. The students will be astonished to find that their teacher stands through much of the lessons, that he keeps them concentrating all the time, that he says less and less and they more and more, that he neither approves nor disapproves but throws them back upon their own tools of judgment, indicating that they must listen better, use their mouths differently, stress here or there, shorten one sound and prolong another. Very soon, the more or less arbitrary conventions he introduces become accepted between himself and his class.

In four or five lessons the vocabulary will have increased very little. The plurals of "rod," of the adjectives (if they exist) and of the pronouns are introduced, plus the conjunction "and," some possessive adjectives, and perhaps one or two demonstrative ones. The numerals "one," "two," and perhaps "three" are added—generally there may be about thirty words in circulation.

These are: one noun: rod; color adjectives: red, green, yellow, black, brown, blue; numeral adjectives: one, two, three; articles: a and the (of one gender or neutral only, in languages that require them); verbs in the imperative: take, give, and perhaps put; personal pronouns: me, him, her, it, them; possessive adjectives: his, her, my; the adverbs: here, there; the preposition: to; the conjunction: and—in all twenty-seven words.

But with them we have heard and understood, and uttered and understood:

take a xxx rod (six or seven colors)
give it to xxx (him, her, me)

and their conjunctions:

take a xxx rod and give it to xxx—
take xxx rods and give them to xxx—

These produce a large number of sentences. Obviously, there are hundreds of different utterances possible, though the general impression is that the number is much smaller because the changes between one phrase and the next may be of only one word. More utterances are easily found if we use the conjunctions as well:

take a xxx rod and a xxx rod and give them to xxx .

The importance of this exercise is that it allows us to work on the formation of a natural way of using the melody of the foreign language. This allows the learners to gain from the start something of the spirit of the language that is usually left for much later in linguistic studies.

It is my contention that we are giving our students something of great value by restricting the vocabulary but extending as much as we can the length of the statements uttered with ease and in the way one uses one's own language.

PERCEPTION*

Caleb Gattegno

The verbs we use in the beginning in all languages are "pick up" or "take," "give," and "put." It is easy to make them plain without words or explanation. The first verb is made clear by saying to a student, *Take a xxx rod,* or *Take xxx xxx rods* and then taking his hand, putting it on top of the rod mentioned, and closing his fingers on it. At once that student is induced by gestures to tell the other student, *Take xxx* (whatever he chooses).

The second student is induced to tell the first another of these forms in the singular, and the teacher, holding his hand out, at once adds the equivalent of, *Give it to me.* Then, turning to the other student, the teacher says, *Take xxx and give it to me.* If this order is executed, he indicates by gesture to that student that he must give such an order verbally to the other student. If it takes place and the rod is received by the speaker, the teacher asks for that rod, and a round of, *Give it to me* is formed. After going around one or two times, the teacher introduces, *Give it to him or her,* or their equivalent forms in that language. The advantage of this new form is that the class as a whole can be involved and can tell any one of the three people at the table: *Take a xxx rod and give it to her (or him)* followed by a round of, *Give it to her (or him).* This can be coupled with the recipient's inserting, *Give it to me,* at the same time as the others make their statement.

We now have a number of options to consider. We can either go to the plural and replace *it* by *them,* if these exist in the language, or ask for a variety of rods to be picked up and given, some to one and some to another, as, for example: *Take three blue rods and two black ones, give a black one to him and a blue one to me.*

This will lead to a situation that forces the introduction of the definite article (if it exists) and a new form such as "give me" instead of "give it to me" (if it exists). The definite plural article (if it exists) can also be introduced by asking for more than one.

---

*An excerpt from *The Common Sense of Teaching Foreign Languages.*

If the class has fewer than twenty students, we can involve each of them individually in telling neighbors to take rods and give themselves or others some of them. We only need to have a box of rods on hand and pass it from one student to the next until it returns to the table. To introduce variety, the teacher can signal to the student ready to speak that he should ask for so many rods to be picked up and this many given to himself and that many to someone else nearby. In larger classes the students called to the table can be replaced at certain intervals by pairs or groups of other students, and the class can learn by proxy when the first personal pronoun is used but speak in chorus in the other cases.

With the verb *put* we can introduce *here, there,* and the demonstrative adjectives and pronouns. For example: *Take seven rods, put one here, two there, and give me three.* It is indicated by pointing where *here* and *there* should be.

After *this, that, these,* and *those* have been introduced with *put,* it is possible to introduce *is* and *are* (if they exist) and obtain sentences such as *This rod is yellow and that one blue.* Or *These rods are these two blue, this one white, and these three black.*

From there we can introduce: *The color of this rod is xxx* or *The colors of these rods are xxx* and start asking questions with *what.*

Possessive pronouns, adjectives, and the verb *to have* (if it exists) can be introduced as a cluster by having a few students and the teacher each holding, first, one rod (each a different color), with the teacher saying *My rod is blue* and each student in turn expressing possession in a similar manner. This is followed by the teacher's putting into circulation the equivalent of *his, her, their, our, your,* and the corresponding forms for the pronouns.

By giving one or two students rods of the same color, we can introduce the equivalent of *too* or *also* with an immediate understanding of what is meant. *So is mine* can also introduce *so,* as an equivalent expression.

Then (or earlier) *another* and *the other* can be introduced, the first with *take,* the second with *give.*

Students can introduce themselves by saying *My name is xxx,* and soon after, their names can be used with personal pronouns, acting as objects in various combinations. Personal subject pronouns and the verb *to be* in the present, for *my name is xxx* can be replaced by the equivalent expression: *I am so and so.* This can be followed by *I am here, you are there* or *we are here and she is there.*

Now or earlier, occasions for the introduction of *not* or the negative form may have been met a number of times: *My rod is blue, it is not red* or *your rod is not yellow, it is orange.*

Yes and *no,* as part of an answer or in apposition, are easily put into circulation via: *Is his rod blue?* If the answer is affirmative, *Yes* is sufficient, while *no, it is yellow,* is the answer required in the negative.

If we think of teaching French, the pronoun *en* can be introduced quite early and be fully understood. In particular *je n'en ai pas,* claimed to be a major obstacle to non-French speakers, becomes obvious when practiced at this level.

Working with situations made with the rods brings to the classroom the naturalness found by babies in the home. The meanings come from the situations, not from words, and students seem ready to ask for the proper forms in the new language to fill in an expectation that somehow what one thinks should be sayable in this language.

The overall result is that there are no really difficult forms which cannot be illustrated through the proper situation involving rods and actions on them about which one makes statements by introducing specific words whose associated meaning is obvious. What teachers must do is to arrange for practice so that students' minds are triggered to use these new words spontaneously.

A rule we have followed in our work is to introduce, whenever possible, one new word or expression at a time and make it become second nature before the next one is introduced. This ensures that retention takes place without drill or idle repetition, that the ground is covered systematically, that more and more of the language is integrated, and that the students use the material freely and correctly, as natives do.

A COMMUNICATIONAL APPROACH: GAMES II

John H. T. Harvey

Many of us can remember a time, not so long ago, when almost everybody seemed to be happy with what was going on in our foreign-language classrooms. What was going on seemed to fit rather neatly with linguistic theory and with psychological theory—at least with American linguistic theory and American psychological theory—and there seemed to be every prospect that it would work.

Nowadays much the same sort of thing is going on in our foreign-language classrooms—most of them most of the time—but hardly anybody seems to be happy with it. For one thing, it no longer seems to be up to date theoretically. For another, it doesn't seem to work very well after all.

But what else is there? One very significant set of alternatives has been discussed in this book. An alternative not yet discussed here, but certainly given sufficient coverage elsewhere to rank as a movement, is individualization.

The alternative I am going to consider is not yet institutionalized enough to be called a movement. It is not yet a tidy body of doctrine. It has hardly begun to become available in the form of materials. But I do think it is a definite trend.

More and more, perhaps starting with John Carroll (1952), people have been saying that *communication* is what is lacking. There has been relatively little effort to define the concept of communication in terms of language and language learning, and not much has been suggested as to how to make communication happen in the classroom. I should mention, parenthetically, that Gerald Dykstra stands out as an exception to both these statements. But the word "communication" is everywhere, and behind the word, I suggest, is an idea whose time has come. I use the cliché deliberately, since I can't think of a better way of expressing the convergence of several lines of thought into an inevitable idea, into an idea which occurs to any number of people at roughly the same time.

Not that the idea doesn't have a history of its own. Like everything else in language learning, it probably has a prehistory. I just think that the present explosion of interest in communication has been set off by fairly recent developments in linguistics and in related sciences. In particular, despite Chomsky's disclaimers, I think it has been inspired by the rise of transformational grammar, which has brought new respect for the depth, complexity, and creativity of language.

Now let me sketch the kind of theory that I think can be developed as a basis for a communicative approach to language learning. Since we are talking about *learning* language, we need some sort of model of learning. The model I propose is essentially contained in a single, simple slogan: learning by doing. There is nothing very novel or particularly sophisticated about this idea, but I think it takes on some novelty and some sophistication if we apply it in a deep sense rather than in a surface sense. In other words, I am not talking about what the student *appears* to be doing, I am talking about what he is *really* doing. And I'm saying that *that* is what he is really learning.

If you ask me whether Jennifer is learning to ride her bicycle, and there she is pedaling along tilted ten degrees off to the right supported by her right training wheel, I say that she isn't. She may be learning to pedal, but she is not learning to balance, which is the whole trick. Now, I will admit—I have to admit for my later argument—that there are degrees of approximation. If Jennifer starts to get up off that right training wheel for a few yards at a time, she is closer to riding a bicycle, and therefore closer to learning to ride it. But we still can't leave that right training wheel out of our analysis of the learning situation. Certainly *she* isn't leaving it out of *hers*.

We want the language learner to use the language. That's how he's going to learn to use it. But we have to be sure that he's really using it, not just appearing to use it.

On the surface level, one student utterance of a given sentence may be roughly equivalent to any other. But we have a pretty good idea of how different they may be on a deep level. One student utterance of the sentence might be repetition after the teacher. Another might be recalled from a memorized dialogue. Another might be manipulation on cue. We can't count these as real use of the language. Then another might be free creation and urgent expression. That's a different matter.

It is true that these differences are differences in what is taking place inside a black box. But that does not mean that they are beyond knowing. If you can hang a man on circumstantial evidence—and I think you can—then you can hang a learning model on what is going on inside the black box, given the inputs and the outputs. With a better idea of what real language use involves, we'll be in better position to make it happen.

We need some sort of model of the performance of the speaker and some sort of model of the hearer—or perhaps, since specialization is seldom carried that far, some sort of model of the performance speaker-hearer. If we consult the linguist and the psychologist, we will come away with something less than a scientific model of performance. But we will not come away empty-handed.

The linguist is likely to insist on components to deal with semantics, syntax, phonology, and lexicon, or some such breakdown. The psychologist is likely to insist on general cognitive components to deal with knowledge, logic, and imagination, at least, and on affective components certainly including drives and inhibitions. Notice that this does not pretend to be an exhaustive listing or a definitive categorization. But it does give an idea of the number and variety of components that will be needed for a working model.

Our consultants will undoubtedly warn, further, that each of these components will be internally complex, and that each of them will be related to each of the models in complex ways. Take the syntactic component of the performance model, for example. We could hardly expect it to be significantly simpler than the syntactic components of current competence models. Again, think back over the debate as to what, if anything, is wrong with one of the highest-frequency sentences in the English language, "Colorless green ideas sleep furiously." We can take the intensity of that debate as a measure of the intimacy of the relations between syntax and semantics, and between these linguistic components and the general cognitive components dealing with knowledge, logic, and imagination. And this is not even to mention the positive and negative affect aroused by that sentence.

Obviously, this performance model is almost as sketchy as my learning model. At the same time, it is overambitious in the present state of the art, and probably will be in any foreseeable state of the art. I am only saying that we must take into account every factor that we know, intuitively, to be important. I don't think that the models of learning and performance explicit or implicit in current language-teaching methods do. I think that they fail to do justice to much of what we know or have reason to suspect about the mind and about language.

One thing we know to be important, or have very good reason to suspect is important, was left out of my performance model. I mentioned earlier that every speaker is a hearer, and vice versa, or that everybody is a speaker-hearer. But I have not mentioned the obvious fact that every speaker requires a hearer, and vice versa, or that every speaker-hearer requires another. In other words, the performance model needs to be expanded into a communication model. There are obvious counterexamples to any claim that language is purely a communicative device, but none of them would seem to weigh heavily against regarding language as first and foremost a communicative device.

The speaker's performance cannot be understood without considering his mental representation of the hearer. I offer two thought experiments to illustrate this. First, imagine yourself writing, "to whom it may concern," a letter explaining why you have decided not to attend the party the Joneses are throwing next Saturday. Don't you find yourself wondering whom it might concern after all? What if it's somebody who has never heard of the Joneses? What if it's the Joneses? Next, imagine yourself conveying substantially the same explanation to your spouse. Would you need to be explicit or so tactful? Would you even need to be articulate?

But it doesn't stop here. The hearer's performance cannot be understood without considering his mental representation of the speaker. Imagine yourself opening a letter. Don't you look at the letterhead or the signature first?

Actually, it doesn't stop here, either. The speaker's representation of the hearer has to include an estimate of the hearer's representation of the speaker. And vice versa. And so on.

Communication is nothing if not a cybernetic process. We have seen that speaker and hearer are looped together in terms of what has been called "feed-forward," that is, in terms of their intentions and expectations. They are also looped together, of course, in terms of feedback. Both speaker and hearer need feedback on the extent to which the message sent was equivalent to the message received. If this feedback doesn't come immediately from what the other party says or does, it should come at some time from some source. Something has to result from what has been said and from how it has been understood, if communication is not to break down.

As soon as we put the subjective performances of speaker and hearer together into a communication model, we realize that there is an objective relationship between them, namely, what *in fact* the speaker communicates to the hearer. This is a function not only of what the speaker says but also of what the hearer already knows. We have arrived, of course, at the basic concept of information theory, in which the *amount* of information is measured by the unpredictability of the message—technically by the number of yes/no questions which the hearer would need to select the message from the array of likely messages.

Notice that his measure of communication means that we cannot judge the performance of the speaker just on the basis of what he says. We have to ask ourselves whether he has really told anybody anything—that is, whether he has told anybody anything they didn't already know. Nor can we judge the performance of the hearer just on the basis of how he responds. We have to ask ourselves whether he could have responded that way anyway. To anticipate, the implications of this for the language classroom are immense. Most of what normally passes for real use of the language fails to meet the test.

Let's trace the path of one communication event through this model, not even trying to touch all the bases.

The speaker starts out with some knowledge of the total situation, including an estimate of what that hearer knows about it. The speaker also has something he wants, something he can get only if the hearer is better informed. He therefore formulates a message—for simplicity let's think of it as prelinguistic, what he wants to say rather than how he is going to say it—shaping this message to fit what he thinks the hearer knows and what he thinks the hearer needs to be told. He then processes the message linguistically, looking up lexical items, applying semantic, syntactic, and phonological rules, to encode it into a signal. For our present purposes we may equate the signal with the surface structure.

The hearer processes the signal linguistically to decode it into a possible message. He checks it against his knowledge of the situation, including his estimate of what the speaker knows, and knows about him. If it doesn't make sense, he may recycle it. If it does, he takes what is *new* to him in the message and adds it to his knowledge. This may in turn affect what he *wants*—as the speaker intended.

But we have not yet completed the path of the communication event. Some clue has to loop back from the hearer to the speaker that the message he sent was the message received, and some clue has to loop back from the speaker to the hearer that the message he received was the message sent.

My essential claim is that students will learn a spoken language in the classroom just to the extent that what they do in the classroom approximates this communication model.

To help in examining this claim, let me extract three key features from the communication model, features I have gotten into the habit of calling *reference, intention,* and *uncertainty.* I think these three features, taken together, most clearly point up what the communicative approach requires and what it offers.

First, the *reference* feature. The reference recognizes that communication, to be communication, must first of all be about something. A word, a phrase, or a sentence has reference if it points to something in particular. There must be a referential framework, a definable state of affairs consisting of everything taken to be the case, a total situation specified by the total information available. Among other things, it must be reasonably clear who is talking to whom, when, and where.

If the learner says, for example, "The book is on the table," we should ask ourselves whether he has in mind any particular book, any particular table, and any particular configuration of book and table. He might not. He might just be producing a well-formed string. If that is the case, it may well be because no universe of discourse including any particular book on any particular table has been established.

Referentiality makes it possible for what is said to be judged true or false, sensible or nonsensical, appropriate or out of place. It insists that what is said be open to confirmation or disconfirmation. It lays the basis for feedback.

When we communicate in our own language, our referential framework is simply the world as we know it, or any part of it. But the world is too wide for the language learner—by definition. If he could talk about anything he might have in mind, he wouldn't be a learner, or at least he would be a very advanced learner. On the other hand, the classroom is too narrow, except for the merest beginner. There just isn't enough there to talk about for very long, or enough the learner needs to learn to talk about. Somehow, then, we have to arrange to bring samples of the world into the classroom, representations of parts of reality which are limited enough not to overchallenge the learner's abilities but rich enough to exploit those abilities.

Most current instruction is based on a script of some sort, a dialogue or narrative which is learned thoroughly and then forms the basis for a certain amount of discussion. This script does provide a referential framework, almost always a carefully limited one, although seldom a sufficiently rich one. Strangely enough, however, it is precisely in those parts of current instruction which aim at communication where the situation is inadequately characterized. In free conversation, for example, more often than not the learner finds himself in a referential limbo.

Recently, in a Chinese class in Washington, I heard the teacher ask a student, "Has your wife come here with you?" It was a question the student could understand—just—and one he knew how to answer in the affirmative or negative. But there was no context whatsoever. If the reference was to the real world, and assuming he had a wife, the student could take "here" to refer to the classroom or to the school or to Washington, each perhaps calling for a different answer, and he had no idea how to give an elaborate answer such as "She came to Washington with me, but she hasn't come to school with me today." If something else was supposed to count as real, what was it? Was he perhaps being cast in the role of Mr. King in the text, whose wife has indeed accompanied him to China? Or was he being invited to cook up an answer? Well, in that case, the affirmative would be much easier.

Whatever was going on in this reference-free exchange, it was certainly not communication.

Next, the *intention* feature. The intention feature recognizes that communication, to be communication, must be purposeful, must be to some end.

There is an obvious affective sense in which unmotivated speech falls short of communication, but there is also a crucial cognitive sense. Just as important as feedback in the communication model—and therefore in the learning—is "feed-forward." The speaker's intentions, and the hearer's expectations, give sharpness and weight to the feedback. There is increasing evidence to suggest that, unless a hypothesis is being tested, the data will seldom surrender or volunteer any meaning.

It would be ideal to be able to harness the learner's real-life intentions, but unfortunately these have little standing in the classroom. There are levels of intention on which this is not true, of course. The learner's intention to learn the language is clearly relevant. His intention to leave when the bell rings is clearly exploitable, perhaps by insisting on a leave-taking ritual. But most of the time, as things stand, the learner *can't* say anything he has any reason to say, and has no reason to say anything he *can* say.

Somehow, then, we must arrange for the learner to have moment-to-moment reasons to use the language he has. By far the simplest way is to give him one big reason and let the small ones follow naturally from it as things develop.

Finally, the *uncertainty* feature. The uncertainty feature recognizes that communication, to be communication, must overcome unpredictability.

If communication is the resolution of uncertainty, there has to be uncertainty to resolve. But if all the information has been made public by the time communication is supposed to begin, if nothing has been withheld, nothing really remains to be said. Behavior superficially resembling communication may ensue, but its redundancy will be nearly absolute. This is the case with most classroom discussion of the classroom. Everybody knows that Mrs. King accompanied her husband to China, and that the book is on the table. Nobody can *inform* anybody of either fact. In a way, we're back to spouse talking to spouse. Speaker and hearer share so much information that there is no point in being articulate. All the machinery of an articulate utterance would be spinning its wheels rather than functioning to convey meaning.

But of course how that machinery functions to convey meaning is precisely what we want the learner to learn, and he will only learn it by seeing it in operation and by operating it. Unless he can observe how form and content depend on one another, unless he gets to try fitting one to the other, he will never work out the complex relationship between sentences and meanings—which *is* the language.

Or, to put it another way, the evidence of the relationship between a sentence and its meaning is no more available in the absence of the meaning than it would be in the absence of the sentence.

The communicative approach offers a simple remedy. It arranges for different people to know different things. The total information about the situation is divided up, perhaps with some overlap, but with everybody screened off from some part of it. At the same time, of course, a requirement is built in for wider distribution of the information. Everybody has a need to know what others know, and has a need for others to know what he knows. It goes without saying that the only licensed channel for the transfer of information is the target language.

My colleague John Francis and I have been working for some time—in connection with the development of a Peace Corps Korean course, a private school program in French and Spanish, a French immersion program, and a government-sponsored Chinese course—to devise classroom activities along these lines. What we have come up with we call *communication games*.

We have some misgivings about the term, despite its inevitability. The word "games" has the drawback of suggesting a lack of seriousness, except perhaps in competitiveness. But our communication games are not intended as diversions from the hard work of language learning, or as rewards for it, but rather as the hard work itself. In fact, if there is one thing about them that is not serious, it is the occasional element of competition. Usually everybody "wins."

These communication games are gamelike in the sense that they simulate purposeful human interaction, and in the further sense that they *are* purposeful human interaction, on a different level. Like games, they are based on made-up situations, with roles to play, rules to follow, and goals to pursue within those situations.

Once taken seriously, communication games often turn out to be diverting and rewarding after all. But it is important to realize, I think, that this windfall profit derives not so much from the situation of reality as from the reality of communication itself. They are games, but they are *communication* games. Success in them hinges on the successful exchange of information. It is not at all a bad feeling to be putting the language to work. It is an even better feeling when, the more you use it, the better you *can* use it. These feelings are nature's way of telling you that you are functioning properly as a language-using, language-learning animal.

Let's take a look at a simple communication game played in the sixth unit of the Chinese course I mentioned. (Incidentally, there are 58 communication games in 39 units, and something like one-third of all class time is devoted to them.) This game is designed to contrast the new expression "to work at (some place)" with the old expressions "to be at (some place)" and "to live at (some place)." This is not a matter of simple lexical substitution, as it appears in English, but rather a matter of three different constructions which cast the same morpheme in the different roles of verb, verbal suffix, and preposition. So it needs work.

Since we aren't actually playing the game—I wish we could—we can cheat and look at the teacher's answer sheet, which represents the total situation. This consists of four copies of a street map showing three named office buildings on one side of the street and three named hotels on the other side. Each of these copies of the map is marked to show where one person works (any of the office buildings), where he lives (any of the three hotels), and where he happens to be now (any of the six buildings). Since this is a game of what we call the "science type," in which the players try to make out significant regularities in the data and base predictions on them, the situation has been rigged: each of the four people is shown as staying at the hotel across the street from his office building, and each of them is at his hotel now.

Now let's look at the worksheets the players are given. There are four different worksheets, one for each group of the four players in a group. Each worksheet is generally like the answer sheet, with four street maps to represent the facts about the four people, except that only one of the street maps—a different one on each player's worksheet—is filled in.

Each player, then, knows about one person and needs to know about the other three if he is to work out the significant regularity in the situation, and the only way he can find out about the other three people is to talk with the other three players. This choreographic pattern, by the way, in which each player pairs off with every other player in turn, is called "milling." Notice that it has the effect that each learner is talking half the time and being talked to the other half.

In the game of the "science" type, each player gathers information using question-word questions, coding it on his worksheet as he goes, until he is able to form a hypothesis about the significant regularity. Then he tests his hypothesis by making predictions with yes/no questions or, better, with slightly more yes than no questions. A hit counts as a hit, a miss as a miss.

I chose a simple example, at the risk of having it appear trivial, although anyone who has been involved in the first fifty or so hours of a language course may recognize that this science game is considerably more demanding than most classwork at that level. It may be worthwhile, now, to suggest what a communication game of the "science" type, but at a much more advanced level, might look like.

Imagine that each player is given a dossier defining his role in terms of socioeconomic background and political opinions, and that he is then to proceed as in my simpler example, this time specifically as a social scientist whose research objective is to uncover correlations such as "well-off people with children eighteen and under tend to favor higher local expenditures for schools, unless they happen to be conversatives." For fun, we might allow him to uncover such idiosyncratic exceptions as one poor and childless citizen who also favors higher expenditures for schools on the grounds that he wishes he had had a chance to go to school himself.

In general, we have found the science paradigm to be extremely productive across all levels and for most kinds of material. Other game types are more restricted in range, all the way down to a one-shot type like 3-D Tic-Tac-Toe, which so far, at least, has only been used to practice giving directions inside a building. Game types differ in many other ways than in range of application. We have identified more than a dozen independent variables which interact to produce a variety we have hardly begun to explore. If you think back over the two versions of "science" I have described, I think you will agree that the reference feature, the intention feature, and the uncertainty feature of the communication approach are all there. The situation is defined by the full set of worksheets. The overall goal, to find the pattern and, implicitly, to help others find the pattern, motivates the production and comprehension of each question and each answer. The division of information is accomplished by the provision of a different worksheet to each of the players.

A workshop would be a better setting for discussion of the nuts-and-bolts aspect of developing and implementing communication games. I would like to mention, however, that each game is preceded by a "briefing," a run-through of a stripped-down version of the game which gives the teacher a chance to demonstrate it to the whole class and to make sure that they are ready for it, and that each game is followed by a "debriefing," a general discussion of the total situation which has been uncovered which gives the teacher a chance to check up on what learning has taken place and to deal with any difficulties which have arisen. I should also mention, although it is perhaps obvious, the very different role of the teacher in this kind of learning activity. Except during the briefing and debriefing, when he has the class in his usual firm grip, the teacher is likely to feel a bit left out. He shouldn't, however. Besides functioning as a roaming linguistic monitor and linguistic resource, he may participate as a player himself and therefore function as a linguistic model for one group at a time, and at all times he remains the classroom manager, which in this case involves trouble-shooting the game.

I would like to close on a more uplifting note. In the Chinese course the games are a follow-through on material presented and practiced earlier in the unit. That's probably the way they should be introduced into classroom practice. In fact, I think their spread into other courses in other languages should probably proceed by piggybacking a game here and a game there onto existing materials. But I would like to think that communication games, despite their undignified name, have a more central role to play. I would like to see a course built around a sequence of communication games, with any other necessary inputs downgraded to the function of priming the learner for the games. I'm not sure that almost all presentation and practice of the material couldn't take place in a communicative context, with a great deal of openness to learner initiative in what gets learned. Anyway, it's worth a try.

GRAMMAR INDUCTION

Robert W. Blair

Many of my colleagues in linguistics are, like myself, keenly interested in the form and structure of language, have studied many languages, and are by training if not also by nature adept at language learning. We are at home with the technical and often esoteric vocabulary used by syntacticians and phonologists—particularly those of our own persuasion in linguistic theory. But we are not always in agreement as to the place of grammar in academic language learning. Some argue that for them an understanding of the grammatical and semantic structure of a language is the most direct and efficient means of learning a language—at least of attaining "linguistic competence." And although they recognize that linguistic competence is not yet communicative competence, they feel that the former is a good bridge to the latter. Some of my colleagues feel that linguistic sophistication is the single best tool for the language student, that scientifically accurate descriptions of grammatical and semantic structure should be a principal part of any academic language course, and that as more and more "powerful" descriptions of grammatical and semantic structures are developed, more and more efficiency in teaching languages will result. One even claims that for a language student to attempt to learn a language without understanding linguistics is like a physics student attempting to learn physics without understanding mathematics; though to some extent it can be done, it is highly inefficient and not to be recommended for the serious student. From that point of view it would seem that just as mathematics is a prerequisite to the study of the physical sciences, so linguistics should be a prerequisite to serious language study.

Although convinced that I myself am in certain ways a more efficient language learner for having acquired some linguistic tools and insights, I am not ready to agree that grammar should have a central place in the first 200 hours of language instruction or that linguistic training should be a prerequisite for language training.

For me there is no question of whether grammar description has a legitimate and useful function in academic language instruction. I think it has. But I feel that much of the attention accorded the form and function of the parts of speech, sentence and pronunciation patterns, and the like has for most students been counterproductive to efficient language learning, more often a barrier than a facilitator. Instructional programs I have seen in textbooks, on wall charts, in computer-assisted instruction, and in classroom presentations have, I think, overplayed grammar description and overloaded students with technical nomenclature. Partly because of this, academic language instruction has for many students been distasteful if not forbidding.

I recognize, of course, the great temptation to talk about form in class, to explain grammar, to provide phonetic descriptions, etc. Some students want it. Given a chance some would turn the classroom into a question-and-answer session on the language. As Krashen pointed out, "cognitive" learning about the structure of a language *feels* good, it holds out false hopes of conquering the language quickly, and it beguiles teacher and student alike with its appearance of an immediate and heavy payoff.

The question I am concerned with is: what is the place of grammar description in the first 100 or 200 hours of language instruction? Can it contribute effectively to the mastery of spoken language? Or is the threat too high that it will get in the way, take time away from more productive activities, convey the wrong impression of what language acquisition is? If it can contribute in a positive way, how?

My present conclusion, shared by many of the authors in this book, is to not deny that the formal study of language structure has value, but to exclude it from the classroom and relegate it to out-of-class study.

The foreign language course that I think best integrates communicative classroom activities with out-of-class grammar study is Alexander Lipson's delightful *A Russian Course*. Its approach to the description of Russian grammar is linguistically sophisticated, but the grammar is not overplayed and is always peripheral to the strong communicational thrust of the course.

Taking part of Lipson's Russian course as a model, I developed a self-instructional grammar-study module in Spanish. It is one of the modules of the integrated acquisition-learning approach discussed below. Prominent features of this grammar module include: (1) a very low rate of vocabulary input—and even that is facilitated through mnemonic priming; (2) an unusually steep rate of climb into complex grammatical patterns (e.g., Spanish verb morphology); (3) a large amount of very simple, self-correcting drills; (4) a simple, nontechnical, and inductively arrived at consideration of generalizations on grammar; and (5) an unusually large amount (for beginning instruction) of very simple text in which selected grammatical patterns occur repeatedly.

Here is a small sampling of parts of the first and fourth lessons. The recommended amount of time devoted to these four lessons is from 10 to 15 hours. Classroom activities I have used with this were inspired by Gomez' participatory learning approach (which combines techniques used by Gattegno with others used by Alexander Lipson). The activities deal with the absurd but attention-engaging "truth values" established in the dialogue. I use sign language and Paleneo (a written sign language) as well as quickly drawn figures in the same way Gomez and Lipson use these.

DISCOVERING HOW SPANISH WORKS

Lesson One

Priming the pump.

Learning to recognize the following words and word roots will make this lesson easy. (Hints to help you remember these are given on the tape.)

reina	queen	cant-	sing	mejor	better
rey	king	toc-	play	peor	worse

Setting: A royal ball is in process at a royal palace. Two servants are observing and commenting.

Instructions: Listen several times to the reading of this dialogue. Pay particular attention to the close correspondence in form and meaning between the English and Spanish sentences. When you can understand the reading fully with eyes closed, you are ready to go on to the next section.

A

— ¿Quién está cantando? — Who is singing?

— El rey. El rey está cantando. — The king. The king is singing.

— ¿Cuál rey? — Which king?

— Aquel que tocaba cantos fúnebres en el tambor. — The one who used to play dirges (funeral songs) on the drum.

— El rey que tocaba cantos fúnebres en el tambor está cantando, ¿eh? — The king who used to play dirges on the drum is singing, eh?

— Sí. Y canta bien, ¿no? — Yes. And (he) sings well, no?

— Canta mejor que toca. — (He) sings better than (he) plays.

(Sections B and C omitted)

Study Task 2

Take a few unhurried minutes now to concentrate on the vocabulary reviewed in the sentences below. Make three passes through these sentences as follows:

(1st pass) Compare the Spanish forms and their meaning with the English. (Read the Spanish out loud; then look away and say it, thinking of its meaning and form. Also without looking at the Spanish see if you can repeat the one just above.)

(2nd pass) Cover the English and see if you can translate the Spanish into English.

(3rd pass) Cover the Spanish and see if you can translate the English into Spanish.

A

1 king and queen   rey y reina
2 queen with king   reina con rey
3 the king and the queen el rey y la reina
4–10

(Sections B, C, and D omitted)

How to turn statements into questions.

Study Task 1. Examine the following sentences. Note how a statement can be transformed into a question by a simple inversion.

1. El rey canta.	The king sings.
¿Canta el rey?	Does the king sing?
2. La princesa cantaba.	The princess used to sing.
¿Cantaba la princesa?	Did the princess used to?

CULMINATING ACTIVITY

Listening In

El rey y la reina están cantando. Están cantando en la torre. Están cantando cantos fúnebres con Polo y Misti (el perro y el gato). Y cantan más o menos bien. El rey canta mejor que la reina, la reina canta mejor que el perro, y el perro canta mejor que el gato. La princesa no está cantando. No canta bien. Canta peor que el perro—pero mejor que el gato.

Questions:

1 ¿Quién está cantando?
2 ¿Cuál rey?
3 ¿Qué está haciendo la reina?
4–15

DISCOVERING HOW SPANISH WORKS

Lesson 4

(The *Listening In* part of the culminating activities of this lesson give an indication of the grammar points and vocabulary covered thus far in the grammar module.)

Listening In.

Hay dos reinas. Una que lloraba en el baño con la princesa, no fumaba, no tomaba, y ahora está cantando con el rey en la torre. (Están cantando cantos fúnebres. Ella está tocando el tambor.) La otra reina vivió diez años en Ojai comprando y vendiendo carros. Ella ya no vive allá y ya no compra y vende carros. Ahora escribe cheques falsos. Es loca, esta reina. De verdad. Completamente loca. Creo que toma. ¿Quién sabe?

Hay dos reyes también. El uno está con la reina en la torre cantando. El no fuma y no toma. En verdad nunca ha tomado y nunca ha fumado. ¿Quién sabe por qué? El es muy inocente . . . y no muy inteligente, creo. Por ejemplo él no sabe que la princesa fuma en la cantina con el príncipe. Y no sabe que el príncipe fuma puros negros y toma tequila en las rocas. Este rey no sabe mucho. No habla chino. No lo entiende tampoco. (Y no le gusta cuando la princesa lo habla en el castillo.) No, el rey habla español. Sólo español. Lo habla con la reina y la princesa, lo habla con los chinos, lo habla aún con el perro y el gato. Habla en español con todos. . . .

Activity

Take the characters depicted in these four lessons and write or tell about their peculiarities.

EASIFICATION

Robert W. Blair

The process of language acquisition for an adult learner involves, among other things, the forging and storing up in the memory of connections or association bonds between meanings and their associated phonic and/or graphic forms. The process by which this is actually done is a hidden one which few teachers or instructional systems pay much attention to. It is generally left up to the individual learner to discover what works for him or her. The job of the instructional system then is generally seen as if it were merely one of dishing up bite-size servings, making the fare nutritious, palatable, and digestible, but not concerning itself with the processes of ingestion or digestion; how the food gets from the plate into the bloodstream is left pretty much to natural processes. Since at the level of forging and storing up association bonds in the memory, learning (like digestion) is a natural process, it is left untouched. People don't need to be taught how to transfer new language data into internal representations and process these appropriately any more than they need to be taught how to digest, it is thought. Yet given a specific learning task, such as memorizing a list of foreign expressions, different people learn at different rates.

In recent years a growing number of people have taken an interest in mathemogenic behaviors, the internal (hidden) behaviors or activities which give birth to learning. And as they have examined these, many have found it logical to suppose that positive mathemogenic behaviors can be enhanced, that certain learning strategies and tactics can be taught, and that perhaps learner differences can be equalized nearer the level of the proficient learners as those with less effective learning skills acquire more effective ones.

In the field of language teaching surprisingly little experimentation has been done on mnemonic training. Reports of research on the use of mnemonics in teaching Russian vocabulary at Stanford University have been published by Atkinson and Raugh. Their aim was to teach only word recognition (Russian to English) rather than active recall (English to Russian). Michael Tatton and Delbert H. Groberg are among the few experimentalists I know of in second language acquisition who have done serious work with mnemonics in teaching active word and text memorization. Andrew D. Cohen, coiner of the term "easification" in language learning, is the contact person of a group of people scattered worldwide who are interested in the subject. It must be added that there are a few studies on easification that come up with the conclusion that attempts to tamper with the learner's learning tactics are not worth the trouble and that prepared mnemonic aids are less effective than learner-invented mnemonics. From experiments conducted at Brigham Young University in these matters, I believe the present evidence contradicts those conclusions.

Let's look at a learner's tactics through the imaginary case of a novice language learner who innocently tries to learn a little bit of a langauge on her own. Jane Brown, an American planning a trip to the Soviet Union, wants to learn to say a few things in Russian; so she buys an inexpensive self-study course complete with cassette recording, and expectantly sets about learning her first Russian words. Anxious to hear what the language sounds like, she listens to the first dialogue. At first hearing, the utterances are perceived only as unanalyzable blurs. Somewhat apprehensively she opens the accompanying booklet, carefully reads the instructions on pronunciation three times, and then looks at the written representation of the same Russian dialogue while she listens to the recording. Here is what she sees written:

| How do you do? My name is Vladimir. | z-DRAHVST-voo-eet-yeh. meen-YAH zah-VOOT Vlah-DyEE-mihr. |
| Very pleasant to make acquaintance with you. | OH-chin pree-YAHT nuh puh-znah-KOH-mee-tsuh s-VAH-mee. |

Simultaneously listening to the dialogue while following the "phonic" representation several more times, she is finally able to associate the sounds with the written representation. What she will do now, she decides, is commit the dialogue to memory, and to do this she plays it over and over, repeating it to herself, then reading it off the page out loud, and finally attempting to say the utterances from memory.

That is when she begins to grapple with a fundamental learning problem. It seems the Russian expressions just don't stick in her memory. She finds nothing to associate them with and therefore no way to cement them in her memory; they just float away. She can listen to the tape with her eyes closed and give the English equivalent of the Russian expressions without trouble, and she can echo the Russian while it is still ringing in her short-term memory, but she cannot look at the English and come up with its Russian equivalent cold. Her self-therapy: more listening; more rehearsal. The result: discouragement and self-incrimination. "Wait a minute, there are only seven new words here! Now why can't I remember them?" Like most diligent language students, she puts in more rehearsal until finally she manages to give the entire dialogue from memory—a somewhat shaky performance, to be sure, but satisfying, nevertheless. She sees that she has invested more than half an hour in that mean little eight-word dialogue. She feels tired and a little deflated, but not defeated. The real test she knows will be seeing if she can remember the dialogue after a break. After a 10-minute rest period she tries to recall the dialogue, but to her utter frustration it has escaped again. "What's wrong with me?" she asks herself. "Am I stupid? At this rate I'll never learn." Then, more analytically: "storage isn't the problem, it's retrieval. How can I learn to retrieve what I store? What does it take to store Russian words in my memory bank so that I can recall them later?"

Deciding to share her frustration, Jane calls her friend Barbara, who recently visited Russia. Barbara nonchalantly tells her that as a matter of fact she learned enough Russian on the flight to Moscow that she was able to say and understand quite a few things in Russian. The following discussion ensued.

How did you learn that much in such a short time?
With my mnemonics.
Mnemonics?
Yeah, little memory tricks. Anybody can learn to use them.
Hey, Barbs, I'm interested, come and show me.
Look, Jane, I'm no language teacher. I don't know the first thing about it. All I can do is show you what worked for me.
Oh, please do.
Okay, but don't laugh.
Don't worry, if it works for me, I won't.

Jane was still smarting from her losing battle with those eight mean Russian words when Barbara came over and laid out on the table an enormous Russian dialogue.[1] "This is what I expect you to master in one hour!"

Hello!	Zdrástvujţe!
Hi!	Priyét!
Where are you going?	Kudá vi?
Over there.	Tudá.
Me too.	Ja tóže.
How about that!	Vot kak.
Let's go together, okay?	Pojdom vméşţe, xorošó?
Okay. Why not?	Xorošó. Počemú ņét?
With pleasure!	S udovólştyijem!
My name is Vladimir.	Meņá zovut Vladímir.
And I am Olga.	A ja Olga.
It's a pleasure to meet you.	Očeņ, prijátno poznakómitsa s vaмį.
For me also.	Mņe tóže.
What are you studying at the university?	Čem vi zaņimájeteş v universiţéte?
Music. I'm a pianist.	Múzikoj. Ja piaņístka.
Interesting, I'm a pianist too.	Interésno, ja tóže piaņíst.
You know, my husband is also a pianist.	Znájeţe, moj muž tóže piaņíst.

Very interesting!	Óčen, intęręsno!
Yes.	Da.
Oh, I forgot.	Ax, ja zabíl.
What?	Što?
Excuse me. It's time for me to go home.	Izvįnįte. Mnę porá domój.
So soon?	Tak skóro?
Yes, unfortunately.	Da, k sožalęniju.
So long then.	Značit poká.
Goodbye.	Do syįdánija.
Till we meet again soon.	Do skórovo syįdánija.[1]

That's what you think I ought to be able to learn in one hour?
Yep.
You've gotta be kidding!
I'm serious.
Then you're crazy, you're utterly out of your mind.
I don't think so, but so what, if it works!
What do you mean "learn" it?
Well, I think that after an hour of study you should be able to recite the entire thing from top to bottom with your eyes closed, translate any line from Russian to English or from English to Russian orally and instantly. It's only got thirty lines and about seventy words!
I couldn't do that in English. I'd have to be a genius to do it in Russian. Do you know how much time it took me to learn just eight words?
I think you can do it, Jane. I really do.
Okay, Barbs, I'll believe it when I see it.
Let's get started then. Take the first line, it sounds like STRAWS TO WITCH YA. Not STRAYS to witch ya, but STRAWS to witch ya. Got that? Imagine people greeting each other by exchanging straws and saying STRAWS TO WITCH YA. It means "hello." Make a sign of greeting now and say it. Now listen to the tape. Did you notice there's only a couple of little differences between the English sound-alike phrase and the native Russian? For example, it is ZDRAWS, not STRAWS.
Got it: ZDRAWS TO WITCH YA.
What does it mean?
"Hello" or "how do you do?"
Right. Now take the next line. It means "My name is Vladimir." It's a self-introduction. Listen: MEAN JAWS A BOOT VLADIMIR. Visualize, if you can, the MEAN JAWS of a great white shark with A BOOT being redeemed by a reDEEMer named Vladimir, who introduces himself to the shark with those words. Got that? Say it. Now listen to the tape: You see, you're already in the ballpark. Now all that's left to do is make a couple of very minor adjustments to move your version over to home plate. For one, ...
That's easy. Let's go on.
All right. Do you remember how to say "hello?" Good. And do you remember how Vladimir introduces himself? Good. This next one is a long one, but it's not hard. It means "Very happy to make acquaintance with you." If you had never met a SWAMI, you would be happy to meet one, right? Say SWAMI. Now, do you know that a comb eats a swami? Say COMB EATS A SWAMI. What eats what? COMB eats a SWAMI. Put PAUSE GNAW in front. Say PAUSE GNAW COMB EATS A SWAMI. Good. Now say YACHT-GNAW, just like a yacht on the ocean, but followed by GNAW. Good. Now put the prefix PRE before YACHT GNAW: say PRE YACHT GNAW. At the very front comes the ocean, say OCEAN. OCEAN PRE YACHT GNAW PAUSE GNAW COMB EATS A SWAMI.

I've got it. What does it mean again?

"Happy to meet you."

Yeah. I'm happy to meet a swami on his yacht on the ocean.

Good. Now listen to the native Russian version and see what slight adjustments you need to make in your pronunciation to shape it up to native level. . . . Fine. Now see if you remember how to say "hello." . . . Good. Do you remember how Vladimir introduces himself? . . . Good. And can you give the Russian for "Very happy to meet you?" . . . Great!

I'm fascinated. It's working. Let's go on. . . .

In about forty-five minutes Jane is able to translate any part of the dialogue from Russian into English or from English into Russian.

Do you think you know the dialogue now?

I know all the lines, I guess, but I couldn't recite it from top to bottom.

If that is something you want to do it's an easy next step. I'll take you on an imaginary trip through the United States. We'll stop in sixteen places and we'll associate each stop mnemonically with a pair of lines from the dialogue. Then all you have to do in order to remember the sequence of lines in the dialogue is recall the itinerary. Simple, isn't it? It's called the locations, or LOCI, method and it's pretty effective. In fact, if you want to recite the dialogue from bottom to top you just think through the itinerary in reverse!

In less than 15 minutes Jane knows the dialogue "backward and forward." More than that, she is confident that she knows it and can retrieve all or any part of it at will—not only while it is still fresh in mind, but an hour later without further review. With periodic review it is hers for an indefinite period. That seems like quite an accomplishment for an hour's work when contrasted with her earlier attempt, or with the initial attempts of most novice language learners to memorize material in a foreign language.

When one undertakes the task of memorizing expressions in a foreign language, a crucial question is: what sort of learning activity will best assure that learning takes place, that information taken in will be precisely remembered, and that the drain on energy and time will not be excessive?

Robert Gagné points out that there are two traditional but opposing views of learning that relate to the question. In the one view it is the amount of practice that establishes the degree of learning or holding power: increasing the number of repetitions at the time of initial learning serves to "strengthen the learned connection" or "reinforce the bond of association" and thus build up resistance to forgetting. On the basis of this notion, Jane's attempts to set the seven Russian words in her memory by massed repetition was justified, each repetition serving supposedly to "hammer it in" just a little farther, until it is embedded permanently.

A more recent view of learning rejects the notion of strengthening learning connections by massed practice. Research has shown that in the kind of learning that involves pairing each one of a series of new stimulus items with an arbitrary response item (as in memorizing a vocabulary list in a foreign language) each pair is learned or not learned on a given trial. In an ideal instructional program, one might suppose, the aim would be to cause each pair to be learned by all subjects on the first trial.

Gagné (1969) explains the mechanics of this view:

Information is first registered by the senses and remains as perceived for an instant. It then enters what is called the short-term memory store where it can be retained for 30 seconds or so. This short-term store has a limited capacity, so that new information coming into it simply pushes aside what may already be stored there. But an important process takes place in this short-term memory. There is a kind of internal reviewing mechanism (a "rehearsal buffer") which organizes and rehearses the material even within this short period of time. Then it is ready to be transferred to the long-term memory store. But when this happens, it is first subjected to a process called coding. In other words, it is not transformed in raw form, but is transformed in some way which will make it easier to remember at a later time.

This process of organizing and storing coded information in the long-term memory is only half of the process, however. It is one thing to put information in; it is another thing to get it out. You will recall Jane's perceptive analysis of her problem:

Storage isn't the problem, it's retrieval. How can I learn to retrieve what I store? What do I have to do to store Russian words in my memory bank so that I can recall them later?

Barbara, of course, provided a way of facilitating the process of storing Russian in retrievable form—in fact a way of enabling Jane to learn each item the first time it was encountered.

A closer look at Jane's two very different experiences in memorizing Russian sentences may be instructive:

1. Presented with a Russian sentence for the first time, her brain had to perceive it as a phonically codable entity before it could store it. At first, as you recall, her perception of Russian sounds registered only a (for her) unpronounceable, unanalyzable, phonically uncodable blur. The first registration of one's perception of the sound in repeatable form presumes an initial phonic coding process.

2. In addition to coding the sounds phonically, since she saw a written representation, she also registered a visual coding:

z-DRAHST-voo-eet-yeh, meen-YAH zah-VOOT vlah-DEE-mir

(It is possible that this visual coding influenced—either facilitated or frustrated—the phonic coding process to some extent.)

3. Informed of the translation equivalent of the Russian dialogue, she had to form a bond or connection somehow between the sound sequences and their meanings. That is, she had to encode the sound-meaning composite. This process we will call the *phonosemantic coding*.

4. After meeting that challenge, what remained to be done was crucial.

a. Provide a retrieval strategy: some way of remembering that the item is on file in the memory, and also a way to give instant access to it on call.

b. File each item or sequence in long-term memory.

c. Practice accessing recall repeatedly and at increasing intervals.

The interesting thing about Barbara's approach to teaching the dialogue is that she consciously attempted to mediate learning at each of the levels of memory processing. (1) At the *phonic coding* level she mediated Russian phrases by means of English sound-alike phrases, and these became the key to memory processing and retrieval. Since speakers of English are quite accustomed to processing English words and sounds, they have no difficulty processing Russian coded initially in this way. The approach ties the unfamiliar to the familiar, and the adjustment from the initial English target to the Russian target is then only a small step. (2) At the *graphic coding* level she mediated Russian by means of a written representation using English words in conventional spelling rather than a string of strange-looking words written by arbitrary conventions. Compare the word for the English reader: (a) STRAWS TO WITCH YA (b) z-DRAHST-voo-eet-yeh (3) At the *phonosemantic coding* level, where the task is to associate the sound sequence with its new meaning, Barbara took the English phrase used in the phonic coding and associated a new meaning with it. She took STRAWS TO WITCH YA, said it was a greeting like "hello," and suggested an imageable picture: "Imagine people greeting each other by exchanging straws and saying: STRAWS TO WITCH YA! (4) To make sure Jane had filed the item and could access it on call, Barbara periodically had her exercise retrieval by asking: Do you remember how to say "hello?" Do you remember how Vladimir introduces himself? Can you say "Pleased to meet you" in Russian?

One other thing Barbara did that goes beyond the ordinary was to mediate the serial learning task. She was aware that memorizing a dialogue entails learning the sequence of lines as well as the pronunciation and meaning of each line. Her use of an imaginary itinerary provided a framework on which to lay the sequence of lines of the dialogue.

It is interesting the objections some language teachers have expressed about the use of mnemonics in language teaching. The most common goes like this: "It is unnatural and unnecessary: why build strange and indirect connections between sound and meaning? For proficient bilinguals there is a direct bonding of meaning with sound; it is not mediated through mnemonic associations. That direct bonding is what must be aimed for from the first in language learning. If someone tries to learn vocabulary by mnemonic means, he will soon be a language cripple, always having to go through his mnemonic scheme to locate his next word. Mnemonics just adds a lot of unwieldy, unnecessary, and unnatural baggage."

Without question Barbara's whole approach to teaching Jane was highly unorthodox, but by most calculations—compared, say, with Jane's earlier attempts on her own or with the amount of Russian ordinarily learned the first hour of a Russian class—the approach was highly successful. At the end of the hour Jane could give the entire dialogue in Russian with eyes closed, and she could translate confidently and without hesitation any of the 30 lines from Russian to English or from English to Russian. Earlier, using a more natural approach, she had difficulty learning a sequence of seven words. Like Annie Sullivan's getting Helen Keller to fold her napkin in *The Miracle Worker,* Barbara's approach may seem wholly misguided, but to Jane it brought order out of chaos.

What then of the objection typically raised that association mnemonics force the language learner to take extra, unnatural steps and in the end only hobble his learning? My answer is that none of the learning researchers I know or have read believe this. M. David Merrill, a noted author in the field of instructional science, explains that the brain seems to use what is called the "push-down" principle where once something is learned, regardless of how it was learned, memory access is "pushed down" to the automatic level. Ultimately there is no difference in access time between one thing learned through association mnemonics and a similar thing learned through other strategies.

EXPERIMENTATION IN MNEMONIC PRIMING

Research at Brigham Young University has focused on the use of carefully contrived mnemonics for teaching active recall of running texts as well as long vocabulary lists in Russian, Chinese, and other languages. In one experiment a mnemonics-mediated list of over 60 Russian words is presented by means of audiocassette and printed supplement to volunteer subjects with no previous knowledge of the language. After little more than half an hour most of the subjects can give the English equivalent for any of the Russian words, or the Russian equivalent of any of the English words. We have concluded that the use of this kind of mnemonic "priming" of vocabulary, leading into illustrated lectures and related activities using this vocabulary, makes possible the early introduction of a large amount of spoken input that would otherwise be forbidding. For many inexperienced learners it can, it seems, serve as a "shoehorn" to slip more language in easily.

Other areas than vocabulary and text memorization, of course, are amenable to mnemonic mediation. Groberg (1969) has experimented with an ingenious mnemonic approach to teaching Japanese grammar, and mnemonic aids to learning foreign writing systems are available. Pioneer work in this was done by Frank Laubach of the Laubach Institute in Syracuse, New York. The influence of Laubach is seen in a short self-instructional program developed at Brigham Young University for teaching how to read and write Russian words. Using this program, students have acquired facility in these basic skills in a fraction of the time it usually takes under conventional instruction.

NOTE

1. This is an actual Russian dialogue developed at Brigham Young University for experimentation in foreign language memorization tasks. With the aid of a tutor many novice language learners with no previous knowledge of Russian are able to memorize this dialogue in one hour.

5

AN INTEGRATED APPROACH

AN INTEGRATED APPROACH

Robert W. Blair

The question remains whether the various approaches discussed above are mutually compatible, whether elements or principles of one cannot be harmoniously and advantageously combined with elements or principles of the others. Of course the originators of some of these approaches caution against mixing and predict that only in its pure form can the full power of their approach be tapped. I agree that each approach needs to be further developed by itself, but at the same time unless it should be agreed that for theoretical or practical reasons the interweaving of features of two or more approaches is without justification, there is no reason to rule out experimenting with combinations of features from various approaches, to try to get the properties of one to complement the properties of another. It may be that no one approach is optimally effective for all learners. What one learner may find effective another may find frustrating.

Claims to the contrary notwithstanding, in no approach do all learners learn equally well. Whether because of differences in learning strategies, innate ability, attitude, motivation, personality, or other factors, in any class some learners perform less well than others.

For many years we have been interested in finding out how to help the below-average language learners, those we call the "forgotten bottom forty percent." Of particular interest to us have been middle-aged learners, because these typically experience great difficulty and frustration in learning a new language. It has been primarily in the interest of finding how to help low-efficiency learners that we have collected, tested, and ultimately adopted many of the ideas and techniques discussed above. Our aim has been to create and experiment with a learner-adaptive instructional system rich enough and versatile enough to accommodate a broad range of learning needs and learning styles—not excluding of course those of the gifted learners. The instructional system will allow teachers or individual students in a class or in self-instruction to make up their own study syllabus from a great variety of possible combinations.

So far materials for this instructional system, called the integrated acquisition-learning approach (or IALA), have been developed and tested only in Spanish, Russian, Chinese, Maya, and Esperanto. A sample of the materials used in one language, an account of what actually went on in one class, a description of the syllabus used for in-class instruction and that recommended for out-of-class study, together with a sample of materials used, will serve to give an idea of our recent experimentation in integrating elements of the approaches discussed above. (We do not claim, of course, that this is the first or the ultimate eclectic integration of approaches to learning and acquisition. We do think, however, that it may be the most versatile one developed so far, the one with the most options and variety.)

First to sketch in a little background and add a subjective assessment of the learning outcomes: In 1980, we taught three Spanish courses using different combinations of techniques from Curran, Lozanov, Gattegno, Terrell, Asher, Burling, Lipson, Gomez, Winitz and Reeds, and others. One of these courses, taught in the winter of 1980, was a noncredit minicourse in beginning Spanish, a typical adult-education group, for a dozen middle-aged people, most of them inexperienced in language learning, frightened, worried, and filled with self-doubts. These were people who would have shied away from conventional language training. They were busy people with work and family responsibilities and without much time or energy to devote to study. The class met 6 hours a week (7 to 10 Friday evenings and 8 to 11 Saturday mornings) for 4 consecutive weeks, for a total (including rest breaks) of about 21 hours of classroom instruction.

The primary aim of the course, on which over two thirds of the class time was spent, was to develop listening and reading comprehension. The secondary aim, to which less than one third of the class time was devoted, was to develop a very modest speaking capability. An overarching aim was to make their learning of Spanish joyful and to make them want to go on and feel confident in themselves as language learners.

Almost anyone observing that class would regard the learning outcomes as extraordinary. Our report on its outcomes will have to be considered impressionistic, of course, since no empirical data were extracted, but we will say that in those 21 hours an almost incredible transformation took place. It was a thing we had seen before, but never without a sense of awe and fascination. Observing that transformation was like observing a butterfly emerge from its immobile chrysalis ready to take flight. In those few hours those people acquired the skill to understand a phenomenal amount of spoken Spanish, the grammatical complexity and vocabulary range of which would be a challenge to many college students well along in more conventional training. In addition they acquired the skill to read and understand previously unseen texts of a level of difficulty equal to that found in second-semester college Spanish textbooks. Also they acquired a rudimentary ability to communicate ideas of considerable length and complexity—quite haltingly to be sure, but without rehearsal or memorization.

These may sound like exaggerated claims, but given the out-of-the-ordinary goal and the unconventional approach used to attain it, the achievements of this class are not, we think, unusual.

The language input from the voluminous materials was enormous in itself, but in addition, during much of the class time a steady stream of fairly sophisticated, grammatically complex Spanish was issued as the teacher elaborated ad lib on the contents of the printed materials and made related commentaries on various and sundry matters. The students were allowed the freedom of using English during times of interaction with the teacher, but the response was always in Spanish.

Central in our mind was the aim of providing them with a large amount of comprehensible input, a "critical mass," while at the same time maintaining the attention and interest of the students. Understanding of the stories and commentary was aided, of course, through the exploitation of linguistic and extralinguistic context, using familiar stories, pictures, cuisinaire rods, and paralinguistic expression. The language was somewhat simplified, of course, but it was far more elaborate than what one ordinarily observes in "teacher talk" at this early stage. Yet despite the relatively high sophistication and great volume of Spanish input in the course, the level of response the students knew was expected of them was such as to keep the anxiety level low. They knew they were expected to focus on meaning and not worry about the details of form.

In order to help maintain communication near the "$i + 1$" level, we provided a feedback device, a gauge by which we could tell more or less the extent of each student's understanding. They were each given two "flags," a red one and a yellow one, with which they could indicate their level of understanding: if over 85 percent, no signal; if between 60 and 85 percent, the yellow signal; and if under 60 percent, the red signal. Part of our strategy was to get the students to tolerate less than full comprehension, to use the flags with discretion.

Because over two thirds of their class time was invested in listening rather than in trying to speak, there was little time spent with students "grinding out" Spanish sentences, memorizing or reciting memory pieces, or rehearsing patterns among themselves. In the comprehension training they heard no "gringo Spanish" from their classmates. The amount of well-formed, sophisticated, yet for them largely understandable Spanish input was thus many times the amount and very much more sophisticated in quality than what is presented in more conventional training.

The secondary aim of the course, on which less than one third of the class time was spent, was to enable the students to develop a rudimentary production capability. For this goal we combined the printed and recorded materials from *Spanish for Pleasure* with elements of the Silent Way, Community Language Learning, Participatory Learning, and other communicative techniques to elicit phychologically real, truth-valued classroom communication.

The achievement of the students in regard to Spanish production might have seemed less impressive to an observer than their achievement in the receptive skills of reading and listening (where the major investment of time was made), but it was sufficiently well-developed, spontaneous, and communicative to lead one to suppose that they had spent more than just a few hours learning the language.

Here is a brief syllabus of the first 6 hours, followed by samples of some of the materials used in that course, and some explanation of their rationale.

Syllabus of First Two Classes (6 Hours)

	Minutes
(in-class activities)	
* How Much Spanish Do You Know? (self-test)	15
† Total Physical Response Training	15
* Priming of Illustrated Lecture	15
Giants and Monsters (Model Illustrated Lecture)	10
David and Goliath (Actual Illustrated Lecture)	5
Ad lib commentary in Spanish	10
†"Silent Way" with charts and rods	30
†Community Language Learning	20
* The Lost Son (familiar narrative)	25
(Script with cassette for home listening)	
* A Gomez Bilingual Reader ("Mi Primera Visita . . .")	20
†Burling Reader	10
* Spanish Sounds and Spelling	20
* The Lost Son (familiar narrative), second reading	20
* Discovering How Spanish Works	20

---

†Illustrated in a previous section of this book
*Illustrated below

SAMPLES OF MATERIALS USED

How Much Spanish Do You Know?
How many of the following words do you recognize?

TEQUILA	FIESTA	BRONCO	SIESTA
TORTILLA	HOMBRE	TACOS	MUCHACHO

You see, you already know quite a bit of Spanish. And fortunately the amount of Spanish you already know—your latent knowledge of Spanish—can make learning more Spanish a delightful experience.

Here is a way to find out how much Spanish you already know.

Directions: Circle A, B or C according to the following judgments: (A) if the expression is totally unfamiliar and foreign; (B) if you think you might know but are not sure what it means; and (C) if you feel you know what it means.

A B C 1 padre y madre	A B C 5 ¡Dios mío!
A B C 2 dos o tres	A B C 6 poco a poco
A B C 3 ¿verdad?	A B C 7 se habla español
A B C 4 blanco y negro	A B C 8 toro y matador
(plus 42 others). . .	

Totaling up your score:
    Total of A's circled—_____ (times 1)—_____ points
    Total of B's circled—_____ (times 2)—_____ points
    Total of C's circled—_____ (times 3)—_____ points

                    TOTAL POINTS—_____

ILLUSTRATED LECTURES (with Mnemonic Priming)

Two of the objectives we aim for in the very first hour of a langauge course
are (1) to convince the learners of the effectiveness of mnemonic facilitators in
learning vocabulary, and (2) to give them the excitement of discovering that
they can understand a great amount of spoken discourse in the language right
off—no matter what the language may be. To achieve these objectives we assign
students an hour's preparatory homework, in which time they are introduced
with the aide of mnemonic "priming" to a recorded and printed illustrated
lecture. The purpose of this is to show them that they can get in mind the
meaning and pronunciation of many words in a short time without strain, that
they can then follow a relatively sophisticated recorded lecture with the aid of a
bilingual script, and that then in the first minutes of the first class, after only the
one hour of preparation, they can follow with comfort and satisfaction a series of
short illustrated lectures. Among other things we give a rather elaborate
rendition of the story of David and Goliath during the first few minutes of the
first class.

Here are a few of the words in the priming section of the first illustrated
lecture and an example of the priming exercise. With mnemonic facilitation
provided on a tape many students are able to experience first-trial learning, and
after only a few moments they can give these Spanish words from memory. Then
in a few more moments of mnemonic priming they learn a similar set of words. In
less than 20 minutes of such priming four to six sets (40 to 60 words) can be
learned easily by most learners.

heart	corazón (core zone)
brains	sesos (say so's)
foot	pie (P.A.)
arm	brazo (emBRACE)
neck	cuello (quail)
back	espalda (scalda your 'spalda)
chest	pecho (pitcher)
beard	barba (barber)
moustache	bigotes (bigots)
blind	ciego (ciego in San Diego)
no one	nadie ("there's nadie like Nadia")

Close cognates used in the lecture such as *elefante* and *gorila* are not presented
in the priming exercise. Nor are all of the noncognates presented, but enough are,
so that on first hearing the students can follow the lecture, inferring the meaning

of some of the unfamiliar parts from context. Most students enjoy the challenge and the novelty of it.

Here is a small part of the script for that first preparatory lecture. Students have the bilingual script as well as a cassette recording of the Spanish part only.

He is a very bad giant.	Es un gigante muy malo.
He is mean.	Es malvado.
His name is Goliath.	Su nombre es Goliát.
Goliath is very tall and very strong.	Goliát es muy alto y muy fuerte.
As tall as a giraffe.	Tan alto como una jirafa.
And as strong as an elephant.	Y tan fuerte como un elefante.
His neck and his shoulders are those of a buffalo.	Su cuello y sus hombros son los de un búfalo.
His back and his chest are those of a gorilla.	Su espalda y su pecho son los de un gorila.
But his heart is very small, and full of hate.	Pero su corazón es muy pequeño, y lleno de odio.
He doesn't like anyone.	El no quiere a nadie.
Not even his mother.	Ni a su madre.
He hates her. He hates the entire human race.	La odia. Odia a todo el género humano.

BILINGUAL STORIES

One of our aims in language teaching is to produce "robust" learners who can and will learn on their own out of class. To promote this we provide copious materials for out-of-class study, including the inductive grammar lessons "Discovering How Spanish Works." Also included are two types of bilingual readers: a Burling reader (described in Part Two above) and another type which we call a Gomez bilingual reader. The small piece of "Mi Primera Visita a México" printed below is an example of a Gomez Bilingual Reader, intended, like the Burling reader, as an initial learning activity for a beginning student. Instructions to the reader suggest: let yourself listen and read through the story, inferring the meaning of the Spanish from the context. Don't expect to understand everything the first time through; just enjoy the story to the extent you can follow it.

MI PRIMERA VISITA A MEXICO
A Bilingual Story
(a section near the beginning)

After enjoying *la música por unos minutos* I walked through *la plaza*, crossed *(crucé) la calle central y entré en un restaurante* next to *El Hotel Casa Blanca.*

I sat down at *una mesa* and was *admirando el vaso de flores en medio de la mesa* when I heard *una voz* behind me which asked:

— *Un menú, señor?*

It was *realmente la voz de un ángel!* I looked and saw *una señorita muy bonita, una princesa encantadora.*

— *No, gracias,* I responded. *Chile con carne, por favor, y papas fritas.*
— *Una botella de vino, quizás? O un vaso de leche pasteurizada?*
— *No, muchas gracias, señorita. Sólo agua purificada.*

— *Perdón, señor, no tenemos agua purificada. Tenemos agua filtrada. ¿Está bien?*
— *Sí, está bien. Y un vaso de agua filtrada, por favor.*
— *Bueno, chile con carne y un vaso de agua. ¿Sólo eso?*
— *Sólo eso, gracias.*

La señorita era muy simpática. She must have had 18 *años.* . .

FAMILIAR NARRATIVES

A prominent feature of instructional materials is the copious use of familiar stories. We use stories from classic children's literature (The Boy Who Cried Wolf, The Little Red Hen, The Three Little Pigs, etc.); also universally appreciated stories from Bible literature (The Prodigal Son, David and Goliath, etc.). Adult students find that these classic stories have both simplicity and emotional power, and serve not only to entertain but to teach in an unforgettable way.

Of course, there is nothing new in using familiar stories. What we do with them, however, may be out of the ordinary. We have cast the children's stories in several versions, each telling the same story from beginning to end, but each adding progressively more detail to the previous version. Before each version we provide a preparatory or "priming" exercise. The first version tells the story in skeletal form, so simply that it can be presented the very first day of class. The final version is sufficiently elaborate to entertain native speakers. The students have both the script and the dramatic recording for out-of-class preparation. In class they hear ad lib versions of the same story—embellished and sometimes twisted a bit to keep the students on their toes. At all stages their familiarity with the story provides a measure of predictability or redundancy that carries understanding a long way. The illustrations and the teacher's paralinguistic expression of course increase the redundancy and can add very much to the enjoyment of the stories.

For what we wish to achieve in the initial thrust into a language we sense that stories constitute a more logical and natural entry point than dialogues. For one thing a story is a gestalt with its own logical progession. It is therefore far easier for the initial learner to learn than an equally long situational dialogue. For another thing the linguistic competence required to tell a story is far less than that required to converse creatively with native speakers. Being a monologue, a story can be prepared in advance and performed without fear of interruption. Furthermore it is easier to find a natural occasion to tell a story out of the classroom than to recite a dialogue. In our thinking the place of concentrated work on situational dialogue in language training is generally after, not before, a foundation has been laid through familiar stories and other materials.

We also suspect that there may even be some incalculable benefit in using stories known to the learners since childhood. It may in some subtle way suggest that as language learners they should become like children, casting off their adult inhibitions against language learning, letting themselves get caught up in these moral and heroic tales, reexperiencing their simplicity, beauty, and power.

Children's Literature

Here is a piece of one of the classic children's stories prepared in progressively more elaborate versions.

LOS TRES COCHINITOS
The Three Pigs
(Skeletal Version)

Priming

house	casa	(La Casa Blanca means the White House)
of straw	de paja	(HAHA! de PAJA!)
sticks	leños	(LANE YOSemite)
brick	ladrillo	(la three-O—la dhree-O)
a pig	un cochino	(COACH INO)
piggy	cochinito	(COACH INITO)
a wolf	un lobo	(LOW BOW)
comes	viene	(VIENE to VIENNA)
leaves	sale	(He will SALE and SALLY forth)
falls	se cae	(SAY CAE from on HIGH)
blows	sopla	(HOOPLA)
escapes	se escapa	
with hunger	con hambre	

1

Three little pigs.   Tres cochinitos.

2

Three houses.   Tres casas.
One house of straw.   Una casa de paja.
One house of sticks.   Una casa de leños.
One house of bricks.   Una casa de ladrillos.

3

A wolf.   Un lobo.
He comes with hunger.   Viene con hambre.
He comes to the house of straw.   Viene a la casa de paja.
He blows.   Sopla.

4

The house of straw falls.   La casa de paja se cae.
But the little pig escapes.   Pero el cochinito se escapa.

5

The wolf comes another time.   El lobo viene otra vez.
He comes to the house of sticks. . .   Viene a la casa de leños. . .

(The beginning of the Intermediate Version)

1

Three little pigs.   Tres cochinitos.
They were brothers.   Eran hermanos.
But they were not the same.   Pero no eran iguales.

2

They want to build their own houses.   Ellos quieren construir sus propias casas.
One sees a man with straw. . .   Uno ve a un hombre con paja. . .

(The beginning of the Advanced Version)

1	
There were once three pigs.	Había una vez tres cochinos.
They were brothers,	Eran hermanos,
but they were not the same.	pero no eran iguales.

2	
One day they were talking. . .	Un día estaban hablando. . .

Bible Literature

The familiar stories from the Bible we treat quite differently. With them we use a quasi-suggestopaedia approach, combined with Community Language Learning techniques. There is no priming in preparation for listening. There is no "wading in the shallow end of the pool" to get the learners used to the feel of the water. Rather we jump right into the dramatic narrative. The scripts are long and elaborated far beyond the original in the source text. In the Bible, for example, the part of the Moses story we have adapted occupies less than a page. Our "Cecil B. DeMille version" extends to almost 20 pages. Reproduced below are two sections of one of the Bible stories.

The full version of this narrative—all 16 pages—as well as considerable other material—was, believe it or not, presented the first day in the 4-week course described above. In the next 3 weeks two other equally long scripts were presented—in addition to a great deal of material of other kinds.

The narrative is intended to be read slowly by the teacher, allowing time for the students to get the meaning from across the page, but with dramatic intensity against a background of classical music. My aim in this (taken from Lozanov) is to produce an intensely felt emotional impact from a powerful story told simply and artistically. I agree with him that art and aesthetic enjoyment and a profound emotional experience can combine to enhance learning.

Students are expected to have the script open to them in the class, and for out-of-class use are given a recording of the dramatic narrative as well, with the suggestion that they listen to it before retiring to bed each night until the next class session.

The narrative serves as the engine from which a great amount of commentary and dialogue is generated through a variety of activities. For example, we tell simply but with much embellishment portions of the story, using mostly words introduced in the original.

It is obvious that, judged by conventional standards, the vocabulary load is simply enormous—many times the amount presented in conventional approaches. Likewise, judged by the same standards, the grammar load is unconscionably heavy. (The story has regular and irregular verbs, for example, in present, past and future tense, preterite and imperfect aspect, indicative and subjunctive modes.) But conventional standards evolved from looking at a very different philosophy of instruction, and they simply are not relevant for judging the kind of instruction that assumes language acquisition to be a natural process that thrives in linguistically rich soil.

Again, the purpose kept constantly in mind is to provide not only comprehensible input at the $i + 1$ level but input that is artistic and emotionally charged. This produces an effect very different from beginning with such conventional alternatives as

This is a pen. That is a table.
Is this a pen?
Yes, this is a pen.
Is this a table?
No, this is a pen. That is a table.

or

My name is George. I live in New York. I am a teacher.

or

Hello. How are you?
I'm fine, thanks, And you?
Just fine.

A subtle suggestion conveyed by this approach is, as Lozanov has suggested, that language is not a formidable enemy to be conquered through an emotionally draining, painful, and drawn-out struggle, or a mountain to be climbed one small, measured step at a time. Rather language acquisition is a natural growth process that is nurtured by contact with the fertile soil of mentally and artistically stimulating communication. Language acquisition is nourished through opportunity to use the language to understand and, with gentle guidance, to communicate meaningfully things that are deeply felt.

In the activities following the presentation of what we call the "drama" (equivalent to the "concert session" in Suggestopedia) the students participate in dialogue at will, using English until ready to launch into Spanish, and the teacher proceeds as if he spoke only Spanish but could understand their English, responding to whatever they communicate, whether it is in English or Spanish, by focusing on its meaning, not its form. Thus we deal with significant literature and we talk meaningfully about human experience and ideas of some consequence right from the first day.

By the second or third session students are invited to role-play imaginary situations based on the narrative—for example, an interview between a traveler and the repentant "prodigal son" on his way home. In these role-plays we use the counsel-learning technique we call the "angel on the shoulder," in which a Spanish model is supplied in the ear of the speaker to match whatever he says in English or in faulty Spanish. Thus we marry a "Lozanov approach" with a "Curran approach." It seems that the power of both is enhanced.

These narratives and accompanying activities serve as the large bulk of materials necessary to form the "critical mass." They provide the principal "gem mine" from which, as the students discover the scope and breadth of expression available therein and move deeper into understanding the idiom, they can pluck their own "gems."

Here are two small portions of the version of "The Lost Son" used in the course described.

EL HIJO PERDIDO

THE LOST SON

(A section near the middle)

Se va a una ciudad lejana.	He goes to a distant city.
En la ciudad, como se pueden imaginar,	In the city, as you can imagine,
pronto se encuentra con malos amigos.	he soon finds himself with bad friends.
Y con ellos vive una vida corrupta.	And with them he lives a corrupt life.
Una mañana se levanta sin dinero y sin amigos.	He wakes up one morning without money and without friends.
No hay nadie quien le quiera.	There is no one that loves him.
Justamente cuando Juanito no tiene más dinero	Just when Johnny has no more money
viene un hambre, una gran escasez de comida en la tierra.	there comes a famine—a great lack of food in the land.
Y Juanito comienza a sufrir.	And Johnny begins to suffer.
Ahora está sucio. Está enfermo.	Now he is dirty. He is sick.
Tiene miedo. Miedo de que va a morir. . .	He is afraid. Afraid he is going to die. .

(A section near the end)

Su papá está parado en una elevación de donde puede ver el camino.	His father is standing on a hill from where he can see the road.
De repente ve la silueta de un joven que viene en el camino.	Suddenly he sees the silhouette of a young man coming down the road.
No lo reconoce por su ropa.	He doesn't recognize him by his clothes.
Pues la ropa está despedazada y sucia.	The clothes are tattered and dirty.
Anda descalzo y cogeando.	He is walking barefoot and limping.
Pero el papá reconoce a su hijo.	But the father recognizes his son.
¡Allí está mi hijo!	There's my son.
¡Juanito ha vuelto a casa!. . .	Johnny has come home!. . .

The following is a sample of a taped module in *Spanish with Pleasure* that was provided as home-study material for the course. Like the grammar induction module which was also provided, obviously this is designed for "formal learning." No time was spent in class on pronunciation drill or explanation or on grammar drill or explanation.

PRONUNCIATION AND READING

Hierarchy of Errors

There are two levels of pronunciation errors that Americans typically make when they are learning Spanish pronunciation:

1. They totally mispronounce some sounds—usually vowel sounds—so that their words are totally incomprehensible.
2. They slightly or seriously mispronounce other sounds—usually consonant sounds—so that their Spanish pronunciation is heavily accented and comprehension is impaired.

Part 1: Spanish Vowels in Contrast to English Vowels

We will focus first on Spanish vowels in contrast to English vowels, since they are most basic to acquiring understandable pronunciation.

In Spanish each vowel letter must be pronounced. Each vowel letter represents only one sound. It may help you to think of the spoken scale: do re mi fa SU, in which each vowel letter represents its proper sound in Spanish.

Presentation and Practice

1. *a* (the vowel sound of *fa*). Note that the letter a represents only the vowel sound of fa. Spanish a is never pronounced as in fat or fate. The sound [a] is never represented in Spanish in any way other than by the letter a.

Repeat: papá, mamá, nana, tata, han, al, hamaca

NOTE: The vowel sounds of the English words pat, pit, put, putt do not occur in Spanish. In pronouncing Spanish words you must learn to avoid these sounds. They characterize a gross "gringo" accent.

Distinguishing Native Pronunciation from a "Gringo" Accent

1. Focus on *a*. Each word will be read on tape, once with a Spanish accent, once with a "gringo" accent. Repeat the pronunciations as you hear them on the tape, then mark which reading, (a or b) is the Spanish one. (Keep in mind that the letter a in Spanish is pronounced always as in wand, never as in band.
    1 Alma   (a)   (b)
    2 Nevada   (a)   (b)

Anticipating the Native Model.

Each number is called on the tape, followed by a short pause, followed by a native Spanish rendition of the given word. In the pause after the number is called, read the Spanish word, taking special care with the pronunciation of a, then listen for and repeat the native Spanish model as many times as it is given.

	(pause)	(native model)	(repeat)
1 Alamo	—	—	—
2 Alaska	—	—	—

From the above some idea can be taken as to how the course was organized and what the materials contained. Incidentally the course contained no word or sentence modeling for repetition, no "pattern practice" or "structural drill," no memorization of dialogues, no translation exercises, and no mention of grammar or use of grammatical terminology in class. On the other hand, a significant amount of the 21 hours was invested in Silent Way, Community Language Learning, Total Physical Response, Gomez' Participatory Learning, and other activities that, it seems, articulate well with or flow naturally from the structured curriculum described.

It is recognized that some regard certain of the principles and practices combined in this course as antithetically opposed to each other. Though recognizing that that may pose a problem in the minds of some of the originators or proponents of one method or another, I am not satisfied that any current view of language learning is sufficiently developed to guide our instructional approach exclusively. I am not satisfied that we fully understand what goes into language learning; hence I do not hesitate to use in one course what may in theory be conflicting principles. In fact the observed results of putting together the various techniques seem very positive.

Granted that one cannot simultaneously be following the techniques or principles of Gattegno and Lozanov, of Asher and Curran, of Terrell or Galyean and Harvey, but one can weave together an instructional program in which the principles and techniques of one are followed for a time and then replaced by the principles and techniques of another. Unfortunately, if the result of a given "mix" turns out well, one cannot identify any one part of the mix as the determining cause. But an important question is whether a "mix" can be superior in some ways or for some purposes to any of the component "methodologically pure" approaches. At present we regard them as not only intercompatible but complementary.

It may be of interest to some readers to see a lesson sequence suggested for the first (approximately) 100 hours of self-instruction in *Spanish with Pleasure*, an IALA course in which each set of materials described above forms a module, each module being made up of several sections: a Burling reader module with several chapters, a pronunciation module, a grammar module, etc. It can be seen here how materials of both orientations are integrated. Those marked with (*) are basically formal-learning-oriented. The others are basically informal-acquisition-oriented. Those marked with (#) combine some of both but are predominantly informal-acquisition-oriented.

It may be noted again that the materials that make up the self-instructional course are both printed and recorded on cassette, and for a 100-hour course, in the interest of providing a "critical mass," their volume is extremely large.

SPANISH WITH PLEASURE
Lesson Sequence

I. Acquaintance Level

A
0   Introduction and Self-Test
1   The Three Little Pigs, Elementary Version (#)
2   Reading and Pronouncing Spanish, Lesson 1 (*)
3   Little Red Riding Hood, Elementary Version (#)
4   La Primera Visita, Part I

B
5   The Three Bears, Elementary Version (#)
6   Burling Reader Chapter 1
6a   Burling Reader Notes (*)
7   La Primera Visita, Part II
8   Discovering How Spanish Works, Lesson 1 (*)
9   The Three Little Pigs, Intermediate Version (#)

C
10   Burling Reader Chapter 2
10a   Burling Reader Notes (*)
11   Illustrated Lecture: "Giants and Monsters" (#)
12   Reading and Pronouncing Spanish, Lesson 2 (*)
13   David and Goliath: Background (#)

II. Familiarization Level

A

1   The Three Billy Goats, Reduced Version (#)
2   Burling Reader Chapter 3
2a Burling Reader Notes (*)
3   Discovering How Spanish Works, Lesson 2 (*)
4   Little Red Riding Hood, Intermediate Version (#)

B

5   The Three Billy Goats, Full Version (#)
6   Burling Reader Chapter 4
6a Burling Reader Notes (*)
7   Chicken Little
8   David and Goliath, Reduced Version (#)

C

9   Little Red Hen, Reduced Version (#)
10 Discovering How Spanish Works, Lesson 3 (*)
11 David and Goliath, Full Version (#)
12 The Three Bears, Intermediate Version (#)

III. Foundation Level

A

1   The Three Little Pigs, Advanced Version (#)
2   Burling Reader Chapter 5
3   Little Red Hen, Full Version (#)
4   The Lost Son

B

5   Little Red Riding Hood, Advanced Version (#)
6   Burling Reader Chapter 6
7   Discovering How Spanish Works, Lesson 4(*)
8   The Blind Beggar

C

9   Burling Reader Chapter 7
10 The Three Bears, Advanced Version (#)
11 Moses I
12 Review of First Illustrated Lecture (#)
13 Review of David and Goliath

D

14 Moses II
15 Review of Little Red Riding Hood; The Red Hen (#)
16 Review of The Lost Son

E

17 Moses III
18 Review of The Blind Beggar
19 Review of Three Pigs; Three Billygoats (#)

Most of the modules are internally graded in difficulty, but each module is independent of the others. Since the suggested sequence is not binding, the individual learner is free to choose among countless alternatives. For example, the learner may like the Burling reader so much he or she will prefer to go through all seven chapters without interruption, and then perhaps go back again for review before starting a second module such as Pronunciation and Reading. And if the learner doesn't feel that that module provides what is most satisfying at the time, he or she may leave it and try another. This is reminiscent of dining at a smorgasbord restaurant. Not only is the instruction self-paced but also its components and their sequence are self-selected.

In summary let me restate that our aim has been to create and experiment with a learner-adaptive instructional system rich enough and versatile enough to accommodate a broad range of learning needs and learning styles, including, of course, those of the gifted learners. The teaching system we have designed and the instructional modules we have developed provide a smorgasbord of choices which allow an experimenter, a teacher, or individual students in a class or in self-instruction to make up their own study syllabus from a great variety of possible combinations.

BIBLIOGRAPHY

Andersen, Roger W. 1978. An implicational model for second language research. *Language Learning*, 28:221–282.

Andersen, Roger W. 1979. Expanding Schumann's pidginization hypothesis. *Language Learning*, 29:105–117.

Asher, James J. 1972a. Children's first language as a model for second language learning. *The Modern Language Journal*, 56:133–139.

Asher, James J. 1972b. Implications of psychological research for second language learning. In Dale L. Lange and Charles J. James (editors), *Foreign Language Education: A Reappraisal* (Britannica Reviews of Foreign Language Education; Volume 4). Skokie, Illinois: National Textbook Company.

Asher, James J. 1977. Children learning another language: A developmental hypothesis. *Child Development*, 48:1040–1048.

Asher, James J. 1981. Fear of foreign languages. *Psychology Today*, 15(8):52–59.

Asher, James J., and B. S. Price. 1967. The learning strategy of the total physical response: Some age differences. *Child Development*, 38:4.

Asher, James J., and R. Garcia. 1969. The optimal age to learn a foreign language. *The Modern Language Journal*, 53:334–341.

Asher, James J., J. Kusudo, and R. de la Torre. 1974. Learning a second langauge through commands: The second field test. *Modern Language Journal*, 58:24–32.

Bailey, N., C. Madden, and S. Krashen. 1974. Is there a natural sequence in adult second language learning? *Language Learning*, 24:234–244.

Begin, Yves. 1971. *Evaluative and Emotional Factors in Learning a Foreign Language*. Montreal, Canada: Les Editions Bellarmin.

Bellamy, Martha M., and Sidney E. Bellamy. 1970. The acquisition of morphological inflections by children four to ten. *Language Learning*, 20:199–211.

Benseler, David P., and Renate A. Schulz. 1980. Methodological trends in college foreign language instruction. *The Modern Language Journal*, 64:88–96.

Bertkua, Jana Svoboda. 1974. An analysis of English learner speech. *Language Learning*, 24:279–286.

Bialystok, Ellen. 1978. A theoretical model of second language learning. *Language Learning*, 28:69–83.

Bloomfield, Leonard. 1942. *Outline Guide for the Practical Study of Foreign Languages*. Baltimore: Special Publication of the Linguistic Society of America.

Bolinger, Dwight. 1970. Getting the words in. *American Speech*, 45:78–84.

Brooks, Nelson H. 1964. *Language and Language Learning Theory and Practice*. New York: Harcourt Brace.

Brown, H. Douglas. 1972. Cognitive pruning and second language acquisition. *Language Learning*, 56:218–222.

Brown, H. Douglas. 1973. Affective variables in second language acquisition. *Language Learning*, 23:231–244.

Brown, H. Douglas. 1980. *Principles of Language Learning and Teaching*. Englewood Cliffs, N.J.: Prentice-Hall.

Burt, M., H. Dulay, and M. Finocchiaro (editors). 1977. *Viewpoints on English as a Second Language*. New York, Regents.

Carroll, John B. 1953. *The Study of Language*. Cambridge, Mass.: Harvard University Press.

Carroll, John B. 1960. Wanted: A research basis for educational policy on foreign language teaching. *Harvard Educational Review*, 30:128–140.

Carroll, John B. 1964. The contributions of psychological theory and educational research to the teaching of foreign languages. *Moderner Fremdsprachenunterricht*. Berlin: Pedagogisches Zentrum.

Carroll, John B. 1966. Some neglected relationships in reading and language learning. *Elementary English*, 43:577–582.

Carroll, John B. 1969. What does the Pennsylvania foreign language research project tell us? *Foreign Language Annals*, 3:194–207.

Carroll, John B. 1974. Learning theory for the classroom teacher. In G. A. Jarvis (editor), *The Challenge of Communication. ACTFL Review of Foreign Language Education*, vol. 6. Skokie, Ill.: National Textbook.

Casey, D. J. 1968. The effectiveness of two methods of teaching English and foreign languages in some Finnish secondary schools. Helsinki: Institute of Education, No. 24.

Celce-Murcia, Marianne, and Lois McIntosh (editors). 1979. *Teaching of English as a Second or Foreign Language*. Rowley, Mass.: Newbury House Publishers.

Chastain, Kenneth D. 1975. Affective and ability factors in second language acquisition. *Language Learning*, 25:153–161.

Cohen, Andrew D. 1975. Error correction and the training of language teachers. *The Modern Language Journal*, 59.8:414–422.

Cohen, Andrew D. 1977. Successful second language speakers: A review of research literature. *Balshanut Shimushit. Journal of the Israel Association for Applied Linguistics*, 1:3–21.

Cook, Vivian. 1969. The analogy between first and second language learning. *International Review of Applied Linguistics*, 7:207–216.

Cook, Vivian. 1973. Comparison of language development in native children and foreign adults. *International Review of Applied Linguistics*, 11:13–28.

Corder, S. P. 1967. The significance of learner's errors. *International Review of Applied Linguistics*, 5:161–167.

Corder, S. P. 1971. Idiosyncratic dialects and error analysis. *International Review of Applied Linguistics*, 5:161–170.

Corder, S. P. 1975. The language of second language learners: The broader issues. *The Modern Language Journal*, 59.8:409–413.

Currie, William. 1975. European syllabuses in English as a foreign language. *Language Learning*, 25:339–354.

Dalbor, J. 1972. *Beginning College Spanish*. New York: Random.

d'Anglejan, Alison. 1978. Language learning in and out of classrooms. In Jack C. Richards (editor), *Understanding Second and Foreign Language Learning: Issues and Approaches*, Rowley, Mass.: Newbury House Publishers.

Diller, Karl. 1971. *The Language Teaching Controversy*. Rowley, Mass.: Newbury House Publishers.

Dubin, Fraida, and Elite Olshtain. 1977. *Facilitating Language Learning*. New York: McGraw-Hill.

Dulay, Heidi C., and Marina K. Burt. 1972. Goofing: An indicator of children's second language learning strategies. *Language Learning*, 22:235–252.

Dulay, Heidi C., and Marina K. Burt. 1973. Should we teach children syntax? *Language Learning*, 23:245–258.

Dulay, Heidi C., and Marina K. Burt. 1974a. Errors and strategies in child second language learning acquisition. *TESOL Quarterly*, 8:129–136.

Dulay, H., and Marina K. Burt. 1974b. A new perspective on the creative construction process in child second language acquisition. *Working Papers on Bilingualism*, 4:71–97.

Dulay, Heidi C., and Marina K. Burt. 1974c. Natural sequences in child second language acquisition. *Language Learning*, 24:37–53.

Eckman, Fred R., and Ashley J. Hastings (editors). 1979. *Studies in First and Second Language Acquisition*. Rowley, Mass.: Newbury House Publishers.

Ellis, R. 1981. The role of input in language acquisition. *Applied Linguistics*, 2:70–82.

Ervin, S. M. 1964. Imitation and structural change in children's language. In E. H. Lenneberg (editor), *New Directions in the Study of Language*. Cambridge, Mass.: MIT Press.

Ervin-Tripp, Susan. 1971. An overview of theories of grammatical development. In D. Slobin, *The Ontogenesis of Grammar*. New York: Academic Press.

Ervin-Tripp, Susan. 1974. Is second language learning like the first? *TESOL Quarterly*, 8:111–127.

Fathman, Ann. 1975. The relationship between age and second language productive ability. *Language Learning*, 25:245–253.

Fillmore, Charles J., editor. 1979. *Individual Differences in Language Ability and Language Behavior*. New York: Academic Press.

Freeman, D. L. 1975. The acquisition of grammatical morphemes by adult ESL students. Paper presented at the annual TESOL Conference, Los Angeles.

Gardner, Robert, and Wallace E. Lambert. 1972. *Attitudes and Motivation in Second Language Learning*. Rowley, Mass.: Newbury House Publishers.

Geno, T H., and J. L. D. Clark, editors. 1980. *Our Profession: Present Status and Future Directions*. Middlebury, Vt.: Northeast Conference Reports (NCTFL).

Groberg, D. H. 1973. *Mnemonic Japanese*. Salt Lake City, Utah: Interac.

Guiora, Alexander Z., et al. 1971. The effects of experimentally induced changes in ego states on pronunciation ability in second language: An exploratory study. (Mimeographed) University of Michigan.

Hanzeli, Victor. 1975. Learner's language: Implications of recent research for foreign language instruction. *The Modern Language Journal*, 59.8:426–432.

Harris, Alan. 1978. "English as a second language, the conflict between harmony and invention, and some implications for an 'old/new' learning." Paper given at the 9th AILA Congress, Montreal, Quebec, Canada.

Hatch, Evelyn. 1974. Second language learning—universals? *Working Papers on Bilingualism*, 3:1–17.

Hatch, Evelyn. 1978a. Discourse analysis, speech acts and second language acquisition. In W. C. Ritchie (editor), *Second Language Acquisition Research*. New York: Academic Press.

Hatch, Evelyn. 1978b. Discourse analysis and second language acquisition. In Evelyn Hatch (editor), *Second Language Acquisition*. Rowley, Mass.: Newbury House Publishers.

Hatch, Evelyn. 1978c. Acquisition of syntax in a second language. In Jack C. Richards (editor), *Understanding Second and Foreign Language Learning: Issues and Approaches*. Rowley, Mass.: Newbury House Publishers.

Hatch, Evelyn. 1979. *Second Language Acquisition*. Rowley, Mass.: Newbury House Publishers.

Hauptman, Philip. 1971. A structural approach versus a situational approach to foreign language teaching. *Language Learning*, 21:235–244.

Henning, C. A. (editor). 1977. *Proceedings of the Los Angeles Second Acquisition Research Forum*. Los Angeles: USC Linguistics Department.

Henzl, Vera M. 1973. Linguistic register of foreign language instruction. *Language Learning*, 23:207–222.

Hill, Jane. 1970. Foreign accents, language acquisition, and cerebral dominance revisited. *Language Learning*, 20:237–248.

Holley, Freda M., and Janet K. King. 1971. Imitation and correction in foreign language learning. *The Modern Language Journal*, 55:494–498.

Jakobovits, Leon A. 1968. Implications of recent psycholinguistic developments for the teaching of a second language. *Language Learning*, 18:89–109.

Jakobovits, Leon A. 1970. *Foreign Language Learning: A Psycholinguistic Analysis of the Issues*. Rowley, Mass.: Newbury House Publishers.

Jakobovits, L. A., and B. Gordon. 1974. *The Context of Foreign Language Teaching*. Rowley, Mass.: Newbury House Publishers.

Jarvis, Gilbert. 1970. *A comparison of contextualized practice with particularized referents versus practice with generic meaning in the teaching of beginning college French*. Unpublished Ph.D. dissertation, Purdue University.

Joiner, Elizabeth. 1974. *Communicative versus noncommunicative language practice in teaching of beginning college French: A comparison of two treatments*. Unpublished Ph.D. dissertation, Ohio State University.

Kelly, Louis G. 1969. *Twenty-Five Centuries of Language Teaching*. Rowley, Mass.: Newbury House Publishers.

Krashen, Stephen. 1973. Lateralization, language learning, and the critical period: Some new evidence. *Language Learning*, 23:63–74.

Krashen, Stephen. 1976. Formal and informal linguistic environments in language acquisition and language learning. *TESOL Quarterly*, 10:157–168.

Krashen, Stephen. 1977a. The monitor model for adult second language performance. In M. Burt, H. Dulay, and M. Finocchiaro (editors), *Viewpoints on English as a Second Language*. New York: Regents.

Krashen, Stephen. 1977b. Some issues relating to the monitor model. In H. Douglas Brown et al. (editors), *On TESOL 77*. Washington, D.C.: TESOL.

Krashen, Stephen. 1978. Individual variation in the use of the monitor. In W. C. Ritchie (editor), *Second Language Acquisition Research*. New York: Academic Press.

Krashen, Stephen. 1979a. The monitor model for second language acquisition. In R. Gingras (editor), *Second Language Acquisition and Foreign Language Teaching*. Arlington, Virginia: Center for Applied Linguistics.

Krashen, Stephen. 1979b. A response to McLaughlin, "The monitor model: Some methodological considerations." *Language Learning*, 29:151–168.

Krashen, Stephen. 1979c. Relating theory to practice in adult second language acquisition. In S. elix (editor), *Recent Trends in Research on Second Language Acquisition*. Tübingen: TBL Gunter Narr.

Krashen, Stephen. 1980. The theoretical and practical relevance of simple codes. In R. Scarcella and S. Krashen (editors), *Second Language Acquisition*. Rowley, Mass.: Newbury House Publishers.

Krashen, Stephen, and P. Pon. 1975. An error analysis of an advanced ESL learner: The importance of the monitor. *Working Papers on Bilingualism*, 7:125–129.

Krashen, Stephen, and H. Seliger. 1975. The essential contributions of formal instruction in adult second language learning. *TESOL Quarterly*, 10:173–183.

Lado, Robert. 1964. *Language Teaching, a Scientific Approach*. New York: McGraw-Hill.

Lamendella, John T. 1977. General principles of neurofunctional organization and their manifestation in primary and nonprimary language acquisition. *Language Learning*, 27:155–196.

Lamendella, John T. 1979. The neurofunctional basis of pattern practice. *TESOL Quarterly*, 13:5–19.

Landes, James Earle. 1975. Speech addressed to children: Issues and characteristics of parental input. *Language Learning*, 25:355–379.

Larsen-Freeman, Diane. 1976. An explanation for the morpheme acquisition order of second language learners. *Language Learning*, 26:135–134.

Lenneberg, Eric. 1967. *Biological Foundations of Language*. New York: John Wiley and Sons.

Lester, Mark. 1970. *Readings in Applied Transformational Grammar*. New York: Holt, Rinehart and Winston, Inc.

Levin, L. 1969. Implicit and explicit (The GUME Project) Gothenburg, Sweden: Gothenburg School of Education.

Macnamara, John. 1973. Nurseries, streets and classrooms: Some comparisons and deductions. *Modern Language Journal*, 57:5–6.

Macnamara, John. 1975. Comparison between first and second language learning. *Working Papers on Bilingualism*, 7:71–94.

McNeil, D. 1966. Developmental psycholinguistics. In F. Smith and G. Miller (editors), *The Genesis of Language*. Cambridge, Mass.: MIT Press.

McNeil D. 1970. The creation of language. In R. C. Oldfield, *Language: Selected Readings*. Baltimore: Penguin Books.

Nida, Eugene A. 1971. Sociopsychological problems in language mastery and retention. In Paul Pimsleur and Terence Quinn (editors), *The Psychology of Second Language Learning*, Cambridge, England: Cambridge University Press, 59–65.

Oller, J. W. 1971. Language use and foreign language learning. *International Review of Applied Linguistics*, 9:161–168.

Oller, John W., and Jack C. Richards (editors). 1976. *Focus on the Learner: Pragmatic Perspectives for the Language Teacher*. Rowley, Mass.: Newbury House Publishers.

Palmer, Harold E. 1917. *The Scientific Study and Teaching of Languages*. Yonkers-on-Hudson, New York: World Book Company.

Penfield, W., and L. Roberts. 1959. *Speech and Brain Mechanisms*. Princeton: Princeton University Press.

Peters, Ann M. 1977. Language learning strategies: Does the whole equal the sum of the parts? *Language*, 53:3.

Ravem, Roar. 1968. Language acquisition in a second language environment. *International Review of Applied Linguistics*, 6:175–185.

Reibel, David A. 1969. Language learning analysis. *International Review of Applied Linguistics*, 7:283–294.

Richards, Jack C. 1972. Social factors, interlanguage and language learning. *Language Learning*, 22:159–188.

Richards, Jack C. (editor). 1974. *Error Analysis: Perspectives on Second Language Acquisition*. London: Longmans.

Richards, Jack C. 1975. Simplification: A strategy in the adult acquisition of a foreign language: An example from Indonesian/Malay. *Language Learning*, 25:115–126.

Richards, Jack C. 1976. Second language learning. In Wardhaugh and Brown (editors), *The Contexts of Language*. Rowley, Mass.: Newbury House Publishers.

Richards, Jack C. 1978. *Understanding Second and Foreign Language Learning*. Rowley, Mass.: Newbury House Publishers.

Rivers, Wilga M. 1964. *The Psychologist and the Foreign Language Teacher*. Chicago: University of Chicago Press.

Rosansky, Ellen J. 1975. The critical period for the acquisition of language: Some cognitive developmental considerations. *Working Papers on Bilingualism*, 6:92–102.

Savignon, Sandra. 1972. *Communicative Competence: An Experiment in Foreign Language Teaching*. Philadelphia: Center for Curriculum Development.

Scarcella, Robin, and S. Krashen (editors). 1980. *Research in Second Language Acquisition*. Rowley, Mass.: Newbury House Publishers.

Schulz, Renate. 1974. *Discrete point versus simulated communication testing on the development of communicative proficiency in beginning college French classes*. Unpublished Ph.D. dissertation, Ohio State University.

Schumann, John H. 1976a. Second language acquisition: The pidginization hypothesis. *Language Learning*, 26:391–408.

Schumann, John H. 1976b. Second language acquisition research: Getting a more global look at the learner. *Language Learning*, Special Issue No. 4:15–28.

Schumann, John H. 1976c. Social distance as a factor in second language acquisition. *Language Learning*, 26:135–143.

Schumann, John H. 1978a. The acculturation model for second language acquisition. In R. C. Gingras (editor), *Second Language Acquisition and Foreign Language Teaching*. Arlington, Virginia: Center for Applied Linguistics.

Schumann, John H. 1978b. Second language acquisition. In Jack C. Richards (editor), *Understanding Second and Foreign Language Learning: Issues and Approaches*. Rowley, Mass.: Newbury House Publishers.

Schumann, John H., and Nancy Stenson (editors). 1974. *New Frontiers in Second Language Learning*. Rowley, Mass.: Newbury House Publishers.

Scovil, Thomas. 1978. The effect of affect on foreign language learning: A review of the anxiety research. *Language Learning*, 23:129–142.

Seliger, Herbert W. 1979. On the nature and function of language rules in language teaching. *TESOL Quarterly*, 13:3.

Selinker, Larry. 1972. Interlanguage. *International Review of Applied Linguistics*, 10:201–231.

Slobin, D. 1969. Questions of language development in cross cultural perspective. In *Structure of Linguistic Input to Children*, Working Paper Number 14, Language Behavior Research Laboratory, University of California, Berkeley.

Smith, Frank. 1975. *Comprehension and Learning: A Conceptual Framework for Teachers*. New York: Holt, Rinehart and Winston.

Smith, Frank. 1977. Making sense of language learning. In John F. Fanselow and Ruth H. Crymes (editors), *On TESOL 76*, Washington, D.C.:TESOL.

Smith, P. D., Jr., and Helmut Baranyi. 1968. *A comparison study of the effectiveness of the traditional and audiolingual approaches to foreign language instruction using laboratory equipment*. Final Report Project No. 7–0133, U.S. Office of Education.

Smith, P. D., Jr., and Emanuel Berger. 1968. *An assessment of three foreign language teaching strategies utilizing three language laboratory systems*. Final Report Project No. 5–00683, U.S. Office of Education (ERIC Document No. ED 021512).

Snow, Catherine, and Charles A. Ferguson. 1977. *Talking to Children: Language Input and Acquisition*. Cambridge: Cambridge University Press.

Sorenson, Arthur. 1967. Multilingualism in the northwest Amazon. *American Anthropologist*, 69:670–684.

Spolsky, Bernard. 1969. Attitudinal aspects of second language learning. *Language Learning*, 19:271–283.

Spolsky, Bernard. 1970. Linguistics and language pedagogy—applications or implications. *Monograph on Languages and Linguistics*, 22 (Report of the 20th Annual Round Table Meeting, Georgetown University).

Stauble, Ann-Marie E. 1978. The process of decreolization: A model for second language development. *Language Learning*, 28:29–54.

Stern, H. H. 1970. *Perspectives on Second Language Teaching*. Toronto: Ontario Institute for Studies in Education.

Stevick, Earl W. 1973a. A riddle, with some hints for its solution. *Program and Training Journal*. Washington, D.C.: Peace Corps.

Stevick, Earl W. 1973b. Before linguistics and beneath method. In Kurt R. Jankowsky (editors), *Proceedings of the Georgetown Round Table on Language and Linguistics*. Washington, D.C.: Georgetown University School of Languages and Linguistics.

Stevick, Earl W. 1974a. The meaning of drills and exercises.. *Language Learning*, 24:1–22.

Stevick, Earl W. 1974b. Language teaching must do an about-face. *Modern Language Journal*, 58:379–384.

Stevick, Earl W. 1976a. English as an alien language. In John F. Fanselow and Ruth H. Crymes (editors), *On TESOL 76*, Washington, D.C.: TESOL.

Stevick, Earl W. 1976b. *Memory, Meaning and Method: Some Psychological Perspectives on Language Learning.* Rowley, Mass.: Newbury House Publishers.

Stevick, Earl W. 1978. Toward a practical philosophy of pronunciation: Another view. *TESOL Quarterly,* 12:146–150.

Stevick, Earl W. 1981. *Teaching Languages: A Way and Ways.* Rowley, Mass.: Newbury House Publishers.

Taylor, Barry. 1974. Toward a theory of language acquisition. *Language Learning,* 24:23–36.

Taylor, Insup. 1978. Acquiring vs. learning a second language. *The Canadian Modern Language Review,* 34:455–472.

Titone, Renzo. 1968. *Teaching Foreign Languages: An Historical Sketch.* Washington, D.C.: Georgetown University Press.

Tucker, G. R., E. Hamayan, and F. H. Genesee. 1976. Affective, cognitive, and social factors in second language acquisition. *The Canadian Modern Language Review,* 32:214–226.

Valdman, Albert. 1975. Error analysis and grading in the preparation of teaching materials. *The Modern Language Journal,* 59:422–426.

Wagner-Gough, J., and Evelyn Hatch. 1975. The importance of input data in second language acquisition studies. *Language Learning.* 25:297–308.

Walsh, Terence M., and Karl C. Diller. 1978. Neurolinguistic foundations to methods of teaching a foreign language. International Review of Applied Linguistics. 15:1.

Wardhaugh, Ronald. 1976. *The Contexts of Language.* Rowley, Mass.: Newbury House Publishers.

Wardhaugh, Ronald, and H. Douglas Brown. 1976. *A Survey of Applied Linguistics.* Ann Arbor: University of Michigan Press.

Wilkins, D. A. 1972. *The Common Core in the Unit/Credit System.* London: British Council.

Wilson, Virginia, and Beverly Wattenmaker. 1973. *Real Communication in Foreign Language.* Upper Jay, New York: The Adirondack Mountain Humanistic Education Center.

Wolfe, David, and Philip Smith. 1972. Teacher education for new goals. In Dale Lange and Charles James (editors), *Foreign language education: A reappraisal. ACTFL Review of Foreign Language Education,* vol. 4. Skokie, Illinois: National Textbook Company, 97–126.

THE EVOLUTION OF THE COMPREHENSION APPROACH

Listening Comprehension

Three primary sources of information on varieties of listening-comprehension training and materials are: James Asher, Department of Psychology, San Jose State University, San Jose, California; James Nord, Learning and Evaluation Services, Michigan State University, East Lansing, Michigan; Harris Winitz, Department of Psychology, University of Missouri at Kansas City.

Asher, James J. 1965. The strategy of the total physical response: An application to learning Russian, International Review of Applied Linguistics. 3:291–300.

Asher, James J. 1966. The learning strategy of the total physical response: A review. *The Modern Language Journal,* 50:79–84.

Asher, James J. 1969a. The total physical response approach to second language learning. *The Modern Language Journal,* 53:1–17.

Asher, James J. 1969b. The total physical response technique of learning. *Journal of Special Education,* 3:253–262.

Asher, James J. 1972. Children's first language as a model for second language learning. *The Modern Language Journal,* 56:133–139.

Asher, James J. 1977. *Learning Another Language through Actions: The Complete Teacher's Guidebook.* 19544 Sky Oaks Way, Los Gatos, California: Sky Oaks Productions.

Belasco, Simon. 1965. Nucleation and the audio-lingual approach. *The Modern Language Journal*, 49:482–490.

Belasco, Simon. 1967. The plateau or the case for comprehension: The "concept" approach. *The Modern Language Journal*, 51:82–88.

Burling, Robbins. 1978. *Machine Aided Instruction in Aural Comprehension of Indonesian:* Final Report to the U.S. Office of Education.

Davies, Norman F. 1976. Receptive versus productive skills in foreign language learning. *The Modern Language Journal*, 60:440–443.

Davies, Norman. 1978. *Putting Receptive Skills First: An Investigation into Sequencing in Modern Language Learning.* Institutionen för Språk och Litteratur, Linköping University: Linköping, Sweden.

Dye, J.C. 1976. *The use of body movement to facilitate second language learning for school students: Listening and speaking—A teacher's guide.* Ph.D. dissertation, Department of Curriculum and Teaching, The City University of New York.

Gary, Judith Olmstead. 1975. Delayed oral practice in initial stages of second language learning. In M. K. Burt and H. C. Dulay (editors), *New Directions in Second Language Teaching, Learning and Bilingual Education.* Washington, D.C.: TESOL.

Gary, Judith Olmstead. 1978. Why speak if you don't need to? The case for a listening approach to beginning foreign language learning. In W. C. Ritchie, *Second Language Acquisition Research.* New York: Academic Press.

Gary, Judith Olmstead. 1981. Caution: Talking may be dangerous to your linguistic health. *International Review of Applied Linguistics*, 19:1–14.

Gauthier, Robert. 1963. Tan-Gau—a natural method for learning a second language, *Teacher's Guide to Accompany the Tan-Gau Method.* Toronto: W. J. Gage.

Kalivoda, T. B., G. Morain, and R. J. Elkins. 1971. The audio-motor unit: A listening comprehension strategy that works. *Foreign Language Annals*, 4:392–400.

King, J. K. 1976. Language for communication—A report on the University of Texas experiment. Department of Germanic Language, the University of Texas: Austin, Texas.

Newmark, Leonard. 1966. How not to interfere with language learning. *International Journal of American Linguistics*, 32(1): part II (January).

Newmark, Leonard. 1967. Notes on the study of language acquisition. *Actes du Xe Congrès International de Linguistes*, III:245–250.

Newmark, Leonard, and David A. Reibel. 1970. Necessity and sufficiency in language learning. *International Review of Applied Linguistics*, IV:2.

Ney, J. W. 1976. Review of Harris Winitz and James Reeds, *Comprehension and Problem Solving as Strategies for Language Training. TESOL Quarterly*, 10.

Nida, Eugene A. 1958. Some psychological problems in second language learning. *Language Learning*, 6:1.

Nida, Eugene A. 1971. Sociopsychological problems in language mastery and retention. In Paul Pimsleur and T. Quinn (editors), *The Psychology of Second Language Learning.* Cambridge, Cambridge University Press, 59–65.

Nord, James R. 1975a. A case for listening comprehension. *Philologia*, 7:1–25.

Nord, James R. 1975b. The Sens-it-Cell. *System*, 3:16–23.

Nord, James R. 1975c. The importance of listening. *Eigo Kyoiku: The English Teachers Magazine*, 24:34–39.

Nord, James R. 1976. Shut-up and listen, a case for listening comprehension. ERIC Document Reproduction Service No. ED 122839.

Nord, James R. 1977. Error recognition as a self-monitoring skill. *System*, 5:158–164.

Nord, James R. 1978. Developing listening fluency before speaking: An alternative paradigm. Paper presented at the Fifth World Congress of Applied Linguistics, University of Montreal, Montreal, Quebec, Canada, August 1978.

Pimsleur, Paul, and T. Quinn (editors). 1971. *The Psychology of Second Language Learning.* Cambridge: Cambridge University Press.

Politzer, Robert L. 1965. *Foreign Language Learning: A Linguistic Introduction.* Englewood Cliffs, N.J.: Prentice-Hall.

Postovsky, Valerian A. 1970. *The effects of delay in oral practice at the beginning of second language teaching.* Unpublished Ph.D. dissertation, University of California at Berkeley.

Postovsky, Valerian A. 1975. On paradoxes in foreign language teaching. *The Modern Language Journal,* 59:18–22.

Postovsky, Valerian A. 1976. The priority of aural comprehension in the language acquisition process. *Proceedings of the 4th AILA Congress,* Stuttgart.

Sutherland, Kenton. 1978. Review of James J. Asher, *Learning Another Language through Actions: The Complete Teacher's Guidebook.* In *TESOL Quarterly,* June 1978.

Taylor, Barry. 1974. Toward a theory of language acquisition. *Language Learning,* 24:33–36.

Winitz, Harris. 1973. Problem solving and the delaying of speech as strategies in the teaching of language, *American Speech and Hearing Association,* 15,10.

Winitz, Harris, and James Reeds. 1973. Rapid acquisition of a foreign language (German) by the avoidance of speaking. *International Review of Applied Linguistics,* 11:295–315.

Winitz, Harris, and James Reeds. 1975. *Comprehension and Problem Solving as Strategies for Language Training.* The Hague: Mouton.

Winitz, Harris. 1981. *A Comprehension Approach to Foreign Language Teaching.* Rowley, Mass.: Newbury House Publishers.

Woodruff, M. 1976. Integration of the total physical response strategy into a first-year German program: From obeying commands to creative writing (Mimeo). Paper presented at the Spring Conference of the Texas Chapter of the American Association of Teachers of German, 1976.

Reading Comprehension Approaches

Burling, Robbins. 1968. Some outlandish proposals for the teaching of foreign languages. *Language Learning,* 18:61–75.

Burling, Robbins. 1978. An introductory course in reading French. *Language Learning,* 28:105–128.

Swaffar, J. K., and M. S. Woodruff. 1978. Language for comprehension: Focus on reading; a report on the University of Texas German Program. *The Modern Language Journal,* 62:27–32.

APPROACHES TO A RICH ACQUISITION ENVIRONMENT

Integrated Acquisition-Learning Approach (IALA)

The primary source of information on IALA is Robert W. Blair, Linguistics Department, Brigham Young University, Provo, Utah 84602.

Counsel-learning/Community Language Learning (C-L/CLL)

The primary source of books and information on C-L/CLL is The Counseling-Learning Institutes, P.O. Box 383, East Dubuque, Illinois 61025.

Brady, Thomas, 1975. *A study in the application of a counseling-learning model for adults.* Ph.D. dissertation: Walden University, Florida.

Brown, H. Douglas. 1978. Some limitations of C-L/CLL models of second language teaching. *TESOL Quarterly,* 11:365–372.

Curran, Charles A. 1966. Counseling in the educative process: A foreign language learning integration. (Unpublished manuscript.)

Curran, Charles A. 1968. *Counseling and Psychotherapy: The Pursuit of Values.* New York: Sheed and Ward.

Curran, Charles A. 1972. *Counseling-Learning: A Whole-Person Model for Education.* New York: Grune and Stratton.

Curran, Charles A. 1976. *Counseling-Learning in Second Languages.* Apple River, Ill.: Apple River Press.

Czarnecki, Karen E., and Joseph A. Ramos. 1975. Counseling-learning: A holistic view of the learner, *TESOL Newsletter,* December.

Gallagher, Rosina. 1973. *Counseling-learning theory applied to foreign language learning.* Ph.D. dissertation, Loyola University, Chicago.

LaFarga, Juan. 1966. *Learning foreign languages in group-counseling conditions.* Ph.D. dissertation, Loyola University, Chicago.

LaForge, Paul G. 1971. Community language learning: A pilot study. *Language Learning,* 21:45–61.

LaForge, Paul G. 1975a. *Research Profiles with Community Language Learning.* Apple River, Illinois: Counseling-Learning Institutes.

LaForge, Paul G. 1975b. Community language learning: The Japanese case. In F. Peng (editor), *Language in Japanese Society: Current Issues in Sociolinguistics.* Tokyo: The University of Tokyo Press.

LaForge, Paul G. 1977. Uses of social silence in the interpersonal dynamics of Community Language Learning. *TESOL Quarterly,* 11:373–382.

LaForge, Paul G. 1979a. The epigenetic principle in Community Language Learning. *JALT Journal,* 1:7–21.

LaForge, Paul G. 1979b. Reflection in the context of Community Language Learning. *English Language Teaching Journal,* 33:247–254.

Rardin, Jennybelle. 1971. *Task-oriented counseling experiences for slow-learning third graders.* Ph.D. dissertation: Loyola University, Chicago.

Rardin, Jennybelle. 1976. A counseling-learning model for second language learning. *TESOL Newsletter* 10 (April 2):21–22.

Rardin, Jennybelle. 1977. The language teacher as facilitator. *TESOL Quarterly,* 11:383–388.

Stevick, Earl W. 1973. Review of Charles A. Curran, *Counseling-Learning: A Whole-Person Model for Education. Language Learning,* 23:259–271.

Stevick, Earl W. 1976. *Memory, Meaning and Method: Some Psychological Perspectives on Language Learning.* Rowley, Mass: Newbury House Publishers.

Stevick, Earl W. 1979. An experience with CLL. *Cross Currents,* 6:1–14.

Stevick, Earl W. 1980. *Teaching Languages: A Way and Ways.* Rowley, Mass.: Newbury House Publishers.

Tranel, Daniel. 1970. *Counseling concepts applied to the process of education.* Ph.D. dissertation, Loyola University, Chicago.

Suggestopedia and Lozanovian Approaches

Journals and Information Sources Devoted to Suggestopedia

Lozanov Learning Institute, Inc. 1110 Fidler Lane, Suite 1215, Silver Spring, MD 20910.

Language in New Dimensions, 80A Museum Way, San Francisco, California 94114.

The Society for Suggestive-Accelerative Learning and Teaching, Inc. (1976–present). P.O. Box 1216, Welch Station, Ames, Iowa 50011.

Suggestology and Suggestopaedia Institute for Scientific Research in Suggestology. Sofia, Bulgaria: Ministry of People's Education.

Suggestopaedia Canada (1975–present). Aselford-Martin Building, 1725 Woodward Dr., Ottawa, Ontario, KLA OM7, Canada.

Books and Articles

Popular articles on Suggestopedia have appeared in *Psychology Today* (August 1977), *Parade Magazine* (March 1978), *New West Magazine* (July 1977), *Training Magazine* (1976), and *New Age* (November 1979).

Bancroft, W. Jane. 1972a. The psychology of Suggestopedia or learning without stress. *The Educational Review.*

Bancroft, W. Jane. 1972b. Foreign language teaching in Bulgaria. *The Canadian Modern Language Review,* 28:9–13.

Bancroft, W. Jane. 1973. *Suggestology and Suggestopedia—The Theory of the Lozanov Method.* ERIC Microfilm ED 132 857 FL 008 259.

Bancroft, W. Jane. 1979. The Lozanov method and its American adaptations. *The Modern Language Journal,* 62:167–175.

Bushman, Robert W. 1976a. Relaxation as an instructional variable in foreign language teaching. in *Deseret Language and Linguistics Society Symposium Papers.* Provo, Utah: Brigham Young University.

Bushman, Robert W. 1976b. Effects of a full and modified suggestopedic treatment in foreign language learning. Unpublished M.A. thesis. Provo, Utah: Brigham Young University.

Bushman, Robert W. 1978. *An intuitive versus a cognitive presentation mode in foreign language instruction.* Unpublished Ph.D. thesis. Provo, Utah: Brigham Young University.

Bushman, Robert W., and Harold S. Madsen. 1977. A description and evaluation of suggestopedia—a new teaching methodology. Paper presented at the annual Deseret Language and Linguistic Society Symposium, Provo, Utah, 1977.

Bushman, Robert W., and Harold S. Madsen. 1978. Lozanov's suggestopedic method: What it is and how it works. A paper presented at the annual convention of TESOL, New York, 1976.

Caskey, Owen L., and M. H. Flake. 1976. Adaptations of the Lozanov method. Unpublished paper.

Lindeman, Mary L. 1976. Suggestion in education: The historical path of suggestopedia. (Unpublished paper, language and culture center, University of Houston.)

Lozanov, Georgi. 1973. Foundations of suggestology. in *Problems of Suggestology: Proceedings of the First International Symposium on the Problems of Suggestology.* Sofia: Research Institute of Suggestology.

Lozanov, Georgi. 1975a. The nature and history of the suggestopaedic system of teaching foreign languages and its experimental prospects. *Suggestology and Suggestopaedia,* 1:5–15.

Lozanov, Georgi. 1975b. Outline of suggestology and suggestopaedia. Paper presented at the Second International Congress of ATESOL.

Lozanov, Georgi. 1978. *Suggestology and Suggestopedia: Theory and Practice.* Paris: United Nations Educational, Scientific and Cultural Organization.

Lozanov, Georgi. 1979. *Suggestology and Outlines of Suggestopedia.* New York: Gordon & Breach Science Publishers, Inc.

Ostrander, Sheila, and Lynn Schroeder. 1970. *Psychic Discoveries behind the Iron Curtain.* Englewood Cliffs, N.J.: Prentice-Hall.

Ostrander, Sheila, and Lynn Schroeder. 1979. *Superlearning.* New York: Delacorte Press.

Philipov, Elizabeth R. 1975. *Suggestology: The Use of Suggestion in Learning and Hypermnesia.* (Unpublished Ph.D. dissertation) United States International University.

Racle, Gabriel L. 1975. *A Teaching Experience with the Suggestopaedic Method: Reports, Studies, Conferences and Round Table with Dr. Lozanov.* Ottawa: Public Service Commission of Canada.

Racle, Gabriel L. 1979. Can Suggestopaedia revolutionize language teaching? *Foreign Language Annals,* 12:39–49.

Robinett, Elizabeth A. 1975. *The effects of Suggestopedia in increasing foreign language achievement.* Lubbock, Texas: Texas Technical University Ph.D. dissertation (unpublished).

Schuster, Donald H., Ray Benitez-Bordon, and Charles A. Gritton. 1976. *Suggestive, Accelerative Learning and Teaching: A Manual of Classroom Procedures Based on the Lozanov Method.* Des Moines, Iowa: Society for Suggestive-Accelerative Learning and Teaching.

Shearer, Brooks. 1978. Suggestive learning. *TESOL Newsletter,* 12 (April 2).

Stevick, Earl W. 1980. *Teaching Languages: A Way and Ways.* Rowley, Mass.: Newbury House Publishers.

Turkevich, Ludmila B. 1972. Suggestology. *Russian Language Journal*, 26:83–84.
Yotsukura, S. 1975. *Suggestology and Language Teaching*. Washington D.C.: Mankind Research.

Natural Approach

The primary source of information on the Natural Approach is Tracy D. Terrell, Department of Spanish and Portuguese, University of California at Irvine 92717.

Barrutia, Richard. 1977. Método nuevo, pues natural. *Hispania*, September 1977.
Christensen, Clay B. 1975. Affective learning activities. *Foreign Language Annals*, 8:211–219.
Christensen, Clay B. 1977. *Explorando: Affective Learning Activities for Intermediate Students*. Englewood Cliffs, N.J.: Prentice-Hall.
Terrell, Tracy D. 1976a. Acceptability in the acquisition and learning of Spanish pronunciation— the Natural Approach. Paper presented at the annual meeting of the AATSP, Atlanta, Georgia, December 1976.
Terrell, Tracy D. 1976b. The interplay between acquisition and learning in a natural approach to second language teaching. Paper presented at the annual meeting of the AATSP, Atlanta, Georgia, December 1976.
Terrell, Tracy D., J. Egasse, and W. Voge. Techniques for a more natural approach to second language teaching. Workshop paper presented at the annual meeting of ACTFL, San Francisco, California, December 1977.
Terrell, Tracy D., B. Baycroft, and C. Perrone. 1980. Teaching the Spanish subjunctive: an error analysis. To appear in *International Journal of American Linguistics*.
Terrell, Tracy D. 1980. A natural approach to the teaching of verb forms and function in Spanish. To appear in *Language Annals*.
Terrell, Tracy D. (with S. Krashen and W. Voge). *A Natural Approach to Language Teaching: The Monitor Model in the Classroom*. In preparation—to be published by Newbury House Publishers.
Voge, Wilfried. 1979. A more natural approach to the teaching of German. Paper presented to the joint meeting of northern and southern AATC, November 1979.

Confluent Approach

The primary source of information on the Confluent Approach is Beverly Galyean, 767 Gladys Ave., Long Beach, California 90804.

Background

Alschuler, Alfred. 1973. *Developing Achievement Motivation in Adolescents*. Englewood Cliffs, N.J.: Educational Technology Publications.
Borton, Terry. 1970. *Reach, Touch, and Teach*. New York: McGraw-Hill.
Brown, George. 1971. *Human Teaching for Human Learning*. New York: The Viking Press.
Combs, Arthur. 1975. The personal approach to good teaching. In Donald A. Read and Sidney B. Simons (editors), *Humanistic Education Sourcebook*. Englewood Cliffs, N.J.: Prentice-Hall, 249–261.
Combs, Arthur, Robert Blume, Arthur Newman, and Hannelore Wass. 1974. *The Professional Education of Teachers: A Humanistic Approach to Teacher Preparation*. Boston: Allyn and Bacon, Inc.
Hawley, R., and E. Hawley. 1975. *Human Values in the Classroom: A Handbook for Teachers*. New York: Hart Publishing Company.
Patterson, C. H. 1973. *Humanistic Education*. Englewood Cliffs, N.J.: Prentice-Hall.
Perls, Frederick. 1973. *The Gestalt Approach and Eye Witness to Therapy*. Palo Alto, California: Science and Behavior Books.

Raths, L., M. Harmon, and S. Simon. 1975. *Humanistic Education Sourcebook*. Englewood Cliffs, N.J.: Prentice-Hall.

Rogers, Carl, and Barry Stevens. 1967. *Person to Person: The Problem of Being Human*. Lafayette, California: Real People Press.

Weinstein, Gerald, and Marlo Fantini. 1972. *Toward Humanistic Education: A Curriculum of Affect*. New York: Praeger Publishers.

Description and Evaluation of the Confluent Apprroach

Galyean, Beverly. 1975. *Report on Research in the Confluent Teaching of Language*. Santa Barbara: Confluent Education Research Center.

Galyean, Beverly. 1976. *Language from Within*. Santa Barbara: Confluent Education Research Center.

Galyean, Beverly. 1977a. *The Effects of a Confluent Language Curriculum on the Oral and Written Communication Skills, Self Identity and Esteem, Attitudes, and Interpersonal Relationships of Junior and Senior High School French and Spanish Students*. Confluent Education Research Center, Santa Barbara.

Galyean, Beverly. 1977b. *The effects of a confluent language curriculum on the oral and written communication skills, and various aspects of personal and interpersonal growth, on a college French level one class*. Unpublished Ph.D. dissertation, University of California at Santa Barbara.

Galyean, Beverly. 1979. A confluent design for language teaching. *TESOL Quarterly*, 11:143–156.

Galyean, Beverly, and Lucille Rader. 1974. *Survey of student attitudes toward high school classes*. Los Angeles and Santa Barbara, Joint Report: Immaculate Heart College and Confluent Education Research Center.

The Silent Way

The primary source of information on the Silent Way is Educational Solutions, 80 Fifth Avenue, New York, N.Y. 10011.

Educational Solutions Newsletter. 1970–present. New York: Educational Solutions.

Diller, Karl C. 1975. Some new trends for applied linguistics and foreign language teaching in the United States. *TESOL Quarterly*, 9:65–73.

Fanselow, John F. 1973. The Silent Way: A new look at language teaching. *Idiom*, fall 1973.

Fanselow, John F. 1977. Review of C. Gattegno, *The Common Sense of Teaching Foreign Languages. TESOL Quarterly* 11.

Gattegno, Caleb. 1963. *Teaching Foreign Language in Schools the Silent Way*. New York: Educational Solutions.

Gattegno, Caleb. 1976. *The Common Sense of Teaching Foreign Languages*. New York: Educational Solutions.

Olsen, Judy E. 1977. *Communication Starters*. San Francisco: The Alemany Press.

Selman, Mary. 1977. The Silent Way: Insights for ESL. *TESL Talk*, 8:33–36.

Stevick, Earl W. 1974. Review of *Teaching Foreign Languages: The Silent Way. TESOL Quarterly*, 8:305–314.

Stevick, Earl W. 1975. One simple visual aid:A psychodynamic view. *Language Learning*, 25:63–72.

Stevick, Earl W. 1976. *Memory, Meaning and Method: Some Psychological Perspectives on Language Learning*. Rowley, Mass.: Newbury House Publishers.

Stevick, Earl W. 1980. *Teaching Languages: A Way and Ways*. Rowley, Mass.: Newbury House Publishers.

APPROACHES TO A RICH LEARNING ENVIRONMENT

Atkinson, Richard C., and M. R. Rough. 1974. *An Application of the Mnemonic Keyword Method to the Acquisition of a Russian Vocabulary.* ERIC 096841.

Ball, John P. 1973. *An experimental comparison of elaborative prompt utilization by learners of different aptitude levels in foreign language vocabulary learning.* Unpublished M.A. Thesis, Brigham Young University.

Boon, H., Y. Davrou, and J. C. Maquet. 1976. *La Sophrologie.* Edition Retz.

Caycedo, A. 1979. *L'aventure de la sophrologie,* propos recueillis par Y. Davrou, Edition Retz.

Groberg, Delbert H. 1972. *Mnemonic Japanese.* Salt Lake City: Interac.

Lipson, Alexander. 1971. Some new strategies for teaching oral skills. In Lugton (editor), *Toward a Cognitive Approach to Second Language Acquisition.* Philadelphia: Center for Curriculum Development.

Ott, C. E., D. Butler, R. Blake, and J. Ball. 1973. The effect of interactive-image elaboration on the acquisition of foreign language vocabulary. *Language Learning,* 23:197–206.

Ott, C. E., D. Butler, R. Blake, and J. Ball. 1975. Mnemotechnics in second language learning. *American Psychologist,* 30:821–828.

Ott, C. E., D. Butler, R. Blake, and J. Ball. 1976. Implications of mental elaboration for the acquisition of foreign language vocabulary. *International Review of Applied Linguistics,* 14 (March):37–48.

Ott, C. E., D. Butler, R. Blake, and J. Ball. 1976. Recent research on mnemonic techniques for learning foreign language vocabulary. *Educational Technology,* 16 (August):43–44.

010133|3|85